WITHDRAWN

HOUSEHOLDS
AND THE WORLD-ECONOMY

EXPLORATIONS IN THE WORLD ECONOMY:
Publications of the Fernand Braudel Center

Series Editor:
Immanuel Wallerstein
*Fernand Braudel Center for the Study of Economies, Historical Systems,
and Civilizations*

Volumes in this series:

1. *WORLD-SYSTEMS ANALYSIS: Theory and Methodology*
   edited by Terence K. Hopkins, Immanuel Wallerstein and Associates

2. *LABOR IN THE WORLD SOCIAL STRUCTURE*
   edited by Immanuel Wallerstein

3. *HOUSEHOLDS AND THE WORLD-ECONOMY*
   edited by Joan Smith, Immanuel Wallerstein, Hans-Dieter Evers

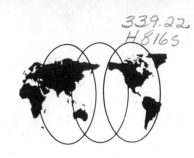

Explorations in the World-Economy:
Publications of the Fernand Braudel Center
Volume 3

HOUSEHOLDS AND
THE WORLD-ECONOMY

Joan Smith
Immanuel Wallerstein
Hans-Dieter Evers
Editors

SAGE PUBLICATIONS
Beverly Hills   London   New Delhi

For information address:

SAGE Publications, Inc.
275 South Beverly Drive
Beverly Hills, California 90212

SAGE Publications India Pvt. Ltd.
C-236 Defence Colony
New Delhi 110 024, India

SAGE Publications Ltd
28 Banner Street
London EC1Y 8QE, England

Printed in the United States of America

Library of Congress Cataloging in Publication Data

Main entry under title:

Households and the world-economy.

(Explorations in the world-economy ; v. 3)
1. Households—Economic aspects—Addresses, essays, lectures. 2. Capitalism—Addresses, essays, lectures.
I. Smith, Joan, 1935-   . II. Wallerstein, Immanuel Maurice, 1930-   . III. Evers, Hans-Dieter. IV. Series.
HB199.H645   1984   339.2'2   84-4875
ISBN 0-8039-2290-6

FIRST PRINTING

Contents

Introduction

Everyday language and terminology, the unavoidable tools of social science, can at times become more of a burden than a boon. The transhistorical and static character of most concepts in current usage render the classification of historical differences extremely difficult. Though attempts to distinguish the empirical variations of states, classes, races, or households over time are occasionally made, the continued use of the same terminology eventually suggests the continuity of a genus or type rather than the emergence of radically different social institutions.

If we assume, however, that the modern world-system is radically different from other historical systems, the use of transhistorical concepts can be profoundly misleading. It leads us to think that states, classes, ethnic groups, and households were somehow in existence as primordial institutions that changed under the pressure of a reified phenomenon, e.g., "capitalism".

Not only is this a misleading description of historical reality, but it also tends to lead us to classify particular subvarieties of these institutions as progressive or backward, meaning they have or have not "changed" in response to "capitalism". Thus a state in the core is "modern" because it has an efficient bureaucracy, but one in the periphery is "backward" or has undergone a "distorted development" because corruption is rampant.

Nowhere are these biases more deep-set than in the discussion of those small groups in which we band together to reproduce our social existences— the family and/or the household. The nuclear, wage-earning household is thought to be "modern", while a non-nuclear, "subsistence" household is the primordial type out of which the modern form evolved. Thus the transfer of functions from households to organizations in industrial societies has been a favorite topic of generations of sociologists of the family. The changing authority relations of the nuclear family have equally been attributed to the transformation processes said to be associated with modernity.

The authors in this volume start with a different set of assumptions. We believe that the form of "households" as we know them today—whatever they are, and, as the reader will see, this is a central matter of our internal debate—are not "responses" to a capitalist world, but part and parcel of that world. Households are seen neither as isolates nor as small units of social organization related to national economies, but instead as basic units of an emerging world-system.

The chapters here are products of the collaboration of two institutions: the Research Working Group on Households, Labor Force Formation, and the World-Economy of the Fernand Braudel Center at SUNY-Binghamton in the U.S., and the Sociology of Development Research Center at the University of Bielefeld in Germany. We each started with a different initial concern. The Binghamton group was puzzled by the persistence of radical disparities in payments for parallel kinds of wage labor in different parts of the world and centered its attention on the long-term development of households. The Bielefeld group was puzzled by the manifold unexpected linkages of small, largely subsistence "peasants" throughout Asia, the Middle East, Africa, and Latin America with the world of large-scale commodity production and thus focused on the in-depth comparative study of households in the Third World.

Both groups found the traditional descriptions and explanations for household transformations empirically untrue and theoretically unsatisfactory. Both groups were particularly unhappy with the understanding of gender relations as part of this picture. Both groups had come to the view that understanding the "household" was a crucial nexus in the explanation of empirical reality.

What kind of answers have we found? We maintain that a substantial part of labor power in the capitalist world-economy is not generated through exchange in a labor market but through a system of reproduction that at first sight does not seem to be part of the capitalist production system at all; and this is not accidentally but necessarily so (see, in this volume, Evers, Clauss & Wong; Wallerstein). The processes and relationships that compose these systems of reproduction of labor power are structured by and subject to the laws of capitalist accumulation on a world scale but are not themselves exclusively defined by relationships of exchange. We call these systems "households". They are systems that are able to provide labor to capital precisely because they ensure the combination of income from wage labor with that from non-wage labor so as to form an adequate pool of resources guaranteeing the replenishment of labor power. Apparently non-capitalist relationships and processes are responsible for a substantial supply of the world's labor force and thus are at the very heart of capitalism. Rather than being vestiges of some distant past conveniently articulated with a capitalist mode of production, they have everywhere been reconstituted in quite fundamental and decisive ways.

The households are neither the lineage systems of some earlier period nor the kinship systems of a later one, although lineage and kinship may play both an ideological and material role in their structure and functioning. Sometimes kinship is a component of household relationships and sometimes not. That is to say, the set of functions satisfied by households are sometimes but not always the work of kinship, but they can be satisfied by other relationships as well. Elwert, for example, argues that the notion of household as a definitive group of people who bear a kin or lineage relationship to each other makes little sense among Ayizo in Benin. The units of sharing are quite different from what can be called "households" or "families" in the conventional sense. Elwert shows that these alternative processes of sharing are highly complex systems that are today subject to deep-seated disturbances that are leading to their transformation.

Similarly households, in the views advanced here, cannot be equated with co-residential groups. Augel, for example, shows the importance of collective consumption, that is collectively provided goods that are not distributed via the market and do not therefore require an equivalent of wage labor. Wong provides examples from West Africa showing that instances of consumption limited to the residential unit are rare and that reproduction is ensured only by a network of solidarity. Data from a Malaysian village shows a great number of residential units depending on transfers from others. Units of consumption are thus much larger than individual dwelling units.

The view we are advancing here is that the fast and increasing incorporation of labor into low-wage sectors is absolutely conditioned upon the persistence of these alternative relationships, networks, and activities (Wong). The only form of lifetime security such low-wage workers have and thus, from the point of view of capital, the only way their continued availability is guaranteed is precisely that which the dualists and others have argued are non-capitalist modes of production. These so-called non-capitalist modes of production are indeed to be found in core (industrialized) countries as well as the periphery. In fact, the paradox of vast numbers of immigrants entering an area of high employment in the core is precisely explained by the use to which non-wage remuneration and corresponding non-wage relations are put in counteracting falling rates of profit. Even in areas that are quintessentially "core"—New York City, for just one example—apparently non-capitalist modes of production are growing and in doing so accommodate a new and distinctive round of investment even when old capital is flowing out at ever-increasing rates.

But does this mean perhaps that there exists in New York City a distinctive and autonomous mode of production—a non-capitalist mode? By no means. Processes associated with and only intelligible through the world-system called these relationships into being, and it is the state—another structure of the world-economy—that will limit their role, should their existence prove all too tempting to enterprises that wish to dig too deeply into their reservoir of what would be additional sources of cheap labor.

The structures associated with the reproduction of low-wage labor are crucial in shaping the capitalist labor process itself. Thus there is a particular irony, as Baerga points out, that the needleworkers were isolated from a labor movement that sought to organize the sugar cane workers whose very labor was deeply dependent on the labor of their wives. Work that is short-term and cyclical, and that thus engendered high turnover rates, requires the presence of structures that keep the erstwhile wage worker alive during periods of unemployment.

As areas within the core itself become dominated by these "marginalized" labor processes we can expect to see greater dependence on these apparently anomalous structures. The irony of course is that these ostensibly irregular structures are then used as "evidence" of racial and ethnic inferiority of those involved in them and serve to underwrite the racism that is the ideological counterpart to the politics of wage inequalities (Dickinson).

How does our view relate to the so-called domestic labor debate, which centers on the role of housework in the capitalist world-economy? It is the apparent persistent presence and indeed growth of non-wage labor that has triggered this particular controversy (Davin, Bennholdt-Thomsen). The particular questions raised in the domestic labor debate are similar to those raised here: What is the relationship of non-wage housework to the reproduction of the capitalist system, and how are hierarchical relationships that are secured by non-wage structures to be understood? That is, what are we to make of the housewife and her labor under capital?

In the rapidly growing number of texts dealing with the role of housework in the capitalist economy there is the implicit and quite often explicit recognition that housework somehow lies outside the law of value. Because it does, it is argued in much of that literature, housework in particular and unwaged reproductive labor in general constitutes a separate and distinct mode of production adhering to its own logic and rules. The view adopted by the pieces to follow is quite different.

The reproduction of non-wage labor—including that form that falls under the heading of housework—depends upon the logic of the world-economy itself (Smith, von Werlhof). In fact non-wage labor is intelligible only from the perspective that sees it as itself a constant feature of the capitalist world-system. Domestic work, no matter what its form, has no autonomous existence, but is everywhere subject to the dynamics inherent in the world-system. This is not to argue that the world-economy is to operate within the law of value but merely to suggest that the world-economy as it is presently constituted creates mechanisms that act as a barrier to the full realization of that law. That is to say, one of the contradictions of capitalism is that the optimal functioning of the law of value seems to require that it *not* be universally applied. It is for this reason that the set of relationships that guarantee non-wage labor are themselves predicated on the world-economy.

As soon as waged labor is created, so too must be non-waged work. The sets of particulars within which this work is carried out are historically variable and must be studied in their own right. The concept of the household, as we are defining it here, cannot be of help in that task. Nor is it meant to be. Nevertheless, a few general remarks can be offered concerning the historical forces to which non-wage labor is subject.

As we have argued, the preservation or recreation of non-wage labor forms—provided they are such that they make available sufficient quantities of labor for waged work—is the necessary condition for the vast disparities in wages as well as in products (Schiel) or in savings (Barbosa) that are integrated into the circuits of capital. Yet, at the same time, these non-waged activities signal to the individual firm or enterprise an area of untapped but potential commodity production and/or a potential for what appears to be an unlimited supply of labor. Thus at any given moment the relationship of households to the owning class as a whole is subject to the pressures exerted by individual members of that class. The working-out of these contradictory pressures depends in the last analysis on the results of the class struggles of the proletariat throughout the world-economy.

While setting out the theoretical framework, the chapters that compose Part I of the volume raise a series of questions that remain to be resolved by future research. What is the relationship between the processes of commodification, crisis, and the formation of households? One would think that the current crisis, for example, would enhance the formation of households that have as a major part of their necessary resources increased access to non-wage labor. Yet apparently every crisis over the past 100 years or so has resulted in more rather than less proletarianization. As capital avails itself of so-called marginal workers—workers who are produced and reproduced outside of the wage per se—what specifically happens to household structures? As Evers, Clauss, and Wong argue, the existence of rural and urban subsistence production shapes the character of society in peripheral areas, but what set of specific structures guarantees the reproduction of these subsistence sectors?

Given that the expansion of world capitalism depends upon increasing effective demand and thus decreasing the degree to which labor is reproduced and maintained outside of the wage, while the continual reproduction of unequal exchange between trading partners depends upon the preservation of relationships that guarantee extraordinarily low wages by providing a consumption fund satisfied by non-waged activities, what factors are responsible for one of these pressures to dominate the other? Friedman's paper begins to specify the particular set of parameters that must be studied closely to answer this question. Wong of course raises an important issue when she suggests that the household, if defined primarily as a co-residential unit, is not an adequate unit of analysis in attempts to account for the reproduction of the labor force. She suggests that rather than an individual belonging to a coherent "household", he or she is more appropriately thought of as belonging to a network determined in part by the kinds of goods and services required.

That households are not appropriately considered "primordial" units is certainly indicated by the analysis found in Schiel's chapter and in part is an answer consistent with that offered by Stauth to his own question concerning "what is primordial about the household"? Finally, the section is concluded by a debate between Smith and von Werlhof concerning whether or not all labor that is not directly waged can be grouped together under the same conceptual apparatus. Smith suggests that entirely different forms of non-wage labor emerge under increases in relative surplus value and are not to be confused with those that are engaged in subsistence production. Conversely, von Werlhof would argue that housewives in the core and women and peasants in subsistence production in the periphery find themselves in similar relationships to capitalist accumulation.

The next two sections of the volume raise very particular questions concerning the relationship of households to the state on the one hand and to their internal structures on the other. Precisely because capitalist accumulation is a process constructed out of contradictory relationships, households are always and everywhere under contradictory pressures that have a tendency both to reinforce them and to erode them as major institutional structures in the world-economy. Thompson in his chapter on the People's Republic of China demonstrates how this process is just as true when it is the state that organizes production as when it is organized via privately owned firms. Of course, for many, the reconstitution of the unequal relationship within the household even within the People's Republic has led to the conclusion that internal household inequalities reflect indeed something quite primordial. Nevertheless, when we consider the chapters in Part II in their totality, the very strong impression emerges that households are reconstituted under very different historical circumstances resulting in very different sorts of structures and are thus vulnerable to different sorts of pressures. Part of those pressures result in specific forms of labor obligations that are organized via gender and age. The concluding section of the volume raises the questions of how the internal structure of households can be considered in an historical context ultimately shaped by the constraints of the world-economy.

The perspectives offered here speak to the very important debate concerning the nature of patriarchy. If the household and the internal relationships that compose it came into existence under particular constraints of the world-economy, then the patriarchical hierarchy that is their principal feature is neither a remnant of an earlier period in fundamental contradiction with the contemporary capitalist mode of production nor a product of a putative universal male urge to dominate. Rather, the views advanced here suggest that patriarchy is an entirely modern affair and is one of the fundamental political components of the modern world-economy. Male dominance within household relationships ceases to be a relationship external to world capitalism but can be seen as very much part of its everyday operation. Thus our reconceptualization of the household places the questions of the subordination of women at the center of any account of accumulation on a world scale.

Systems of reproduction are, metaphorically speaking, created by the modern world-economy. As more and more labor in both the core and the periphery is the product of workers who from the immediate point of view of capitalists just appear at the factory gates, the sets of relationships that guarantee the social existence of a growing portion of the working class become both historically and analytically crucial in the operation of the world-economy. The chapters presented here should be considered a preliminary exploration into the nature of these systems.

Acknowledgments

The research conducted by those participants coming from the Fernand Braudel Center was assisted by a grant from the National Endowment for the Humanities. The colloquium was made possible by a grant from the Volkswagen Stiftung and the Zentrum für Interdisciplinäre Forschung of the Universität Bielefeld. We thank the university authorities of Bielefeld as well for their hospitality. We thank Darrell Colombo for his extensive editorial assistance on this book, and Anna Davin for her help as well.

Joan Smith
Immanuel Wallerstein
Hans-Dieter Evers

I

Households, Subsistence, and the Capitalist World-Economy: Theoretical Perspectives

1

HOUSEHOLD STRUCTURES AND LABOR-FORCE FORMATION IN THE CAPITALIST WORLD-ECONOMY

Immanuel Wallerstein

Fernand Braudel Center
State University of New York—Binghamton

Households make up one of the key institutional structures of the capitalist world-economy. It is always an error to analyze social institutions trans-historically, as though they constituted a genus of which each historical system produced a variant or species. Rather, the multiple institutional structures of a given historical system (a) are in fundamental ways unique to that system, and (b) are part of an interrelated *set* of institutions that constitute the operational structures of the system.

The historical system in this case is the capitalist world-economy as a single evolving historical entity. The households located in that system can most fruitfully be understood by analyzing how they fit into the set of institutions of that system rather than by comparing them to hypothetically parallel institutions (often bearing the same nominal designation) in other historical systems. Indeed, one can reasonably doubt whether there was anything parallel to our "household" in previous systems (but the same could be said of such institutional concepts as "state" or "class"). The use of such terms as "households" transhistorically is at best an analogy.

Rather than compare putative sets of characteristics of possibly parallel institutions, let us rather pose the problem from inside the ongoing capitalist world-economy. The endless accumulation of capital is the defining characteristic and *raison d'être* of this system. Over time, this endless accumulation pushes towards the commodification of everything, the absolute increase of world production, and a complex and sophisticated social division of labor. The objective of accumulation presupposes a system of polarizing distribution in which the majority of the world population serve as a labor force producing surplus-value, which is somehow distributed among the remaining minority of the world population.

From the point of view of the accumulators of capital, what problems are posed by the ways in which this world labor force is produced and reproduced? I think the accumulators can be seen to have three main concerns:

(1) They benefit by having a labor force whose use is variable in time. That is to say, individual entrepreneurs will want to have expenditures only directly related to production and therefore will not wish to pay a rental fee for future option on unused labor time. On the other hand, when they wish to produce, they also wish to have persons willing to work. The variation in time may be decade to decade, year to year, week to week, or even hour to hour.

(2) They will benefit by having a labor force whose use is variable in space. That is to say, individual entrepreneurs will wish to locate or relocate their enterprises according to some considerations of costs (the costs of transport, the historical costs of labor power, and so on) without being unduly constrained by the existing geographical distribution of the world's labor force. The variation in space can be continent to continent, rural to urban, or one particular immediate locus to another.

(3) They will benefit by having the cost-level of the labor force as low as possible. That is to say, individual entrepreneurs will want their direct costs (in the form of wages, of indirect monetary payments, and of payments in kind) to be minimized, at least over some middle run.

Each of these preferences to which individual entrepreneurs must adhere (on pain of their elimination from the economic arena through bankruptcy) lies in partial contradiction with the interests of the accumulators of capital as a world class. As a world class, accumulators need to ensure that the world labor force be reproduced at a numerical level related to the level of world production, and that this world labor force not so organize itself as a class force that it will threaten the existence of the system as such. Thus, as a world class, certain kinds of redistribution (to ensure an adequate level of worldwide effective demand, to ensure long-term reproduction of the world labor force, and to guarantee an adequate political defense mechanism for the system by allowing cadres to receive a part of the surplus) all may seem necessary steps.

The problem then is what kinds of institutions would, from the point of view of the accumulators of capital (in their contradictory capacities as a set of competing individuals and as a collective class), be optimal in terms of labor-force formation? We shall suggest several ways in which the historical development of "household" structures have been consonant with this objective. The contradictory needs of entrepreneurs as individuals and entrepreneurs as a class can best be reconciled if the determinants of labor-force supply have a molasses-like consistency: the institutions ooze (that is, they respond flexibly to various pressures of the "market") but they ooze slowly. The "household" as it has historically developed under capitalism seems to have precisely this character. Its boundaries are malleable but have nonetheless a short-run firmness embedded in both economic self-interest and the social psychology of its members.

There are three major ways in which the boundaries have been kept gently malleable. First of all, there has been a steady pressure to break the link between household organization and territoriality. In the early phase, this was the pressure, long observed, to detach more and more people from a commitment (physical, legal, and emotional) to a particular small unit of land. In the second phase, usually temporally later, this has been the pressure to diminish but never entirely eliminate co-residentiality as the basis of the legal and socio-psychological commitments to a pooled income structure. (It is this phenomenon that has been perceived, largely incorrectly in my view, as the rise of the nuclear family.)

Secondly, as the capitalist world-economy has evolved over time, it has become more and more clear that the social division of production has been predicated on a partially waged world labor force. This "partialism" was double. (a) There was a dispersion of the world's households along a curve representing the percentage of total productive work that was remunerated by wages. I suspect that a proper statistical analysis for the world-economy as a whole would show that this curve has gotten less skewed and more bell-like over historical time. (b) Virtually no households inside the capitalist world-economy have been located on the far ends of the curve. This means that virtually every individual household's mode of remuneration was that of "partial" wage labor.

Thirdly, the households' forms of participation in the labor force were stratified, and increasingly so, in terms of ethnicity/peoplehood and gender. But the ideology of equal opportunity was simultaneously increasingly asserted and implemented. The way these two thrusts were reconciled was that the actual stratification was flexible, since the boundary lines of ethnicity (including the rules for endogamy) were themselves malleable. While the boundary lines for gender were less malleable than those for ethnicity, it was nonetheless possible to redefine constantly which occupational roles fell on each side of the gender-stratification dividing line.

Note that, in each of these aspects (territoriality, wage labor, and ethnic and gender stratification), the structure was one involving a tension—the break from territoriality but some role for co-residentiality, a waged labor system but only a partial one, ethnic and gender stratification system but one moderated by an ideology of equal opportunity. It is precisely this tension, this "intermediateness", that enabled the accumulators to manipulate (but only up to a point) the world labor force. It was the very same tension that created both the vigor and the ambiguities of the response of the world labor force—their response in terms of social consciousness (loyalties to a people, a class, a household) and in terms of political consciousness (involvement in movements).

The efficacy of the household from the point of view of the accumulators can be seen if it is contrasted with two hypothetical alternatives as an income-pooling unit (commensality in the figurative sense). One is a "community" (a commune) of 50 or 100 or even more persons. The second is an isolated very small unit (a single person; a nuclear family counting no children of adult status). The community was of course a frequent unit of social reproduction in prior historical systems. There have been occasional (mostly unsuccessful) attempts to replicate units of such size within the capitalist world-economy. The very small units of course occurred but seemed also to be strongly resisted as somehow "unviable".

It is empircally the case that actual income-pooling households have tended to be intermediate in size. In order to avoid too small units, households have often moved beyond the kinship networks to incorporate non-kin. In order to avoid the too large units, both social and legal limits to mutual obligations have grown up. Why should such a tendency to inter-mediateness—in size as well as composition—have prevailed?

The chief disadvantage, it would seem, of the too small units was that the level of wage income necessary to ensure collective reproduction was clearly higher than for the intermediate units. Where the level of wages was too low, the households themselves sought to enlarge their boundaries for survival. But this was clearly in the interest of the accumulators as well.

The chief disadvantage, it would seem, of the too large units was that the level of work output required to ensure survival was too low. On the one hand, accumulators did not like this because it diminished pressure to enter the wage-labor market. On the other hand, members of the labor force found that it created a strain between those members of the community who felt they could profit from some immediate mobility and those who did not. One could "move" a household. It was very difficult to "move" a community.

Institutional structures are not givens. They tend to be loci of, indeed objects of, contradictory attempts to shape them. There were two primary struggles surrounding the institution of the household. The first was the frequently opposed interests of the workers grouped together in a household and the accumulators who had power in a given locality and/or state. The second was the contradiction between the objectives pursued by the accumulators in terms of household structures and their frequent need to engage in behavior that undermined these objectives. Let us consider each in turn.

The household as an income-pooling unit can be seen as a fortress both of accommodation to and resistance to the patterns of labor-force allocation favored by accumulators. As more and more responsibility for reproduction of the work force moved away from the "community" towards the "household" as constrained by the "state", the very malleability of the institution (in terms of membership, boundaries, combination of forms of labor, and location), which was so useful to capitalists, was also useful in resisting or circumventing the pressures over short runs. Indeed, until the rise of the movements, and even after that, household decision-making was perhaps the principal everyday political weapon available to the world's labor force. What have frequently been analyzed as atavistic thrusts were often sociopolitical parries in defense of given use-values or simply efforts to minimize the rate of exploitation. The fact that the demands of the households varied erratically (e.g., sometimes in favor of more women moving into waged labor, sometimes against it) can in fact be readily explained if we look on such demands as tactical rather than strategic, as immediate responses to an immediate political situation.

The actual forms of conflict between the household as a locus of political resistance by the world labor force and the accumulators controlling economic and state structures, and how this varies systematically over time and place, is a topic worthy of much elaboration. I shall not do it here. Rather I would turn to the impact of the contradictions within the basic economic mechanisms of capitalism itself. Capitalism involves commodification, but as we have emphasized, only partial commodificiation. However, further commodificiation has in fact been a regular mechanism of getting out of the cyclical stagnations of the world-economy. The result can be summed up as follows: Despite themselves, and against their own long-run interests, accumulators constantly push to the commodificiation of everything, and in particular of everyday life. The description of the secular process of the commodification of everyday life has comprised a large part of social science efforts for two centuries. In the long run, this secular process guarantees the demise of the system. In the meantime, it gets translated into household structures whose internal dynamics have been, are increasingly, commodified, from the preparation of food, to the cleaning and repair of home appurtenances and clothing, to custodial care, to nursing care, to emotional repair. With the increasing commodification of everyday life has gone a decline in co-residentiality and kinship as determinative of the boundaries. The end point of this secular pressure is not, however, it seems to me, the "individual" or the "nuclear family" but a unit whose cohesiveness is increasing predicated on the income-pooling function it performs.

Marshall Berman has used as the title of his recent book (1982) on the experience of modernity Marx's metaphor in the *Manifesto*: "All that is solid melts into air." This comes as the conclusion of Marx's analysis of the relentless "revolutionizing" of the means and relations of production. The passage continues, "all that is holy is profaned", and then culminates in what I think is the most relevant passage for us in the context: "and man is at last compelled to face with sober senses his real conditions of life and his relations with his kind." In many ways this has just begun to happen. It is the income-pooling lifetime proletarian household—torn from its once indissoluble link to territory, to kinship, and to co-residentiality— that does the most to strip bare the real conditions of life. That is why it becomes politically impossible to keep them at this minimum level. The very expansion of commodification is itself the most profound politicization. If all that is holy is profaned, then there remains no justification for the unequal distribution of reward. Even the individualistic reaction of "more for me" translates into "at least my fair share." This is the most radical political message imaginable.

In this way, it becomes clear why the efforts of the accumulators have always been to create an "intermediate" household—to break with the older "community" forms of labor-force organization to be sure, but still to retard the inexorable if slow pace of proletarianization. It is no accident therefore that today issues surrounding family life, gender rights, and the organization of everyday life remain central political issues. Indeed, these issues are becoming more acute precisely because of the secular advance of proletarianization, which is regarded with deep distrust by the accumulators but often also with confused dismay by the world's work forces, whose social movements have developed such ambivalent positions on the subject. And yet it is the key in many ways to the structuring of class consciousness and therefore to the potential of these movements themselves.

2

SUBSISTENCE REPRODUCTION
A Framework for Analysis

Hans-Dieter Evers
Wolfgang Clauss
Diana Wong
Sociology of Development Research Center
University of Bielefeld

An understanding of complex social and economic systems, let alone their processes and ways of change, cannot be achieved solely by an economic analysis that relegates society and politics to the shadow world of "ceteris paribus". On the other hand, a purely sociological analysis of societies that does not take account of the interaction of man and nature, i.e., the economics of procreation and survival, remains similarly incapable of revealing what keeps societies going. In an age in which attention is focused on development and change, up to a point at which the destruction of mankind becomes a distinct possibility, it may be useful to return to the issue of the maintenance of life and society.

The stress on production and progress has diverted attention from reproduction and procreation; the fascination with money and markets has repressed first-hand experience on non-market exchange and work without pay.

In the social science literature, particularly in economics, the sphere of "production" is usually stressed together with the sphere of "circulation" or the market. The system in which production and circulation take place is taken as fixed; but in order to "produce", a socio-economic system has to be "reproduced", itself, over time. Economic theory takes account of this by emphasizing savings, depreciation, and investments. But on a more general level we should consider the reproduction of the economic and social formation as whole, which of course includes much more than savings and reinvestments. The basis of all reproduction of any socio-economic formation is after all the maintenance of human life—of the working population to ensure the continued input of labor. Work is the basis of production, and it permits, via the appropriation of surplus value, the accumulation of capital. The maintenance ("reproduction") of the labor force is the mainstay of any economy, and this means that the satisfaction of basic needs to reproduce human life should also be the basic consideration in the construction of any social or economic theory. It is a paradox at best, an obscenity at worst, that economic theorists and policy makers have tended to neglect this basic aspect and have concentrated on capital formation or, particularly in treating problems of economic development in underdeveloped areas, the importation of capital or foreign investment.

The reproduction of human life and the reproduction of society are thus closely interrelated. For analytical purposes we should, however, distinguish between a *primary reproduction* (i.e., the reproduction of labor power and human life in general) and *secondary reproduction* (i.e., the reproduction of the social and economic order in such a way as to ensure either its continued existence as a definite social formation or its propitious transformation).

Primary Reproduction

Primary reproduction, i.e., the reproduction of the labor force, is a fairly complex process that includes the production of food and its processing, education, running a household management, the provision of housing, and many other additional aspects. Households may combine various sources of income in order to provide for their reproduction requirements. It is important however, that a large part of this reproduction takes place as directly connected production and consumption *outside* the market economy. Many activities in the sphere of reproduction are carried out by unpaid labor, and many products are used that have not entered the sphere of circulation or the markets at all. Consequently, a major part of the reproduction process does not enter government statistics, government planning, and government concern, and is therefore not easy to capture statistically; it does not even seem to "exist" officially.[1]

This direct production-consumption pattern is usually referred to as typical for a "subsistence economy". In the rural sector, particularly of underdeveloped countries, this pattern is often seen as an important though vanishing form of production. Peasants produce their own foodstuffs and partly their own clothing, tools, and utensils, which they consequently use themselves without channeling them through the market. Less recognized are the facts that a similar process takes place in the urban economy and that similar principles apply there as well as in the rural sector. These assumptions warrant some explanation.

In an analysis of the basic needs of a population, we have to consider not only the production of food, but also its processing. In advanced capitalist societies, this processing is done, of course, partly commercially but largely as part of household activities, mainly by women. Before rice, potatoes, or noodles, that have been purchased in the market, can be consumed, considerable labor has to go into preparation to make them fit for consumption. This process takes place in almost every household even in the most highly developed capitalist economies. Short of eating in a canteen or shoving a TV dinner into an oven, a large proportion of the population (which is typically not listed as economically active in census statistics) is occupied in carrying out exactly this task. A large part of the "subsistence production" work is done by unpaid family labor, primarily female.[2] The social organization of this type of work often takes the form of a household or a kin-group. The boundaries of these groups are, however, different in different historical periods and in different societies. Nevertheless, we shall avoid the issue at this stage and treat the household (whatever may be its social structure) as the basic unit of reproduction.

Short for "subsistence production for the reproduction of households or families", we use the term "household subsistence reproduction" to describe this process. Another important part of subsistence production is the production of living space (habitat subsistence reproduction). In many societies, particularly in rural areas, houses are often built by villagers themselves, which means the provision of housing is again part of direct subsistence production. In urban areas, but also in villages, houses may be built by building contractors using wage labor, in which case housing is provided by normal capitalistic production. But the provision of housing does not end here; after a house has been built it is necessary to reproduce a "habitat". A house has to be cleaned, repaired, and maintained in order to provide continuous living facilities. This can be done by a straightforward production of living space as is the case with hotel or boarding-house wage laborers like waiters, maids, and craftsmen who are employed to maintain and reproduce living space continuously. But more common is, of course, the form of direct subsistence reproduction, in which the family, especially women, produces and consumes the habitat continuously, very much in the same way as a rural family in a subsistence economy produces and consumes rice, vegetables, and other food stuffs.

Labor that goes into subsistence reproduction is often seen by economists and government servants as "unproductive" because no goods enter the market and no income is earned. Left out of these accounts, therefore, is a big, undefined "black" area in the economy of any society that is frequently exempted from government policies designed to stimulate economic development. We would take the opposite position: Subsistence production in its forms of household subsistence reproduction and habitat subsistence reproduction is very productive in the sense that it allows, in the long run, the accumulation of surplus value, profits, and capital.[3] It is easy to understand that without this labor, "productive" in a sense much more basic than bourgeois economists allow, any economy would collapse, and that a fully automated economy is a utopia.

There are, however, many intermediate steps or analytical leaps between primary reproduction and the ultimate level of societal reproduction (Evers & Schiel, 1979: 285-87). An important level is the reproduction of the particular structure of households, families, and kinship systems.

The system of control of women, the original producers of human life and of labor power, is reproduced within the household and kinship structure of a particular society. In other words, to ensure the supply of labor power, a definite family and household structure must be maintained.

In a capitalist mode of production the domination of women by men and the use of unwaged female labor to reproduce men and male labor of relatively low value seem to be essential features of household structure and family relations—essential for the reproduction of capitalist society in general (von Werlhof, 1980). How they developed over time, together with or at the base of the capitalist world-economy, remains an open question.

Secondary Reproduction

The reproduction of social formations can be properly conceived only in a historical perspective as a dynamic process. Since the colonial era, the dominating factor in the development of these formations has been the expansion of capitalism on a worldwide scale. As a result of their incorporation into the world capitalist system, contemporary Third World social formations integrate capitalist and noncapitalist forms of production such as subsistence production, petty commodity production, and capitalist commodity production.

The debate over the concept of articulation of modes of production, while still being far from agreement on the definition of central concepts such as mode of production and social formation (see Wolpe [1980] for a discussion of the "state of the art"), has helped to shed light on the complex ways in which various relations of production are being combined within different economic systems in different historical periods.

As to the relationship between these forms, two main differing views can be identified within the current discussion. One claims that

> the world-economy is shaped by a single rationality (attributed to capitalism), that rationality is diffused to all enterprises within the system and all economic forms must be shaped to perform the single function of off-setting the declining rate of profit, supplying cheap labor, maximising capitalism's total surplus, etc. (Kahn, 1980: 204).

Consequently, it is assumed that either pre-capitalist forms are purposefully preserved in order to ensure the supply of cheap labor, or the capitalist mode of production transforms all non-capitalist relations (i.e., the capital-labor relation) into capitalist ones, even though some may still appear to be non-capitalist on the surface.

The other position maintains that the capitalist mode of production and other modes/forms are related in one way or another, but that not all of the latter are necessary for the reproduction of the capitalist mode (Wolpe, 1980: 1-42).

In any case, to assume a priori from a functionalist perspective that all forms of production within a social formation are articulated in such a way as to serve ultimately the sole purpose of reproducing capitalism, would be to underestimate or even to neglect the internal dynamics of forms of production and their potential resistence to transformation (Bradby, 1980; Evers & Schiel, 1979).

The expansion of capitalism on a world-wide scale has led to the destruction of "natural economy" (i.e., economies with dominating use-value production and limited trade relations) "reproductive forms of subsistence production" (Elwert & Wong, 1980) in Third World countries.

The most important mechanisms of this destruction have been

— interventions of the colonial state;
— the internal monetarization of traditional social relations;
— an increasing dependency on industrial products substituting traditional self-produced goods;
— the development of new needs;
— the destruction of the ecological equilibrium;
— the disintegration of the domestic economy, social obligations and traditional forms of reciprocal and collective labor (see Elwert & Wong, 1980).

Not all of these mechanisms have always and in all places worked simultaneously because of the specific internal structures and dynamics of particular precapitalist social formations. Nevertheless, some of them are closely interrelated.

The commercialization of peasant agriculture, the development of estate agriculture, industrialization and urbanization on the national level in Third World countries, and an increasing international division of labor have created a complex network of exchange relations.

While direct forms of appropriation through tenancy relations, wage labor, and the bureaucracy (taxation, corruption) are relatively easy to identify, the theoretical discussion regarding the nature of the other forms still shows considerable confusion, e.g., in the seemingly endless debate over unequal exchange and value transfer. Any empirical analysis of the articulation of different forms of production within a social formation will have to examine the flow or non-flow of goods and services between sectors, identifying the mechansims by which surplus is appropriated from the direct producer (including relations of power that ensure this appropriation).

It is certainly not sufficient to examine statistics on income distribution, nor is it satisfactory to deduce theoretically that class contradictions do exist. A dynamic analysis of group and class formation, which must include an analysis of the various levels of societal reproduction down to the primary reproduction level, will be necessary to enhance our understanding of long-term processes of societal development.

The Interrelation of
Subsistence and Market Production

As has been noted above, subsistence production is neither a relic of the past nor a form of underdeveloped agriculture but a part and precondition of any economy and society.[4] Peasants and proletarians, craftsmen and professionals, sweepers and executives are enmeshed in a complex system of subsistence production and reproduction. The way production is organized and how much subsistence production contributes differ, however, from society to society.

Labor is, of course, reproduced not only through subsistence production but also through market production. In Third World cities the "informal sector" of hawkers, food vendors, and small-scale food processing and service establishments takes a leading part in this reproduction. As those who work in the labor-intensive informal sector have to be reproduced in turn, a cumulative effect swells the ranks of the urban proto-proletariat[5] but also increases the relative importance of subsistence production.

The working class in developing countries spends up to one-quarter of its income on housing and rent, i.e., in our terminology, on habitat reproduction, and two-thirds or more on food, i.e., on household reproduction (Evers, 1981a; 1981b). Large parts of the urban and rural economy are thus determined by the primary reproduction sphere. Though the income utilized for household reproduction circulates largely amongst the "proto-proletariat" of hawkers and market vendors, wholesalers eventually establish the connection with the other capital-productive circuit of the urban economy. As recent studies have argued (e.g., Santos, 1979), surplus value is siphoned from the reproduction sector into the productive sector through these channels provided by commerical, particularly wholesale, establishments.

This combination of subsistence production and small commodity production in the informal sector is typical of the social structure of Third World cities. It also provides the basis for production in the formal sector, including industrial production. Labor can be employed in the formal sector at low wages because the reproduction costs of labor are kept low. In fact, subsistence production can be said to subsidize wage labor, as becomes even more clear when we consider rural-urban migration. In the countryside, human beings are reproduced with the help of a large contribution of rural subsistence production and migrate to urban areas as soon as they are productive and exploitable. A large part of their reproduction costs is thus born by the rural subsistence sector.[6]

This observation is, however, not confined to the urban economy: Plantations, transmigration, and settlement schemes all utilize labor power that has been produced and reproduced elsewhere. Examples of large-scale international migration, such as the transfer of indentured labor from India and China to colonial Southeast Asia, and the temporary migrant workers in free production zones *(Gastarbeiter)* in Western Europe have to be seen in this light.

For peasants, the maintenance of subsistence production of foodstuffs is often of vital importance as an insurance against the risk involved in cash-crop production: In cases of deteriorating prices on the cash-crop market, subsistence production alone guarantees the survival of the producer. At the same time, commodity production is again subsidized through subsistence production, in that a substantial part of the reproduction of peasant labor force is provided for outside the market (Elwert & Wong, 1980).

It is, therefore, not the "unlimited supply of labor" analyzed by Lewis (1954) but the existence of rural and urban subsistence production that, from our point of view, determines the structure of economy and society in underdeveloped areas on the periphery of the capitalist world-economy.

Subsistence production and market production are not stages in a process of development but closely interrelated and mutually determined aspects of a single process (Wallerstein, 1974: 389). There is practically no "subsistence economy" in which all that is produced is consumed by the producers, nor is there a "market economy" in which all goods and services are distributed through market channels. No society can function without subsistence production. Charlie Chaplin's nightmare of *Modern Times* in which he, as an industrial worker, is fed by a feeding machine, is as utopian as Robinson Crusoe's island subsistence economy.

The Organization of Primary Reproduction

Peasant Reproduction

The organization of peasant reproduction is determined by factors both internal and external to the households of which the domestic development cycle is the most important. Changes in the composition of the household influence the volume of the requirements for reproduction as well as the size of the labor force. Reproduction requirements have sometimes been analytically defined in terms of physical need (e.g., the minimum caloric intake necessary for survival). This approach may be useful for certain purposes, but we prefer to conceive those requirements as historically and socially defined.

The allocation of a household's labor force depends to some degree on the working capacity of its members, the culturally defined, internal division of labor, and the development of the productive forces. In Chayanov's theory of peasant economy, the labor-consumer balance is the key to the logic behind the family farm's economic activities. While drawing attention to important aspects of the internal dynamics of the domestic unit, Chayanov fails to develp an adequate conceptualization of the relations between households and also between individual households and the wider economy. The more recent approach of "New Household Economics" likewise focuses on the household's economic behavior on the micro level. Applying models of micro-economics originally developed in the context of advanced capitalist countries to developing societies, New Household Economics concentrates on the analysis of income, consumption, nutrition, fertility, and time allocation among rural households (Binswanger et al., 1980). Data on time allocation in particular have helped shed new light on the importance of household work rated as "unproductive" in conventional economic approaches. Apart from its undebatable merits, New Household Economics likewise does not adequately capture the external determinants of household economic behavior, such as differential access to means of production, and does not develop a time perspective.

Peasant reproduction does not take place in isolated units independent of each other but in households tied together through kinship, cooperative and reciprocal arrangements, and sometimes tenancy or wage-labor relations; and the conditions of reproduction are to a large extent determined by the "outside world" through the market and political structures. Any analysis of peasant reproduction that neglects these factors must remain inadequate.

The expansion of capitalism has profoundly changed the organization of peasant reproduction. Peasants have become linked to the market in several ways, namely through both the sale of part of their produce and the purchase of items of production consumption (agricultural inputs) and individual consumption such as food, clothes, and other household consumption items:

[T]he destruction of the conditions of natural economy simultaneously creates some of the social conditions of commodity production. ... As far as the peasantry is concerned, its simple reproduction comes to include the consumption of commodities to meet needs previously satisfied by the production (and simple exchange) of use-values. New needs also develop simultaneously with the erosion of an entire culture of production based in the previous systems of natural economy. Many traditional production skills, particularly in non-agricultural activities, become lost over time in the face of the pressures exerted by the process of commoditization (Bernstein, 1979: 424).

Destruction of the "peasant economy" does not necessarily imply a weakening of the basis for reproduction of peasant households. This may well occur if cash crops are introduced by force and replace or compete with staple food crops previously grown. In that case, deteriorating market conditions may immediately threaten the peasants' very existence. The situation is different if cash crops are grown through the mobilization of previously unused production capacties (land and labor reserves, "offseasons"). Then, the combination of subsistence production of foodstuffs and agricultural commodity production ("mixed production") is more likely to extend the peasants' reproduction basis.

Mechanisms of destruction of the peasant economy may pave the way for an increasing differentiation of peasantries.

Advantages in the conditions of production which are initially distributed randomly (household size and composition in terms of productive members, more fertile land, better access to sources of irrigation or transport, savings acquired from wage labor) can contribute to class differentiation, but this is by no means a necessary development. Differentiation in the materialist sense is tied to the conditions in which wealth becomes capital, when it is not consumed individually but productively through investment in means of production. It is this which gives a content to the classification of "poor", "middle", and "rich" peasants in terms of the relations of production (Bernstein, 1979: 430).

"Poor" peasants do own a plot of land, but regularly have to engage in wage labor to secure their reproduction because either their means of production or their family labor power are insufficient. "Middle" peasants reproduce themselves mainly through family labor on their own land, but in specific relations with other forms of production; they may also seasonally employ wage labor. "Rich" peasants are able to initiate and maintain a cycle of extended reproduction based on accumulation: They can afford to invest in means of production and employ wage labor (Bernstein, 1979: 431).

However, this classification appears to be too rough to examine adequately differentiation processes on the village level. For instance, it ignores the develoment of "occupational multiplicity", i.e., an increasing number of different economic activities by members of the households, which contribute substantially to their reproduction (White, 1976; Hartmann, 1981). The dynamics of the process of differentiation depend on a number of interrelated preconditions, the most important of which are differential access to land, employment opportunities for wage labor, and opportunities for the realization of capital.

Limited access to land or loss of land through indebtedness make peasants dependent on wage labor. Should employment opportunities be limited, these peasants may eventually be forced to emigrate. The emergence of a class of rich peasants, on the other hand, depends on actual opportunities for investing any surplus.

> [A]n understanding of the dynamics of peasant communities, requires an examination of the uses to which the surplus product which is the property of peasant A, can be put. In more isolated peasant areas there would be little or no opportunity for productive investment by peasant A. The family's only options would include increased consumption and ceremonial expenses. . . . The point is that investment is an option for some peasants (type A peasants) in noncapitalist areas incorporated within the capitalist system (Roseberry, 1976: 52f.).

The peasant might become a part-time trader, functioning as a "broker" between peasants and the capitalist system. Profits accumulated in the sphere of circulation might be invested in trading again, eventually making the peasant a "capitalist" trader, or in means of agricultural production, eventually turning the peasant into a capitalist farmer (Roseberry, 1976).

Urban Subsistence Production

The destruction of pre-capitalist subsistence production in rural areas has been a slow process that has never been completed. In fact, there are indications that a new type of subsistence production has arisen. This is most clearly seen in urban areas where subsistence production has become a major contributing factor in securing the survival of the urban masses (Evers, 1981a; 1981b). Having access to the means of reproduction, particularly urban space and urban housing, equals in importance the access to means of production, i.e., land in rural areas. The creation of a livable environment through personal work and the utilization of urban waste also opens access to trading in small commodity production and wage labor in the urban economy. Urban households, therefore, tend to be volatile: They have to adjust to a rapidly changing environment; they change in size and composition through the arrival of migrants from rural areas; and they have to adjust the distribution of their labor power to make use of suddenly arising opportunities to increase incomes from formal, informal, and subsistence sector activities.

The resulting units of reproduction are very complex, indeed, and cannot be described in simple demographic terms. Average figures on household size and household composition are particularly misleading. As internal migration within cities tends to be high either through "urban renewal" or the pressure of incoming migrants, it is difficult to establish the link between primary subsistence reproduction and the urban social formation on a macro level.

Methodological Problems in the
Analysis of Primary Reproduction

Determining the Unit of Analysis

The unit of analysis employed for the analysis of primary reproduction is usually the household, for statistical purposes, determined as the co-residential unit. This co-residential unit is then presumed to function as a unit of production and consumption, since, ultimately, it is taken to be the unit of reproduction. This procedure, however, is not entirely unproblematic; some households may indeed function as units of production and consumption, but others may not. To maintain, for example, that the household is the unit of consumption would imply two things: first, that consumption takes place within the boundaries of the household, and secondly, that income is, in fact, pooled and not consumed individually. In certain village societies, consumption at kinship, neighborhood, or village-level feasts may account for a significant percentage of total consumption, the unit of consumption thereby being a unit greater than the household. Neither can income-pooling within a household be presumed a priori (Wong, 1982).

Furthermore, even for peasant households, it is doubtful that the household can be unproblematically conceptualized as a unit of production. The central assumption of the model of the family farm, namely that of the absence of wage labor, does not hold true of the farm operations of many households today.

For purposes of empirical data collection, household-centered data have to be collected. Careful attention, however, should also be paid to the internal structure of power and distribution within the household, as well as to the way and the extent to which other households impinge on the household processes of production and consumption. Research should not be restricted to the household as *the* unit of analysis but should be directed to the identification of the different units (household, neighborhood, village, and so on) that may be constituted for different kinds of consumption and different reproduction needs.

Measuring Subsistence Production in Relation to Other Economic Activities

Attempts to measure subsistence production in quantitative terms are faced with serious problems. Two alternative (or perhaps complementary) measures appear to be available: the time spent on certain activities, and an assessment of the returns to these activities.

As to time budget studies, detailed records of the time spent by members of a domestic unit on different activities do help to gain insight to the internal organization of household reproduction. But there are problems with this approach when it comes to the assessment of the "value of time". To give just one simple example: Are the three hours the head of a household spends transplanting rice for wages more or less valuable to the family than the one hour one of his children spends collecting firewood to cook the evening meal?

Imputations of money values of subsistence goods (and services) are equally problematic. For one thing, these goods do not have an exchange value per definitonem; and calculations of costs of production for these goods apart from actual money inputs (e.g., fertilizer for food crops) finally lead back to the problem of measuring the value of time.

While the consideration of "shadow prices" for goods alternatively available on the market may be justifiable, the assignments of such prices for other goods are somewhat arbitrary. Finally, it appears to be almost impossible to determine the money value of household services such as food preparation (although in urban contexts one might use "shadow wages" based on wages paid to the servants who might alternatively perform these tasks) (Evers, Betke & Sundoyo, 1982).

The choice of techniques of measurement will have to be determined with regard to the specific goals and context of a particular study (and the working capacity and budget of the researcher). In any case, too strong an obsession with quantitative measurement alone is very likely to distract attention from more central questions of evaluation.

Stating that, for instance, subsistence production accounts for x percent of a household's total budget, represents a value of y dollars, and requires z percent of the household's labor time can help to substantiate, but never replace, another kind of argument; what matters is that the subsistence share may keep the urban slum dweller alive in the absence of other sources of income or may prevent the peasant from loosing his land through indebtedness or keep him from starving in case of a cash-crop failure (this is what we prefer to call the "strategic" importance of subsistence production).

Arguments of that kind, in turn, can be based only on an examination of both internal and external factors that determine the options households have in organizing reproduction.

NOTES

1. For an attempt to evaluate subsistence production, see Evers, 1981a; 1981b.
2. Research in the Sociology of Development Research Center, Faculty of Sociology, University of Bielefeld, has concentrated on subsistence production for some time. Several studies are found in: Arbeitsgruppe Bielefelder Entwicklungssoziologen, 1981, as well as in a number of papers by Veronika Bennholdt-Thomsen, Georg Elwert, Hans-Dieter Evers, Georg Stauth, Claudia von Werlhof, Tilman Schiel, Diana Wong, and other members of the SDRC.
3. Note, however, the debate initiated by Tilman Schiel (1977) over the conceptual usage of the term "value" in Marxist theory. According to Schiel, the precise formulation of the phenomenon observed should take the form not of the generation or transfer of surplus value but of the external savings according to capital.
4. The theoretical implications of the maintenance of subsistence production are elaborated in Evers and Schiel (1979).
5. This term has been used by McGee (1976) to designate those who work in the informal sector without being integrated into a formal wage-labor structure typical for proletariat-capitalist relations.
6. This thesis was particularly put forward in the discussion on migrant workers in Africa (see Meillassoux, 1975). Whether or not this thesis holds true is an empirical question that cannot be answered without referring to empirical data.

REFERENCES

Arbeitsgruppe Bielefelder Entwicklungssoziologen (1979). *Subsistenzproduktion und Akkumulation*, Bielefelder Studien zur Entwicklungssoziologie, Vol. 5. Saarbrücken: Breitenbach.
Bernstein, Henry (1979). "African Peasantries: A Theoretical Framework," *Journal of Peasant Studies*, VI, 4, July, 421-43.
Binswanger, H. P. et al., eds. (1980). *Rural Household Studies in Asia*. Singapore: Singapore Univ. Press.
Bradby, Barbara (1980). "The Destruction of Natural Economy," in H. Wolpe, ed. *The Articulation of Modes of Production: Essays from Economy and Society*. London: Routledge & Kegan Paul.
Elwert, Georg & Wong, Diana (1980). "Subsistence Production and Commodity Production in the Third World," *Review*, III, 3, Win., 501-22.
Evers, Hans-Dieter (1981a). "The Contribution of Urban Subsistence Production to Incomes in Jakarta," *Bulletin of Indonesian Economic Studies*, XVII, 2, 89-96.
Evers, Hans-Dieter (1981b). "Subsistence Production and Wage Labour in Jakarta," Working Paper No. 8, Forschungsschwerpunkt Entwicklungssoziologie, Univ. of Bielefeld, Fakultät für Soziologie.
Evers, H.-D., Betke, F. & Pitomo, S. (forthcoming) "The Complexity of Basic Needs: A Study on Poor Urban Households in Jakarta."

Evers, H.-D., Betke, F. & Sundoyo (1982). "A Survey of Low Income Households in Jakarta: Selected Summary Tables," Working Paper No. 17, Forschungsschwerpunkt Entwicklungssoziologie, Univ. of Bielefeld, Facultät für Soziologie.

Evers, Hans-Dieter & Schiel, Tilman (1979). "Expropriation der unmittelbaren Produzenten oder Ausdehnung der Subsistenzproduktion," in Arbeitsgruppe Bielefelder Entwicklungssoziologen, *Subsistenzproduktion und Akkumulation*, Bielefelder Studien zur Entwicklungssoziologie, Vol. 5. Saarbrücken: Breitenbach, 279-332.

Hartmann, J. (1981). *Subsistenzproduktion und Agrarentwicklung in Java/Indonesien*, Bielefelder Studien zur Entwicklungssoziologie, Vol. 13. Saarbrücken: Breitenbach.

Kahn, J.S. (1980). *Minangkabau Social Formations: Indonesian Peasants and the World-Economy*. Cambridge: Cambridge Univ. Press.

Lewis, W. A. (1954). "Economic Development with Unlimited Supply of Labour," *The Manchester School of Economic and Social Studies*, XXII, 2, May, 139-91.

McGee, T. G. (1976). "The Persistence of the Protoproletariat: Occupational Structures and Planning for the Future of Third World Cities," unpubl. ms., Canberra, Australian National Univ., Dept. of Human Geography.

Meillassoux, Claude (1975). *Femmes, greniers et capitaux*. Paris: Maspero.

Roseberry, William (1976). "Rent, Differentiation, and the Development of Capitalism among Peasants," *American Anthropologist*, LXXVIII, 1, Mar., 45-58.

Santos, Milton (1979). *The Shared Space: The Two Circuits of the Urban Economy in Underdeveloped Countries*. London: Methuen.

Schiel, Tilman (1977). "Einige kritische Anmerkung zu zentralen Aussagen: Meillassoux 'Die wilden Früchte der Frau'," Teil II, "Die Ausbeutung der haüslichen Gemeinschaft," unpubl. ms., Univ. of Bielefeld.

Wallerstein, Immanuel (1974). "The Rise and Future Demise of the World Capitalist System: Concepts for Comparative Analysis," *Comparative Studies in Society and History*, XVI, 4, Sept. 387-415.

Werlhof, Claudia von (1980). "Women's Work: The Blind Spot in the Critique of Political Economy," *Jornadas d'Estudi Sobre el Patriarcat*, Barcelona.

White, B. N. F. (1976). "Production and Reproduction in a Javanese Village," Ph.D. diss., Columbia Univ.

Wolpe, Harold (1980). "Introduction," in H. Wolpe, ed. *The Articulation of Modes of Production: Essays from Economy and Society*. London: Routledge & Kegan Paul.

Wong, Diana (1982). "The Household as a Unit of Analysis," unpubl. working paper, Univ. of Bielefeld.

3

HOUSEHOLDS AS INCOME-POOLING UNITS

Kathie Friedman

Fernand Braudel Center
State University of New York—Binghamton

Few categories of social science have been endowed with the special property or secret of being the foundation for the organization of social life.
Two come to mind: "value" and "household" (or "family"). It is the latter with which we are concerned. That household/family initially appears
here as a couplet is not incidental. Debates questioning the empirical and
analytical distinctiveness of each concept continue.[1] Yet, what remains particularly unacceptable is that a key edifice of social organization (building
block, as it were) such as the household/family should contain within its
boundaries all manner of unspecified material to such an extent that it is
often invoked as the "ultimate" explanation without itself being explained.

This chapter is a contribution to the discussion on households in the
capitalist world-economy, more precisely on the relationship between
household organization and the composition and structure of the labor force
in the world-economy. As such, it is a very specific intervention into the
efforts to unlock the "secret" of capitalist social organization, comprising
at once a narrow intent across the broad terrain of social science disciplines.

The first section begins with a brief review of three sets of literature
that relate to one aspect or another of labor-force patterns and household
organization: the sociology of the family/family history, women's studies,
and the literature on labor-force formation in the world-economy. This
review is not meant to be thorough or exhaustive; rather, it is an attempt
to highlight the themes of these literatures in order later to contrast and
to clarify a view of households and labor-force patterns emerging within
the Fernand Braudel Center's Research Working Group on Households,
Labor-Force Formation, and the World-Economy. The concern here is with

the intellectual problems posed by each set of literature, its theoretical concerns, and also debates within each set, since the three broad groupings tend to obscure considerable diversity. While the reference point of each set may be, in its own terms, the "household", all may be concerend with different objects, and hence each may ultimately have a different problem in mind. There is thus more at stake here than mere terminological ambiguity or confusion. There are, no doubt, more problems with these sets of literature than mere shortcomings or oversights. Part of the purpose of this section is to sort out what is useful from what is not and to illuminate where and possibly why critical gaps exist.

The second section of this chapter will focus on the discussions we've had in the Households Research Working Group. More specifically, the object there is to clarify how we have moved from certain observations about labor-force patterns in the capitalist world-economy to a concern with households as income-pooling units, and what we believe we can explain with this emerging conceptual tool. Our definition of household and its varying dimensions will be explored there.

The conclusion of the chapter will introduce several of the ongoing debates, controversies, and research problems that our new view of "households" has evoked within the Research Group itself.

Three Relevant Literatures

A.

Beginning in the 1950's, the sociology of the family/family history had increasingly turned its attention to the relationship between industrialization and changes in the structure and functioning of the family. This body of scholarly literature stressed four major aspects of the modern family.

(1) Following Talcott Parsons (1959) the form of the modern family was explained in terms of the manner in which it adapts to meet the needs of industrial society. This historical tendency of "structural differentation" was said to induce the family to perform its core/universal function, which had been obscured in previous societies. The modern family thus completely loses its "productive" functions and becomes a unit of socialization that is organized around reproduction, including consumption (see also Smelser, 1959; 1968). Industrialization is the independent variable, in this view, and the family is the dependent (passive) variable.

(2) The modern family becomes increasingly structurally isolated, nuclear in form, and more specialized or atomized in function. The material support for this group was assumed to be strictly endogamous, with little if any support for the unit being provided by individuals outside of it.

(3) Male and female tasks become more specified with industrialization. These structurally differentiated roles mean distinct, yet "complementary", male and female personality types. These roles are based on women's non-productive nurturing obligations on the one hand, and, on the other, the provision of the family's material needs primarily through the wage provided by men.

(4) These three changes in the family indentified in traditional family literature—the loss of "productive" functions; the universal nuclearization of the unit; and a strict division of labor between "non-produtive" women and fully waged men—are the effects of industrialization and occur wherever and whenever industrialization takes place.

This causal sequence, or evolutionary model, has been increasingly challenged since its formulation. William J. Goode suggests that the resultant conjugal family system may not be so fully in harmony with industrialization as the above account claims, and he notes several significant areas of a lack of adjustment between the needs of the modern family and those of the industrial system (1963: 12-17). He points to the theoretical possibility that the emergence of the conjugal family system—possibly in the fifteenth or sixteenth century in England—was itself an independent facilitating factor for industrialization, rather than the other way around.

Tamara Hareven (1975a) argues that the family and the industrial system were interacting partners in modernization. At certain stages of their developmental life cycle families were more independent than at other stages (see also Hareven, 1974; Glick, 1947; Glick & Park, 1965). Governed by their own demographic/internal rhythms, traditional families could make their own labor-force decisions and maintain controls over the careers of their members. At other points of their life cycle, the behavior of families was predominantly conditioned by the pressures and requirements of the industrial system. Contrary to previously cited studies, Hareven suggests that the most flexible/adaptable family form in the new industrial system was the extended family rather than the isolated nuclear/conjugal family. Nonetheless, on the model of the family cycle she proposes, the family appears as a *process* over time, rather than as a static unit within certain time periods. It assumes that individual families evolve through a variety of patterns of family and household organization during different stages of their life cycle. This perspective demands that historians of the family pursue longitudinal analysis (diachronic analysis), rather than the conventional "snapshot" cross-sectional analysis, which obscures considerable diversity and transformation (synchronic analysis). This is the predominant line of criticism directed against Peter Laslett and others in the Cambridge Group (Laslett & Wall, 1972; for critiques, see Anderson, 1971; Berkner, 1972; 1975; Hareven, 1975b). Drawings on statistical studies of early censuses,

Laslett concluded that since at least the sixteenth century the predominant, if not universal, family/household form has been nuclear (in terms of mean household size), both cross-culturally and over time. There is so little evidence of extended or stem-family households in the past that theories claiming a shift to a nuclear pattern with industrialization cannot be empirically validated. In other words, the existence of the nuclear family and its remarkable uniformity in size and composition in the centuries prior to the Industiral Revolution explode the idea of any functional interdependence between family/household and industrialization. The household emerges as a relatively autonomous and resilient social unit with regard to social change.

As mentioned, the work of Laslett and the Cambridge Group has not emerged without opponents. Their concern with establishing constancy in mean household size has obscured important variations among households of the same size and composition, but different in ethnic, class, occupational, or age compositon, to mention only several distinctions. In a similar vein, the Cambridge Group's methods have glossed over significant variations among households of the same size concerning internal allocation of tasks and distribution of resources among members, including the nature of the sexual division of labor within the households. Relations between households have also been overlooked. Only one section of the family, namely its co-residential unit, can be studied within the confines of the household as Laslett defines it. Significant kin networks linking households are ignored. "Because historians have tended to measure family 'extension' only by the presence of kin inside the household, they have imposed artificial boundaries on the family. The myth about the isolation of the 'modern' family is partly the result of this entrapment in the household cell" (Hareven, 1975b: 243).[2]

The notion of the developmental cycle of the household (or family life cycle) was formulated, in part, as a resolution of these problems. Yet this conceptual tool has been subject to many of the same criticisms it was developed to counter.

> Functional developmental theories have been based on a static ''domestic group'' composition which contains a more or less constant set of roles, functions, and purposes. These theories tend to assume a predictable, cyclical process of inner change from generation to generation which is closely associated with procreation, and which largely ignores changes in the surrounding society, the sources of those changes, and changes in external pressures that house organization and the systems it contains experiences (Woodford-Berger, 1981: 29).

B.

The growing body of literature associated with "women's studies", through its challenges to traditional family sociology, has drawn attention to new and heretofore relatively unexplored aspects of household organization. Among the more relevant questions, for us, raised by recent academic analyses of the situation of women in society are those concerning the following:

(1) the kind of work women perform within the household (alternatively termed the "domestic economy" and the "private sphere");
(2) ways of assessing the relative productive value of that work—the concern of those involved in the "domestic labor debates";[3] and
(3) the consequences such work has for women's relative status in cross-cultural contexts (including both status within the household and that within the waged labor market).

Despite considerable diversity in approach, there is fundamental consensus within this body of literature that the household should *not* be viewed as a cohesive unit. This is in marked contrast to conventional family history/sociology, which implicitly assumes a unity of interests among family/household members. However, mutual dependence does not guarantee lack of internal conflicts or basic differences of interests. In fact, it may well be that historical instances of family solidarity are what must be explained, rather than assumed. This basic consensus within women's studies is premised upon opposition to an additional, but related, aspect of the sociology of the family as it emerged in the 1950's—specifically, the tendency to neglect the increasing participation of women in the labor force and its effects on the organization of the family. Modernization was seen as leading to an egalitarian family life (see Goode, 1963; Gordon, 1978; Shorter, 1975). Insofar as the increasing participation of women in the labor force was noted, it was seen as further proof of this egalitarian trend. Women's earnings were assumed to translate into far greater leverage and independence for them in the family than they had in pre-industrial society. The critics from within women's studies suggested that such economic participation had little effect on the internal decision-making hierarchy within the household, and that, if anything, women's subordination was intensified, if not created with industrialization. Some went further and spoke of the enduring or transhistorical system of "patriarchy", insisting that any analysis of women's subordination centering on the economy inevitably missed this continuing feature of social structure (see, e.g., Hartmann, 1979; 1981).

A basic tenet within women's studies is the rejection of the equation of productive work with waged work. Initial contributors to the field underscored the fact that women throughout history have indeed "worked". This, despite the fact that women's contributions to *total* household income (particularly unwaged domestic labor, but also seasonal, temporary, or part-time waged work) did not show up in many historical documents (e.g., in censuses that use the category "housewives") or even in oral labor history interviews ("No, my wife didn't work" is a typical remark). This early emphasis quickly gave way to the recognition of the significance of women's work and their contributions to total household income, which often meant the difference between the survival of the household unit or its disintegration. Documentation of this aspect was often achieved by simply listing the kinds of activities in which wives and daughters have engaged. One interesting development in this area is the recognition of the centrality of women (and children) in linking sets of "kin-related" households. Such women-centered kin networks significantly affect an individual's or a family's access to economic resources (such as jobs and housing) as well as to community political leaderhsip (see Nieves, 1979; Schildkrout, 1978; Stack, 1974; and Yanagisako, 1977).[4]

For our purposes, the body of literature associated with women's studies has at minimum a dual significance. First, it represents an appreciation for the importance of non-wage forms of labor in the reproduction of proletarian households. (This importance has, implicitly or explicitly, been the subject of numerous articles on the relation of domestic labor and/or the family to capitalism.) Secondly, and related to the first point, this literature has validated the *varieties* of laboring and *remuneration still* available in a capitalist society. Further, it is not simply that this multiplicity or diversity of household income sources *still* exists, as a remnant of the past, so to speak, but that *it is maintained and reconstituted*, and thus it reopens a classical debate on the supposedly homogenizing tendencies of capitalism defined solely on the basis of the exploitation of the wage laborer.

C.

Recent research on the growth of the capitalist world-economy (e.g., Research Working Group on Cycles and Trends, 1977) has indicated that economic development, instead of being a replicable and linear process that takes place within national boundaries, is a complex global process of capital accumulation involving the construction of complementary rather than parallel structures in different zones of the world-economy (i.e., axial divison of labor). Furthermore, successive waves of technological and industrial innovation have marked the growth of the world-system from its genesis onward, successively re-organizing labor practices on a global scale. Within this long-term secular transformation of the content of "industrialization-modernization'' there seem also to be cycles of economic expansion and contraction, 40-60 years in length, (known variously as ''Kondratieffs'', ''A and B'' phases, or ''long cycles''). The relationship between households and labor-force patterns in the capitalist world-economy would then be viewed as shaped by these long-term and undulating economic transformations within which they are situated and to which they are in large measure a response. This is counter to previously mentioned studies on the sociology of families, which view their ''structure and function'' as the consequence of a single straight line of development from the terminus of ''industrialization''.

The growth of the capitalist world-economy is by its very nature uneven and differentiating in effect, and this phenomenon suggests a single worldwide division of labor organically linked via differences in integrated production processes and exchange. The various zones of this world-economy are organized relationally and hierarchically, with some units forming a core, others a semiperiphery, and still others a periphery. Within each of these zones there occur further hierarchical arrangements between high-wage and low-wage groups. The nature of these groups differs by variation in their remuneration as well as by the set of processes that distinguish the zones within which they are found. That is to say, high-wage groups in core areas, for example, will differ as much from the high-wage groups in the periphery as they do from low-wage groups in any of the zones.

Several important features regarding labor-force formation follow from these premises regarding the capitalist world-economy and its development (Wallerstein, 1979; 1981; 1982). Reversing a basic tenet of classical Marxist theory, world-systems theory holds that fully waged labor is *not* the defining feature of the capitalist mode of production, but rather a frequent and growing consequence of its development. That is to say, the existence of a multiplicity of labor forms has accompanied the growth of capitalism since its genesis, both as a cause and consequence. Since wage labor is probably the most expensive mode of labor from the viewpoint of the capitalist, it becomes clear why it has never been the exclusive, and until recently not even the principal, form of labor in the capitalist world-economy.

According to classical Marxist theory, capitalists have sought to increase full proletarianization because that was the source of surplus value, while workers have resisted exploitation. Paradoxically, in practice, capitalists giving priority to optimizing profits have often been led to pursue policies that have the consequence of slowing down full proletarianization. And workers have often, in practice, viewed wage work as preferable to other forms of labor, because it allows them to retain a higher amount of value than they could under other conditions. Another common assumption of classical Marxist theory is that the amount of value retained by the wage worker must be at least the minimum necessary to reproduce the labor force. Otherwise, they would be of no use; they would die, and with them so would the source of all value. But it is not true that employers must pay wage workers the amounts necessary for the reproduction of the labor force; in fact, under certain conditions they pay far less than the costs of reproduction.

This is often the case, particularly if the wage worker is part of a household with multiple sources of income (including subsistence, gifts, transfer payments, rent, profits, and the like), and if wage work is not lifelong, but rather an activity that is part-life-time (whether in terms of hours, months, seasons, years). In this situation the wage worker can subsist even if he or she earns *less* than a proportionate share of the total household's income fund, provided others in the household supplement the worker, or provided the worker, during other periods in his or her work life, contributes more than a proportionate share. What is occurring in this case is a "hidden" transfer of surplus value to the employer of the wage worker. To the extent that this is true (and it is for a large part of the global work force in areas where peripheral economic activities prevail), increased full proletarianization of the work force tends to *decrease*, not increase, the proportion of the surplus value transferred to the individual entrepreneur employing wage labor.

But capitalism is not without its contradictions. If full proletarianization has nonetheless been steadily increasing, it is because of two other aspects of the capitalist world-economy. First, while maximization of profit is best achieved for the individual entrepreneur by reducing labor-costs (i.e., by resisting full proletarianization), for collective capital as a world class, the reduction of wage payments reduces overall purchasing power as well as world aggregate demand, and therefore ultimately affects the realization of profit.

> The ability of the system as a whole to expand (necessary to maintain the rate of profit) regularly runs into the bottleneck of inadequate world demand. One of the ways this is overcome is by the social transformation of some productive processes from non-wage labor to wage labor processes [the full proletarianization of previously partially-proletarianized households]. This tends to increase the portion of produced value the producer keeps and thereby to increase world demand. As a result, the overall world-wide percentage of wage labor as a form of labor has been steadily increasing throughout the history of the capitalist world-economy (Wallerstein, 1979: 290-91).

Secondly, as previously mentioned, semi-proletarianized households have often struggled to achieve full proletarianization so as to retain more of the surplus value they create. The creation of mass workers' organizations—both trade unions and political parties—attests to this.

Each of the three areas of inquiry examined here—the sociology of the family/family history, women's studies, and studies of labor-force formation in the capitalist world-economy—taken individually or collectively, sheds some light upon the connections between the organization of the household and global labor-force patterns.

The following section will track the movement from some observations about the labor force in the world-economy to the Fernand Braudel Center's Research Group's interest in households.

The Relationship between Household Organization and Labor-Force Patterns in the World-Economy

Research efforts by members of the Household Research Working Group at the Fernand Braudel Center were initially motivated by what appeared to be two striking anomalies in the global labor force. First, despite the increasing numbers of people engaged in wage labor, only a minority of the world's population participate in the wage-labor force on a constant basis throughout their adult lives. Most work either part-time throughout their adult life or work full-time only sporadically. Secondly, behind the vast and apparently increasing wage disparities that parallel the growth of wage labor worldwide, one may observe that wage packets in areas of low wages do not approach levels necessary to sustain and reproduce the labor force over long periods of time.

With these observations forming our central problematic, we inaugurated research into the sets of institutional arrangements and social relationships that sustain and reinforce these vast differentials in labor-force particpation and levels of remuneration, especially where these disparities indicate wage levels below what is necessary to replenish the labor force over time (Wallerstein, Martin & Dickinson, 1979; 1982; Research Working Group on Households, 1982). Initial research, based upon the three sets of literature discussed previously and supplemented by anthropological and ethnographic literature, indicates that these labor-force discontinuities are supported through a set of organized practices that are responsible for the immediate sharing of income derived by labor and its products among a limited number of people who have specific responsibilities for the income shared. This sharing has as its explicit purpose the renewal of that capacity to labor on a daily basis and its replacement on a generational basis. More specifically, the observed differentials in both labor-force participation and remuneration can be sustained only under the condition that those receiving wages below what is necessary for full-life-time support have relatively stable and systematic access to support outside their own wage. This stability is assured through the set of relationships that are constituted by sharing obligations.

We have termed the *practices* that compose this sharing and ensure its continuity "householding". In this vein, "households" refers to the *set* of relationships between people that impose sharing obligations.

It should be immediately noted that our conceptualization of household differs quite substantially from the one that is posed in much of the conventional literatures reviewed. One crucial difference concerns the nature of household income, which is commonly understood to be equal to the sum of its parts. That is to say, each component of total household income is generally treated as having a definite and individual value quite independent of the other forms of income with which it is brought into contact via household practices and relationships. We believe that this is a major departure from what actually occurs.[5] In fact, the value of each form of total household income is a product of its being in relation to the other forms of income. The total household consumption fund is composed of a variety of labor relations that are drawn together, put into systematic relationship with each other, and derive significance only from being linked to one another. Householding practices are those which link these in a totality. Furthermore, it is only through this linkage that the resources originating in the different labor relationships have the capacity to sustain that labor and to replenish it across generations. To be quite specific, we posit five sources of income that are pooled into the household's collective consumption fund:

(1) wage labor/capital relationships with remuneration either in wages or in kind (whether these wages are paid in money or in kind makes a difference for the world-economy as a whole, but may not make a great difference to the household consumption fund);
(2) work outside market relations that results in directly consumable goods (these are most often called "subsistence" or "domestic labor" activities);
(3) labor in activities that lead to the sale of commodities on the market (this may be the result of "petty commodity production" or of "petty commerce");
(4) contractual relationships over the use of land, animals, equipment, money, etc., that lead to rental income; and
(5) transfer payments (gifts, subsidies, or any other income received without immediate reciprocal exchange of labor or commodities).

The income that is pooled by a household is normally derived from a multiplicity of labor relations (often all of the above), provided that one calculates income over a long period of time and provided that one takes into account the contributions that "come in" via *all* the members of a household—men and women, adults, children, and the elderly.

Another difference between our reconceptualization of households and the concepts previously attributed to conventional family history will be elaborated upon here. Households are *not* sets of definitive relationships finally shaped by industrialization, nor are they definitive sites. Nor is a household some kind of primordial unit that exists as a universal or trans-historical feature of "society in general", such that it predates the existence of the capitalist world-economy. While many have used the same nominal designation to refer to other units, "household" as we are using it here derives its social meaning from being one of the main institutional spheres of the world-economy. As such it has a genesis; it develops, and it is transformed and reconstituted in accordance with the rhythms of the world-economy. That is to say, households are sets of relationships the boundaries of which are relatively elastic in relation to (a) long-term secular changes of labor and productive processes, (b) medium-term cycles of economic growth and stagnation, and (c) variations between and within zones of the world-economy in which they are located. It thus follows that workers will be located in very different kinds of income-pooling arrangements throughout the world-economy according to these global processes and that it is in reference to such processes that we can determine who is and who is not a relevant contributor and recipient of the household consumption fund.

A third difference between our reconceptualization of households and the concepts of the conventional family/household literatures concerns the composition of the household unit. Quite often it is assumed that the "household" and the "family" refer to the same social unit—or at most refer to different aspects of the same unit. Family historians, sociologists, and anthropologists (although to a lesser degree) who have generally considered small communities, populations, or groups of "related" people who "live" (usually residing under one roof) and/or who somehow "work" together as "basic units" of study analytically and empirically, have typically resorted to the use of a single concept—household—to describe the nature of *the* structure enclosing these various relationships. In the view of the Household Research Working Group—and in the view of numerous critics of this approach—the conflation of the family with household has led to much conceptual confusion in general as well as totally obscuring the income-pooling practices toward which our research is directed (see Note 1 and Yanagisako [1975]).

> A major problem with the household as concept is the conflation of several dimensions into a single term: a physical or spatial dimension referring to a building; a social or demographic dimension which refers to a given population of people who inhabit, occupy, or somehow use the facilities of a spatial unit collectively and/or who interact in terms of certain sets of relationships between and among them, and a conceptual dimension referring to a relative area of being and action within a total system of ideas that together "make sense" of the world for a group of people (Woodford-Berger, 1981: 25).

Attempts to solve these problems of definition, boundary, and composition have led principally in one direction—towards the singling out of the physical or co-residential unit as *the* household—while the criterion for the family remains kinship or biological ties. Of course, physical units that are bounded and clearly discrete spatially are easier to distinguish and to classify. But in its historical usage, the concept of household linked the continuity of the family (kin) with the perenniality of settlement (control over property) in a particular location through the transmission of property rights in family inheritance schemes—thus the later conflation of the terms.

Clearly there are many cases wherein families (as kin-related units) do not share households (as co-residential units) and many more cases wherein households are not composed of families. Innumerable problematic cases in the ethnographic literature illustrate the difficulties in defining the boundaries of households if the sole criterion is residential propinquity. These cases raise questions about how to treat "residential" groupings that move through a seasonal cycle of dispersal and concentration, how to handle the movement of people between dwelling units (particularly in societies wherein there is normally and regularly great mobility between these units), whether to define as a single household the huts or houses that share a common "compound" which may or may not be enclosed from other "compounds" or "clusters", and whether to include servants, apprentices, boarders, and lodgers as members of the household. If the sole criterion in the usage of the term "household" is co-residentiality, there are certainly some discrepancies in its application. If individuals living alone ("solitaries") are generally regarded on this view as constituting households, why are institutions like orphanages, boarding schools, boarding homes, and even army barracks excluded? The emphasis on a single and universal criterion in attempts to define the household and distinguish it from the family easily leads to definitions that are either too restricted or else entirely too broad and all-conclusive.

Unfortunately, for our purposes the above attempts to distinguish family and household from one another and to delimit more clearly their respective boundaries/composition do not sufficiently capture the nature of the unit circumscribing income-pooling relationships. "Family" may or may not imply some sharing obligations. "Household" may imply only the sharing of one source of income. We have thus reconceptualized households not as a determinate set of people but as a set of relationships that impose a mutual obligation to pool resources from a multiplicity of labor forms whether or not one of those resources is a common residence.

We posit that the actual organization of householding practices and thus the structure of the household as an income-pooling unit may vary along the following five dimensions:

(1) the boundaries of membership defined by the operation of income-pooling (in terms of numbers, generations, kin-relatedness);
(2) the percentages of kinds of income-pooled (wages, profits, subsistence, rent, gifts) by age and gender of household members;
(3) the degree to which the household is co-residential;
(4) the allocation of tasks and rewards among household members (by gender and age group); and
(5) the structure of internal decision-making within the household allocation of tasks, allocation of rewards, and collective behavior vis-à-vis the outside world (including political action and investment).

Finally, our reconceptualization of the household, focusing on the set of relationships that arise around and facilitate the pooling of resources in different parts and times of the capitalist world-economy, now makes it possible to address some of the larger theoretical concerns of labor-force formation in the modern world. For example, how are the boundaries of income-pooling relationships—delimiting who is in and who is out—transformed, given changes in the composition of labor force? How do specific changes in the organization and composition of household relationships influence in one direction or another differentiation within households (especially with regard to a division of labor based on age and gender)? How do different boundaries and different constraints associated with the secular development and phases of contraction and expansion of the world-economy lead to householding variations (including divisions based on class and ethnicity) within the same zone or between zones? For example, do periods of contraction lead to an increase in non-wage productive activity and sources of income? Does the expansion of the world-economy increase formal labor-force participation and correspondingly decrease productive activity outside the formal sector of economic life? Are areas of high and low wages correspondingly separated by distinct productive activities dependent upon divergent householding practices? Has the increase in the proportion of the global labor force engaged in wage labor obscured increasing polarization in wage remuneration? If so, is this sustained only by householding activity outside the wage relationship?

The ongoing work of the Household Research Working Group aims at the generation and legitimacy of these types of questions while at the same time seeking their resolution.

Some Debates, Controversies, Research Dilemmas within the Fernand Braudel Center Households Research Working Group

Need it be mentioned that it would be unrealistic and misleading to feign absolute consensus, consistency, and completeness within the Households

Research Working Group regarding the project laid out in the preceding section? While we have every confidence that our reconceptualization of householding practices can lead to fruitful contributions concerning labor-force patterns in the world-economy, we are nevertheless particularly bothered by some questions that have consistently trailed us from nearly the beginning of the project to which we have given inadequate attention and/or never sufficiently resolved. This section poses three such questions for further research and study.

First, in the course of its development, the capitalist world-economy has developed various institutional structures that mediate its operations, one of which is the household. Studies on the world-system lead us to assume, correctly, that the household is in no sense a "primordial" unit; there is no essential, tranhistorical reality to the household that predates the existence of the capitalist world-economy. But are the dimensions we have isolated (particularly the five income sources and the five dimensions along which household organization varies) sufficiently specific to the dynamics and rhythms of the capitalist world-economy? Is there something "primordial" or "universal" about these features or variables we've chosen to concen-trate upon such that we could apply them equally well to social formations predating the emergence of the modern world? Is the obligation of a group of individuals to share resources and responsibilities for the purpose of renewing their capacity to labor on a daily and generational basis sufficiently specific to capitalism?

Preliminary discussions on this question within the working group have been insightful, but not yet satisfying. The following are some general sug-gestions from within the group for distinguishing households in the capitalist world-system from previous modes of social organization. With capitalism, the household becomes "specialized" as a reproductive unit in contrast to the previous existence of much larger units providing for reproduction of the labor force, such as the larger "community". Where units charged with decision-making and labor-allocation tasks were once relatively isolated and autonomous, now they have become integrated relational structures whose operations are subject to the pressures of the world-economy. Increasing commodification has narrowed the unit of reproduction—the unit that *ac-tually* shares obligations for pooling income—making it more geographically and occupationally mobile, which is a requirement of capitalism. Households are small enough and flexible enough in their operational units to ensure/regulate that mobility of resources, especially labor. The ultimate pressures on the individual are transmitted through the households, which ensure the "motivations" for "hard work". Furthermore, the household is the only cradle-to-grave unit reproducing the labor force since the emergence of the capitalist world-economy. Finally, as mentioned in a previous section, the continued expansion of the capitalist world-system requires the existence/re-creation of a multiplicity of labor forms in combination with each other. It is the household that serves to link these different sources of income/labor relationships together.

A second point of contention with the research group concerns the capacity of our household concept to incorporate *change* in household organization. Are we assuming, implicitly, that pressures for change are basically uni-directional—only from macro-social systems to the reorganization of internal household relationships and never vice versa? Do internal household dynamics have significant outward extensions/impacts?

Third, while we have gained much from our focus on the household as an income-pooling unit, as opposed to more conventional conceptualizations limited to either kinship or co-residential ties between individuals, we have consistently run into a problem of household boundaries, membership, and composition—and thus a problem with available data sources. Income-pooling practices clearly extend beyond biological kinship and bind individuals who are dispersed geographically. Consider a current example that is commonly found in very low-waged urban areas in the United States: The individual who eats in one household may sleep in another, and contributes resources to yet another. Can an individual be a member of multiple households? Income-pooling appears to have rather complex, circuitous, and overlapping boundaries. One suggestion from within the research group is to conceive of two types of income-pooling arrangements—one, a long-term household with life-time obligations and rights ensuring exchanges among a core group and the other, a short-term household with less cohesive networks between fictive kin, "friends", neighbors, and co-workers that exist for specific purposes and for a shorter duration.

Obviously these questions can be resolved only partially on an abstract or conceptual level. A more thorough examination of historical and ethnographic material in conjunction with the continual refinement and reassessment of our conceptualizations is in order.

NOTES

1. That the debate over the distinctiveness between "household" and "family" has not yet been conclusively resolved is not for lack of trying. Some noteworthy examples of efforts in this direction include Bender (1967), Flandrin (1979), Goody (1972), Laslett (1972), Rapp (1978), and Woodford-Berger (1981).

In a summary evaluation of these attempts, Prudence Woodford-Berger states

Concepts such as houseful, simple family households, extended family households, multiple family households, nuclear family households, elementary family units, domestic groups, domestic households, dispersed households, domestic communities, household complex, expanded households, household collectivities, and many more—

some of which appear to be bafflingly redundant—are examples of attempts to refine the concepts of family and household in order to describe *where* the people are *who* somehow form a *cohesive group* (in one place or spread out), as well as vaguely *how* we are to infer that they form a group at all (1981: 26).

2. Michael Anderson's (1971) work on kin networks during the height of England's industrialization, indicating the extensive use of kin made by those laboring in the mills (particularly by rural migrants) points to the much longer-term functionality of kin even in an urban-industrial setting. His work suggests, contrary to Laslett, as well as to Parsonian family sociologists, that the size of the household *increased* with industrialization.

3. A large and growing literature, commonly referred to as "the domestic labor debates", has developed in the past nine to ten years. Key works include Anthias (1980), Barrett (1980), Barrett & McIntosh (1980), Beechey (1977; 1978), Coulson, Magas, and Wainright (1975), Dalla Costa and James (1973), Deere (1979), Edholm, Harris, and Young (1977), Fee (1976), Gardiner (1975; 1976), Gardiner, Himmelweit, and Mackintosh (1975), Gerstein (1973), Gough and Harrison (1975), Harrison (1973), Himmelweit (1974), Himmelweit and Mohun (1977), Humphries (1977), James (1973; 1975), Macintosh (1977; 1979), Meillassoux (1975), Molyneux (1979), Seccombe (1974; 1975), Smith (1978), Tilly and Scott (1978), Weinbaum and Bridges (1979), Vogel (1973), and von Werlhof (1979).

4. For an excellent introduction to the analysis of child labor in the world-economy—drawing on and developing, in large part, as a "sub-discipline" of "women's studies"—see Child Labor Workshop (1981).

5. An important exception to the conventional understanding of the nature of household income and organization are the views of Prudence Woodford-Berger, who states,

> The house unit represents a fundamental organizational area for the marshalling and channeling of different kinds of collective resources from and to and through its members. . . . It is within house organization that people's differential options for social action are determined and coordinated. These options are in turn the outcome of a continual assessment of needs and of rights of house members in relation to one another at a particular time (1981:15).

REFERENCES

Anderson, Michael (1971). *Family Structure in Nineteenth-Century Lancashire*. Cambridge: Cambridge Univ. Press.

Anthias, Floya (1980). "Women and the Reserve Army of Labour: A Critique of Veronica Beechey,"*Capital and Class*, No. 10, Spr., 50-63.

Barrett, Michèle (1980). *Women's Oppression Today: Problems in Marxist Feminist Analysis*. London: NLB.

Barrett, Michèle & McIntosh, Mary (1980). "The 'Family Wage': Some Problems for Socialists and Feminists," *Capital and Class*, No. 11, Sum., 51-72.

Beechey, Veronica (1977). "Some Notes on Female Wage Labour in Capitalist Production," *Capital and Class*, No. 3, Aut., 45-66.

Beechey, Veronica (1978). "Women and Production: A Critical Analysis of some Sociological Theories of Women's Work," in A. Kuhn & A. M. Wolpe, eds., *Feminism and Materialism*.London: Routledge and Kegan Paul, 155-97.

Bender, D. R. (1967). "A Refinement of the Concept of Household: Families, Co-residence, and Domestic Function," *American Anthropologist*, LXIX, 3-4, June-Aug., 493-504.

Berkner, Lutz (1972). "The Stem Family and the Developmental Cycle of the Peasant Household: An Eighteenth-Century Austrian Example," *American Historical Review*, LXXVII, 2, Apr., 398-418.

Berkner, Lutz (1975). "The Use and Misuse of Census Data for Historical Analysis of Family Structure," *Journal of Interdisciplinary History*, V, 4, Spr., 721-38.

Child Labour Workshop (1981). "Working Children: An International Perspective," unpubl. report of the Child Labour Workshop held at the Institute for Development Studies, Univ. of Sussex, January 5-8.

Coulson, Margaret, Magas, Branca & Wainright, Hilary (1975). "The Housewife and her Labour under Capitalism—A Critique," *New Left Review*, No. 89, Jan.-Feb., 59-71.

Dalla Costa, Maria & James, Selma (1973). *The Power of Women and Subversion of the Community*. Bristol: Falling Wall.

Deere, Carmen D. (1979). "Rural Women's Subsistence Production in the Capitalist Periphery," in R. Cohen, P. Gutkind & P. Brazier, eds., *Peasants and Proletarians*. New York: Monthly Review Press, 133-48.

Edholm, Felicity, Harris, Olivia & Young, Kate (1977). "Conceptualizing Women," *Critique of Anthropology*, III, 9-10, 101-30.

Fee, Terry (1976). "Domestic Labour: An Analysis of Housework and its Relation to the Production Process," *Review of Radical Political Economy*, VIII, 1, Spr., 1-8.

Flandrin, Jean-Louis (1979). *Families in Former Times*. Cambridge: Cambridge Univ. Press.

Gardiner, Jean (1975). "Women's Domestic Labour," *New Left Review*, No. 89, Jan.-Feb., 47-58.

Gardiner, Jean (1976). "The Political Economy of Domestic Labour in Capitalist Society," in D. L. Barker & S. Allen, eds., *Dependence and Exploitation in Work and Marriage*. London: Longman.

Gardiner, Jean, Himmelweit, Susan & Macintosh, Maureen (1975). "Women's Domestic Labour," *Bulletin of the Conference of Socialist Economists*, IV, 2, 1-11.

Gerstein, Ira (1973). "Domestic Work and Capitalism," *Radical America*, VII, 4-5, July-Aug., 101-28.

Glick, Paul C. (1947). "The Family Cycle," *American Sociological Review*, XII, 2, Apr., 164-74.

Glick, Paul & Park, Robert Jr. (1965). "New Approaches in Studying the Life Cycle of the Family," *Demography*, Vol. II, 187-202.

Goode, William J. (1963). *World Revolution and Family Patterns*. Glencoe, IL: Free Press.

Goody, Jack (1972). "The Evolution of the Family," in P. Laslett & R. Wall, eds., *Household and Family in Past Time*. Cambridge: Cambridge Univ. Press, 103-24.

Gordon, Michael, ed. (1978). "Introduction," in M. Gordon, ed., *The American Family in Socio-Historical Perspective*. New York: St. Martin's Press.

Gough, Ian & Harrison, John (1975). "Unproductive Labour and Housework Again," *Bulletin of the Conference of Socialist Economists*, IV, 1.

Hareven, Tamara (1974). "The Family as Process: The Historical Study of the Family Cycle," *Journal of Social History*, VII, 3, Spr., 322-29.

Hareven, Tamara (1975a). "Family Time and Industrial Time: Family and Work in a Planned Corporate Town, 1900-1924," *Journal of Urban History*, I, 3, July, 365-89.

Hareven, Tamara (1975b). "Review Essay: *Household and Family in Past Time*," *Theory and History*, XIV, 2, 242-51.

Harrison, John (1973). "Political Economy of Housework," *Bulletin of the Conference of Socialist Economists*, III, 1, 35-51.

Hartmann, Heidi (1979). "Capitalism, Patriarchy, and Job Segregation by Sex," in Zillah Eisenstein, ed., *Capitalist Patriarchy and the Case for Socialist Feminism*. New York: Monthly Review Press, 206-47.

Hartmann, Heidi (1981). "The Unhappy Marriage of Marxism and Feminism: Towards a more Progressive Union," in Lydia Sargent, ed., *Women and Revolution*. Boston: Southend Press, 1-41.

Himmelweit, Susan (1974). "Domestic Labour and the Mode of Production," *Bulletin of the Conference of Socialist Economists*, III, 1.

Himmelweit, Susan & Mohun, Simon (1977). "Domestic Labour and Capital," *Cambridge Journal of Economics*, I, 1, March, 15-31.

James, Selma (1973). "Women, the Unions and Work, or . . . What is not to be done," *Radical America*, VII, 4-5, July-Oct., 51-72.

James, Selma (1975). *Sex, Race, and Working Class Power*. Bristol: Falling Wall/*Race Today* Publications.

Laslett, Peter (1972). "Introduction," in P. Laslett & R. Wall, eds., *Household and Family in Past Time*. Cambridge: Cambridge Univ. Press, 1-89.

Laslett, Peter & Wall, Richard, eds. (1972). *Household and Family in Past Time*. Cambridge: Cambridge Univ. Press.

Macintosh, Maureen (1977). "Reproduction and Patriarchy: A Critique of Meillassoux, *Femmes, greniers et capitaux*," *Capital and Class*, No. 2, Aut., 119-27.

Macintosh, Maureen (1979). "Domestic Labor and the Household," in Sandra Burman, ed., *Fit Work for Women*. Canberra: Australian National Univ. Press, 173-91.

Meillassoux, Claude (1975). *Femmes, greniers et capitaux*. Paris: Maspero.

Molyneux, Maxine (1979). "Beyond the Domestic Labour Debate," *New Left Review*, No. 116, July-Aug., 3-27.

Nieves, Isabel (1979). "Household Arrangements and Multiple Jobs in San Salvador," *Signs*, V, 1, Aut., 134-42.

Parsons, Talcott (1959). "The Social Structure of the Family," in R. N. Anshen, ed., *The Family: Its Function and Destiny*. New York: Harper, 173-201.

Rapp, Rayna (1978). "Family and Class in Contemporary America: Notes toward an Understanding of Ideology," *Science and Society*, XLII, 3, Fall, 278-300.

Research Working Group on Cycles and Trends of the Modern World-System (1977). "Patterns of Development of the Modern World-System: A Research Proposal," *Review*, I, 2, Fall, 111-45.

Research Working Group on Households, Labor-Force Formation, and the World-Economy (1982). "Household Structures and the World-Economy," unpubl. ms., Fernand Braudel Center, SUNY-Binghamton.

Schildkrout, Enid (1978). "Age and Gender in Hausa Society: Socio-Economic Roles of Children in Urban Kano," in J. S. LaFontaine, ed., *Sex and Age as Principles of Social Differentiation*. New York: Academic Press, 109-37.

Seccombe, Wally (1974). "The Housewife and her Labour under Capitalism," *New Left Review*, No. 83, Jan. 3-24.

Seccombe, Wally (1975). "Domestic Labour—Reply to Critics," *New Left Review*, No. 94, Nov.-Dec., 85-96.

Shorter, Edward (1975). *The Making of the Modern Family*. New York: Basic Books.

Smelser, Neil (1959). *Social Change in the Industrial Revolution*. London: Routledge and Kegan Paul.

Smelser, Neil (1968). "Sociological History: The Industrial Revolution and the British Working-class Family," in M. W. Flinn & T. C. Smout, eds. *Essays in Social History*, Oxford: Oxford Univ. Press, 23-38.

Smith, Paul (1978). "Domestic Labour and Marx's Theory of Value," in A. Kuhn & A. M. Wolpe, eds., *Feminism and Materialism*. London: Routledge and Kegan Paul, 198-219.

Stack, Carol (1974). *All Our Kin: Strategies for Survival in a Black Community*. New York: Harper.

Tilly, Louise A. & Scott, Joan W. (1978). *Women, Work, and Family*. New York: Holt, Rinehart and Winston.

Vogel, Lise (1973). "The Earthly Family," *Radical America*, VII, 4-5, July-Oct., 9-50.

Wallerstein, Immanuel (1979). "Class Conflict in the Capitalist World-Economy," in I. Wallerstein, ed., *The Capitalist World-Economy*. Cambridge: Cambridge Univ. Press, 283-93.

Wallerstein, Immanuel (1981). "Cities and Socialist Theory and Capitalist Praxis," unpubl. paper delivered to the Tenth World Congress of Sociology, Mexico City, August 16-21.

Wallerstein, Immanuel (1982). "Crisis as Transition," in S. Amin, G. Arrighi, A. G. Frank & I. Wallerstein, eds., *Dynamics of Global Crisis*. New York: Monthly Review Press, 11-54.

Wallerstein, Immanuel, Martin, William G. & Dickinson, Torry (1979). "Household Structures and Production Processes: Theoretical Concerns, plus Data from Southern Africa and Nineteenth-Century United States," unpubl. Fernand Braudel Center Working Paper, SUNY-Binghamton.

Wallerstein, Immanuel, Martin, William G. & Dickinson, Torry (1982). "Household Structures and Production Processes: Preliminary Theses and Findings," *Review*, V, 3, Win., 437-58.

Weinbaum, Batya & Bridges, Amy (1979). "The Other Side of the Paycheck: Monopoly Capitalism and the Structure of Consumption," in Z. Eisenstein, ed., *Capitalist Patriarchy and the Case for Socialist Feminism*. New York: Monthly Review Press, 190-205.

Werlhof, Claudia von (1979). "Women's Work: The Blind Spot in the Critique of Political Economy," unpubl. ms., Univ. of Bielefeld.

Woodford-Berger, Prudence (1981). "Women in Houses: The Organization of Residence and Work in Rural Ghana," *Anthropologiske Studies*, Women: Work and Household Systems, 30-31-1981, Kungl. Univ.; Socialantropologisks Institutiones S-10691-Stockholm, Sweden.

Yanagisako, Sylvia Junko (1977). "Women-Centered Kin Networks in Urban Bilateral Kinship," *American Ethnologist*, IV, 2, May, 207-26.

Yanagisako, Sylvia Junko (1979). "Family and Household: The Analysis of Domestic Groups," *Annual Review of Anthropology*, No. 8, 161-205.

4

THE LIMITS OF
USING THE HOUSEHOLD
AS A UNIT OF ANALYSIS

Diana Wong
Sociology of Development Research Center
University of Bielefeld

The recent revival of interest in the household as a unit of analysis in the social science literature is reflected primarily in two disciplines traditionally separated by their areas of concern as well as by their perspectives and methodologies, namely, economic anthropology and historical sociology. Of central concern to the former was the allocational behavior of the household as a joint unit of production and consumption, and to the other, the structure of the family and its possible changes over time. Underlying both approaches, however, is the shared conception of the household as *the* unit of consumption within which the reproduction of human labor, or of the individual, is assured.

The specificity of the household as a productive unit, as formulated by Chayanov (1966), will not be discussed here. Suffice it to say, in this respect, that the assumptions postulated by Chayanov in his model of the peasant family farm—the absence of wage labor and of land scarcity—no longer hold for the majority of the societies we are dealing with today. Furthermore, his insistence on the household as a unit of analysis led him to ignore the issue of inter-household relations as well as the wider socioeconomic context in which households operate.

This chapter is concerned with the conceptualization of the household as a "unit of consumption and reproduction of the labor force", which also forms the point of departure for models of the household as a unit of production. In fact, the close theoretical association between the production and consumption aspects of the household is seen in the fact that Wallerstein and associates, with their programmatic definition of the household as "the unit that ensures the continued reproduction of labor through the consumption of a collective fund of material goods" (Research Group on Households and Production Processes, 1978: 5), nonetheless add that "the ultimate pressures on the individual are transmitted through the households, the household ensuring the 'motivations' for hard work" (Wallerstein, 1981: 2).

The implicit premise of these approaches, I shall argue, is the misconceived one of a benevolent despotism structuring the distribution of pooled income between household members, so that "households are by definition one-class, since the component members of classes are households and not individuals" (Wallerstein, 1981:2). It is assumed that the survival of the individual is assured through the pooling of income with others within a household unit, with a premium thus attached to larger, extended units for the survival of economically weak individuals.

Income-Pooling, Redistribution, and the Patriarchal Family

"Householding" was identified by Polanyi (1957) as a possible fourth form of economic integration, although he adds that this is merely a subform of redistribution. "The principle remains the same—collecting into, and distributing from, a centre." He goes on to add that "the best known instances are the Central African kraal, the Hebrew Patriarchal household, the Greek estate of Aristotle's time, the Roman familia, the medieval manor, or the typical large peasant household before the general marketing of grain" (Polanyi, 1957:254). Alternatively, as an economist noted, "the presumption of a family utility function. . . [would fit]. . . the male-dominated families of much of the low income world (Evanson, 1976:91).

Indeed, it is evident that income-pooling requires cooperation and that a collective consumption fund requires administration. Households defined in such terms or, more specifically, functioning in such a fashion, can only be based on a structure of authority derived from specific forms of family structure. The propensity for sharing and the existence and acceptability of paternal authority cannot simply by assumed as given.

The struggle over labor-force allocation may thus take place not merely between the household and capitalism, but within the household itself. This inner-household struggle can be seen on two levels. One is the by now fairly often documented attempt to control child labor (see, e.g., White, 1976). The other is the perhaps more fundamental one of who is allowed to reproduce in the first place, i.e., to establish a family and a household. In many systems practicing primogeniture or ultimogeniture, for example, the eldest or youngest child respectively was often the only one able to marry, with the siblings remaining as unmarried members of the household (see Elwert, this volume).

The stability of the household as a unit of consumption and reproduction thus rests to a large extent on the acceptance of an unequal distribution of consumption goods, resting ultimately on the unequal access to productive resources, best exemplified in patriarchally organized nuclear or extended type families.

There is reason to believe, however, that this is not always the case, especially where a multiplicity of income sources accruing to a number of household members individually is characteristic of the "income pool". A study of the household budget of fifteen households in a Malaysian village indicated that separate accounts were strictly adhered to within households with members earning off-farm income (Wong, 1981). Income-earning members often, but not always, contribute a percentage of their income to the family head, or more often, to his spouse, but this has more the character of a gift transfer than of income-pooling.

Even more instructive is the form that household budgeting takes in West Africa. Although they are lineally organized, a decisive element in these societies seems to be the fact that the woman never loses membership in her lineage of origin. Especially in those areas in the south, where petty trading has provided women with an independent income, a situation has arisen where, in principle as well as in practice, husbands and wives maintain separate accounts (Sègbènou; 1982 see also Elwert, this volume). A household with a collective consumption fund to assure the reproduction of its constituent members would be the exception rather than the rule.

Income Pooling and the
Stability of the Household Unit

Closely related to the need for authority centered on the household head, is the need for stability in the constitution of the household unit, should a collective consumption fund be maintained in a viable fashion. Marital instability however, threatens the reproduction of the labor force within stable household units and, in fact, seems to be a widespread phenomenon in many parts of the periphery. Sègbènou (1982), among others, has noted that this is true in West Africa, precisely because the ultimate guarantor of a woman's reproduction is her lineage of origin, and not the household she may only temporarily be married into. In the Malaysian village, where nuclear families were said to be the norm, I found to my surprise a significant number of "denuded" households composed primarily of single, aged females or female heads with a child or grandchild. More than half of those classified as poor households in this village were of this nature, dependent for their reproduction on transfers from other households (Wong, 1981). The same phenomenon is reported in a study of a Peruvian village by Deere, who notes,

> The instability of the household as a unit of production and reproduction is evident in considering the number of abandoned or separated female heads of household residing in the countryside. In the 1976 sample of 105 households, 16% were female headed. Almost half of these were constituted by abandoned or separated women with the remainder, widows....Significantly, all these households belong to the landless and minifundio strata (1978:26).

The instability of the household unit implies that, for the women and children in particular, units other than the household may, in times of crises, be crucial to their survival.

Transfers and Networks

It was noted above that other units may be guarantors of the reproduction of individual members of the household in times of personal life crises. Here, I would like to mention the important role that transfers from other households constantly play in the survival of individual household units.

In the Malaysian household budget study, of the five poor households, three were highly dependent on transfers. In one, it accounted for 13% of the total net income, in another, for 26%, and in the third for 53% (Wong, 1981). This is by no means insignificant, forcing us to look again beyond the household as a unit of reproduction.

Again, the phenomenon of households incapable of assuring their own reproduction does not seem to be an isolated one. It is interesting that Sahlins's formulation of the "Domestic Mode of Production" composed of "subsistence-redoubt households" (Research Group on Households and Production Processes, 1978) includes the element of "household failure" (Sahlins, 1972).

> In any large enough community the several households will show a considerable range in size and composition, range that may well leave some susceptible to disastrous mischance. For some must be favourably composed in the ratio of effective workers to dependent non-producers (mostly children and the aged). Of course others are in this respect more fortunately balanced, even overbalanced, on the side of capable producers. Yet any given family is subject to this kind of variation over time and the domestic growth cycle, just as at any given time certain families must find themselves facing economic difficulties. Thus a third apparent dimension of primitive underproduction:

an interesting percentage of households chronically fail to provide their own customary livelihood (Sahlins, 1972: 74).

In the Malaysian village in which I worked, the constant threat to the household's ability to reproduce itself was met by developing ties of transfer either to close kin or to a patron. Every household, I was told, must have a *tempat orang bergantungan* (place we can depend on). This security of credit was of considerable concern to most household heads and, in keeping with this, loans taken from the urban middleman, for example, were seldom repaid in full in order to maintain one's credit-worthiness.

It may be argued that, because "as a unit of consumption and reproduction of the labor force, the household is differentiated from the family, co-resident dwelling groups, and kinship structures" (Research Group on Households and Production Processes, 1978), and in the face of the above situation, the household should not be limited to the co-residential dwelling unit but extended to cover those units that participate actively in the reproduction of the members of the household. The problem with such a formulation, it seems to me, is that a closer examination of the pattern of transfers and exchange reveals a system more indicative of a network pattern with different rules for different kinds of goods and services than of "isolated", tightly bounded, internally coherent household units with little to do with each other.

Transfer payments between a set of closely related kin groups living in separated residential units do not involve the notion of a collective consumption fund to be shared according to need. Transfers often take the form of provision of a specific good or service made necessary due to extraordinary circumstances, e.g., the payment of taxi rental for transportation of the sick mother to hospital, or payment for the sister's school books. On the other hand, one may not feel obliged to contribute to raising the general level of daily consumption in the kin-related household.

Furthermore, the notion that non-capitalist transfers and non-market social relations are of an egalitarian nature and are diametrically opposed to principles of capitalist accumulation should be discarded. As I have tried to show in another paper (Wong, 1982), the internal dynamics of the system of inheritance and usufruct over land and labor can be and were used for accumulative purposes and account for a large part of the social differentiation between households in the village today. In a similar vein, it was noted that for the largest wedding feast that took place in the village in 1980, which involved a total expenditure of 4000 Malaysian dollars, 3000 was raised via transfers while the household head incurred cash expenses of not more than 628 dollars. To a large extent, these transfers were a kind of loan, to be reciprocated on the occasion of some other person's wedding feast. With the aid of these transfers however, the household head was able to devote his own resources to the renting of an additional 3 re. of land during that season.

The notion of the household as an income-pooling unit tends to see the household as an isolated entity and to deny the significance of inter-household relations. Thus, Wallerstein and the rest of the Fernand Brandel Center's Research Group on Households and Production Processes argue that

> Social networks (such as kin networks), which in subsistence redoubt areas provide support for the household processes of consumption and reproduction, come increasingly under attack after incorporation of peripheral zones. This occurs despite vigorous attempts to retain non-market methods of the distribution of goods and non-market social relations (i.e., the principles of capitalist exchange and production increasingly penetrate the arenas of social interaction)" (1978: 7).

Against the notion of non-capitalist sharing networks having given way in the periphery to isolated household units, empirical field research suggests the following:

(1) Non-market methods of the distribution of goods and non-market social relations may have a supportive role to play in surplus accumulation, not merely for the capitalist center, but also within and between households.
(2) Processes of consumption and reproduction are not necessarily confined to the isolated household as a self-sufficient unit.

It is at this point, I think, that we see the limitations of an analysis in terms of *units* (entities). The complicated pattern of transfers, which can be identified not only for many societies in the present periphery but also for present-day core countries in the earlier years of their development (see Davin, this volume), suggests that the *extensional* character of network ties is as crucial (if not more so) to the reproduction of the individual as to the *inclusion* principle of bounded units.

Households and Classes

The same critique against Chayanov's treatment of the household as a unit of production and consumption thus also applies to current attempts to treat it as a unit of reproduction. The household is seen as an internally coherent, tightly bounded entity whose internal dynamics have to be examined but whose reproduction takes place essentially without any reference to other households. Insofar as Wallerstein locates the household within the capitalist world-economy, account is taken in this case of the wider social-economic context in which households have to operate, but the same indifference is exhibited towards inter-household relationships. Thus the research procedure spelled out in the 1978 paper of the Research Working Group on Households and Production Processes calls for research into four areas— time-allocation studies, household budget studies, shifting boundaries and size of the household, and finally the mobility of households and household members—all within the household and its defined boundaries.

It seems to me that it is this emphasis on the household as *the* unit of analysis that has led to the tremendous difficulties faced in the issue of differentiation, for example, in the field of peasant studies. Given its basic premise—that of an economically viable coherent entity—one can only argue that households are homogeneous or are class-differentiated, both positions being essentially the opposite faces of the same coin. The implications are clearly stated by Wallerstein: "Households are by definition one-class, since the component members of classes are households and not individuals" (1981: 2). The question is, Are households, as they are presently constituted, component members of classes, i.e., are the reproduction chances of the household members determined entirely by their position within the household? Especially when a long-term time perspective is taken into account, most of us are left with the uncomfortable feeling that the units observed were neither class-differentiated nor homogeneous. Closer attention to the nature of inter-household relations (without the a priori assumption that these are non-market social relations and therefore egalitarian) should help clarify the issue.

Conclusion

Underlying recent interest in the household as a unit of analysis is its conceptualization as an internally coherent, clearly bounded entity (unit) within which the process of reproduction occurs, and via which labor force participation is regulated. The fundamental fallacy in this conceptual approach lies in its methodology—that of an analysis built around a unit defined a priori rather than analytically derived concepts that would focus attention on processes. Reproduction has to be maintained (see Evers, Clauss & Wong, this volume), both at the primary and secondary level. The actual processes involved, however, may rest on principles of extension (network) or inclusion (unit). The theoretical option for inclusion, in the definition of the household as an income-pooling unit functioning as the "basic building block" of the system (Research Working Group on Households and Production Processes, 1978) is one that households themselves, apart from the patriarchally organized ones mentioned above, may not yet have taken. Furthermore, it prevents the really critical question from being posed: When and why does the locus of reproduction become centered on the household as an income-pooling unit? An adequate answer will certainly have to look beyond the level of the household unit, to structures of reproduction of institutions such as the state.

REFERENCES

Chayanov, A. V. (1966). *The Theory of Peasant Economy*. Homewood, IL: Irwin.

Deere, Carmen (1978). "The Differentiation of the Peasantry and Family Structure: A Peruvian Case Study," unpubl. paper presented at the IDS Conference, Brighton.

Evanson, R. A. (1976). "The New Household Economics," *Journal of Agricultural Economics and Development*, VI, 1, Jan., 87-103.

Polanyi, Karl (1957). "The Economy as Instituted Process," in K. Polanyi, C. Arensberg & H. Pearson, eds. *Trade and Marketing in the Early Empires*. Glencoe, IL: Free Press, 243-70.

Research Working Group on Households and Production Processes (1978). "Households, Labor-Force Formation and Production Processes in the Capitalist World-Economy," Fernand Braudel Center Working Paper, SUNY-Binghamton.

Sahlins, Marshall (1972). *Stone Age Economics*. Chicago: Aldine.

Segbenou, R. (1982). "Grundlage zum Verstandnis des Frauenproblems im sudlichen Teil Westafrikas," unpubl. ms., Univ. of Bielefeld.

Wallerstein, Immanuel (1981). "How to Conceive our Intellectual Task: Memo to the Research Working Group on Households, Labor-Force Formation, and the World-Economy," unpubl. memo, Fernand Braudel Center, SUNY-Binghamton.

White, Benjamin (1976). "Production and Reproduction in a Javanese Village," unpubl. Ph.D. diss, Columbia Univ.

Wong, Diana (1981). "The Household as Unit of Analysis: Results of 15 Household Budgets in a Kedah Village," unpubl. ms., Univ. of Bielefeld.

Wong, Diana (1982). "Households and the Domestic Development Cycle," unpubl. ms., Univ. of Bielefeld.

5

NONWAGE LABOR AND SUBSISTENCE

Joan Smith

Fernand Braudel Center
State University of New York—Binghamton

Introduction

Capitalism and Labor Control

The essence of capitalism—at least in theory, and in contrast to other modes of production—is the following: Workers increasingly lose any alternative but to sell their labor in return for wages; wage labor becomes the predominant form of work because it can be purchased for an amount that is less than the value of what it produces but sufficient to replenish the labor force (the difference being the basis of accumulation); and, finally, the subordination of the working class is exclusively a matter of the operations of the market and the organization of production. That is to say, the more survival is assured through the purchase of goods and services, the more the general population is dependent on employers offering wage work. Further, production is increasingly organized so that both its initiation and its continuation are outside the control of the labor force itself and exclusively in the control of employers. Thus, it is only through their "daily reappearance at the factory gates" that the general population can guarantee its survival and eventual reproduction (Burawoy, 1978: 3-4).

Yet, everywhere we look, the description does not fit. Our home, the favellas, urban ghettos and working class suburbs, the Bantustand—on and on—belie the classical description of capitalism. Moreover, the discrepan-

AUTHOR'S NOTE: This chapter grows out of many hours of conversation with my colleagues in the Household and Domestic Labor Seminar, Department of Sociology, Spring 1982. I want to give notice that unlike others who absolve their colleagues of mistakes in a piece of work, I hold all of us collectively responsible. This chapter's errors and omissions call for more collective work.

cy between theory and practice appears to be not narrowing but growing. Nonwage work is becoming more the rule than the exception to it.[1]

Forms of work organized outside of the direct subsumption of capital are springing up in urban centers, not only in peripheral areas of development and unequal exchange (Amin, 1976; Emmanuel, 1972), but in the middle of core, industrial states as well. Peasant subsistence agriculture continues to contribute substantially to the tables of the poor in both rural and urban areas in the periphery (and increasingly so in the core), and when subsistence agricultural production is dissolved, other forms of nonwaged activities arise in their place (de Janvry, 1974).

In these nonwage sectors we find not only the exchange of services that are absolutely necesssary for the reproduction and daily survival of the work force, but also an economy proper, involving the actual sale of services and goods (Arizpe, 1977). Repairs of appliances, automobiles, and homes (not to mention home construction); the manufacture of everything from furniture to shoes; the provision of charcoal and wood for fuel; backyard production of foodstuffs for weekend sales, not only in the countryside but in urban areas—all testify that an economy is growing in importance behind capital's back. Or so it would appear.

These activities are so organized as not just to be relatively immune from the direct domination of capital but to be relatively invisible to capitalist accounting procedures. Their very existence and operation in the interstices of the formal economy prevent them from being subject to the ordinary methods of accounting for labor activities. Their invisibility, rather than being a mere methodological problem for social scientists who have come to rely on official government reports, is essential to their nature. That they are neither recognized by governments nor subject to government regulation is key to their success.[2]

The Extent of Nonwage
Labor Activities

While such labor activities may be a good deal less common in the core than in the periphery, there is little doubt that in both, labor that is not directly organized by the wage is on the increase. According to some reports, nonwage labor accounts for 60% of the national total in many areas of the periphery (Portes & Walton, 1981). Keith Hart (1973) estimates that half of the urban labor force in Ghana falls outside the official labor market. In poverty areas in the United States, nonwage labor is equally extensive though less frequently reported (Stack, 1975). In any case, a rough estimate of these sorts of activities in nonwage economic sectors would set their level at a minimum of 30% of the total labor activities in the world capitalist system. Some authors indeed predict that, within two decades, even in the United States the formal economy will account for no more than 50% and perhaps as little as 25% of economic activity (Burns, 1977). If we recall that the direct production of goods—industrialized labor—constitutes a good deal less than 50% of even the formal economy (in the United States by 1970 less than 29%, down from close to 40% in 1946 [Bureau of the Census, 1975: 138]), the importance of nonwage labor activities can be fully appreciated.

But yet another kind of labor activity has to be figured into the picture. Of course, I am referring to housework,[3] but more on that later.

The growth of nonwage labor raises serious questions about what had been presumed to be the increasing homogeneity of productive relations. The perserverance of so-called noncapitalist sectors, however, initially captured the attention of only those studying Third World economies (Frank, 1967).[4] The street-corner manufacturer of shoes from old tires in Accra was a more exotic figure, perhaps, than home workers in Vermont knitting hats on a piecework basis or, for that matter, women shopping in a local warehouse such as a retail outlet in Detroit. Yet each of these labor activities equally takes place outside of the factory gates.

Rethinking Capitalist Labor Control
and Nonwaged Activities

From the viewpoint supplied by either the macro level of the world-system or the micro level of the household, it is abundantly clear that the prevailing mode of production takes place via the *combination* of waged and unwaged work (Laclau, 1972). The importance of nonwage labor has not gone unrecognized in recent attempts to account for the nature of capitalism; yet a series of important questions remain to be answered. In what follows I simply want to raise those questions, with no illusion that I am addressing them adequately.

First, there is a serious question whether or not all nonwaged labor activities share fundamentally similar characteristics—whether they are shaped by the same historical processes and subject to the same forces for change. I will suggest that housework and subsistence-sector labor are far from being activities displaying features more similar than different; they are in fact totally different kinds of labor relations. They are subject to different historical and material circumstances and will react in altogether different ways to the same set of circumstances (von Werlhof, 1979).[5]

Secondly, the prevalence of unwaged labor certainly leads one to conclude that the labor force, rather than being reproduced via wages, exists through labor activities that are increasingly unwaged. Nevertheless, enthusiasm for this recent "discovery" of nonwaged labor should not lead one in the opposite direction of de-emphasizing the importance of wage relationships, in shaping nonwage activities, as it does Immanuel Wallerstein (1981). I will attempt to illustrate that reproductive activities—even those that apparently fall outside of the wage—are possible only insofar as they come in contact with the capitalist wage relationship. The conjunction of waged and nonwaged activities is responsible for the major share of reproduction of labor supplies, and that conjunction is both brought into being and reshaped by dynamics that grow directly out of the capitalist wage relationship.

Thirdly, since labor increasingly cannot be reproduced solely by one or another productive relationship but only by a multiplicity of labor forms, the very life of the working class depends upon bringing together, in a relatively stable manner, resources generated in a variety of productive relationships. Contemporary households, wherever they may be found in the world capitalist system, are similar in that they perform this function. Nevertheless, we can expect them to vary widely depending upon the nature of the labor relations they conjoin and the cultural prescriptions that are invoked to accomplish the conjunction. Precisely because these multiple labor forms are subject to very different kinds of contradictory pressures, there is always the tendency for the household to dissolve as the primary site of reproduction. In addition, because of the different labor relations that constitute the household, the ways they tend to dissolve and the mechanisms employed to recompose the household will vary widely.

In what follows I want to raise briefly these issues and to suggest the kinds of problems and investigations they prompt:

(1) Is there not a distinction between housework and other forms of nonwage labor activities?
(2) To what sorts of pressures is each subject, and what is the nature of their link to capitalist production and formal sector dynamics?
(3) How do these pressures affect the composition and dynamics of different household relations wherein the resources from the various labor forms are conjoined to guarantee the reproduction of the labor force?

Surplus Labor and Unwaged Work

The Extraction of Surplus and Formal Labor Control

Since the publication of Harry Braverman's book, *Labor and Monopoly Capital* (1977), social scientists and political activists alike have redirected their energies toward understanding the forms of control that grow out of the specific problems associated with accumulation under the formal control of capital. As Burawoy puts it, "It is one thing to speak of a potential to produce more than one consumes; it is quite another matter to realize that potential" (1978: 264).

The manner in which that potential is realized distinguishes capitalism from all prior modes of production. The industrialized work place appears to be the *sine qua non* of capitalism precisely because, in the absence of extra-economic coercion ruled out by capitalism itself, labor must be brought under the more or less direct control of individual employers. Presumably, lacking that control, workers will produce only enough to guarantee their own subsistence needs and fail to produce beyond that point, that is, they will fail to produce at a rate consistent with the needs of expanding accumulation.

The social relationships between labor and capital that have become the primary candidate for scholarly attention were those that guaranteed production beyond what was necessary for the survival of the working class (Noble, 1977; Edwards, 1980; Burawoy, 1980). Neglected in this recent and manifestly important theoretical enterprise, however, were relations that determined the extent to which the wage would satisfy established levels of consumption.[6]

This neglect is curious. The level of surplus is not just the degree to which workers can be cajoled into producing beyond what is necessary, but the degree to which what is necessary can be met—all else being equal— by nonmarket structures.

Because the United States by the mid-1950's was actually producing at a level higher than ever known before, the problem appeared to be one not of reducing the amount of subsistence met by the wage but, in fact, of increasing consumption. Starting with Baran and Sweezy (1966) and continuing through an entire generation of social scientists they influenced, the real crisis for capitalism was believed to be realization. In plain English, how were firms to get rid of products that resulted from solving the problem of extracting so much surplus from workers?

Reducing Wage Dependency

Reducing the consumption of workers—or at least consumption paid for out of the wage—appeared to be a solution neither to the analytical problem posed by market constraints of capitalism nor to the practical problems faced by marketing departments of oligopolist firms, advertising agencies, credit corporations, or other financial institutions.

Paradoxically, while most attention among U.S. scholars continued to be directed towards the so-called realization crises, U.S. firms were increasingly engaged in searching out and securing areas of investment in which subsistence costs to be met exclusively through wages were considerably lower. Through this well-rehearsed strategy, domestic production in high-wage areas could be cut back even while profit levels were maintained or enhanced.[7] While academics were continuing to concentrate on the problems of increasing accumulation at given levels of subsistence, U.S. firms (and those of other industrialized areas of the world) were taking steps not to enhance productivity at a given level of subsistence but to actually decrease the level of subsistence that the overall wage packet was expected to cover.

This movement of capital has had three important consequences for U.S. workers. The first is a substantial shift in the distribution of wealth. The most conservative estimate shows a net loss to U.S. labor of 35% each year and a net gain to capital of 10%. (These estimates use as a baseline the figures for 1968; in the context of rapidly growing foreign investment and rising inflation, the loss to workers is in all likelihood substantially more [Portes & Walton, 1981: 158-61]).

Secondly, and perhaps more importantly over the long run, the loss of jobs has progressively weakened union bargaining power and forced workers to accept major wage cuts.

Thirdly, the movement of capital increasingly creates a working class (in both the core and the periphery) of which only a small portion can enjoy such high wages as to cover full subsistence costs by a single wage. Needless to say, the exact form of this effect differs according to political and geographical units on the one hand and strata within the working class on the other.

Distinguishing between Different Forms of Nonwage Labor—A Preliminary Excursion

Since the function of the periphery is to drain off capital at a rate higher than that which would occur if production took place in the core, it is precisely its place in the world-system that establishes fetters on domestic accumulation. The existence of these fetters has in large measure led to an informal economic sector—a sector capable, for all intents and purposes, of producing, distributing, and exchanging goods and services apparently (but only apparently) outside the sway of capitalist relations.[8]

While there has been an astounding growth of nonwaged labor activities in the core—an underground economy—its existence cannot be accounted for on the basis of the same set of mechanisms that are responsible for generating such activities as in the periphery. Harlem is in this sense inadequately described as a "colony", albeit an internal one. Further, the processes of accumulation characteristic of the core have led to two opposing phenomena. On the one hand, women are being drawn into the wage labor force at an unprecedented rate. On the other, ironically, both the labor processes in which they engage as wage workers and the composition of the labor force reinforce rather than reduce their nonwage role. While the hours spent on this nonwage labor have not substantially diminished with the addition of wage labor to their activities, the flood of women into the labor force does substantially challenge the material base upon which nonwage labor has been predicated in the past (Smith & Mellor, 1982).

In either case—that of the periphery where wage pressures result in externalizing both production and reproduction, and that of the core where these same kinds of pressures simultaneously threaten disintegration of the material basis of housework on the one hand, and a rejuvenation of an informal economy on the other—the result has at least temporarily been the same: Social structures and relationships that regulate the wage quite independent of the market have been recomposed while, paradoxically, the struggles between capital and labor continue to be centered exclusively in market relationships.

The gap between what the overall wage covers in theory and what it actually covers in practice—between what Portes and Walton call theoretical subsistence costs and actual subsistence costs (1981: 87 ff.)—is dramatically linked to the two forms of labor that are considered to be outside of the formal mechanisms of labor: that is, housework on the one hand, and unwaged subsistence labor activities on the other. Yet, as I suspect and will attempt to show in what follows, there are important distinctions to be made between housework, informal market activities in the periphery, and the "same" sort of activities in the core. Each arises under different circumstances and is subject to different constraints.

The existence of practices that guarantee informal economic sectors and unwaged family labor provides the necessary conditions for reducing the actual amount of subsistence covered by the wage but, as I will argue, in totally different ways. The actual amount of labor time during which waged workers across the globe are working under the direct subsumption of capital to produce their own subsistence can be reduced: first, to the extent that the goods and services necessary for survival and replenishment are available at a price less than what the formal market establishes; secondly, to the extent that there is systematic access to income derived from these less than formal economic structures and activities; and thirdly, to the extent that nonwage labor is used as a substitute for labor for which the production process would normally call.

THE CASE OF HOUSEWORK

Nonwage Labor and Commodification

The previous, very preliminary discussion has the merit of locating in one framework the increasing prevalence of nonwage labor across the world capitalist system. The similarity between nonwaged activities in the periphery and the core and the unwaged work of housewives everywhere in the world has been noted by von Werlhof:

> But who are these "non"capitalist producers, those people who do not produce commodities for a wage? They are the majority: housewives in the whole world, peasants of both sexes producing for their own subsistence mainly in the Third World, and the army of male and female so-called marginalized people also living to a great extent in the Third World (1979).

As a good number of observers are increasingly pointing out, one of the features of capital appears to be the multiplicity of ways survival is accomplished outside the wage. At one level it is necessary to see the similarity between, for example, subsistence farming in a South African protectorate and housework in a working class suburb of Detroit, as does von Werlhof, but at another level the comparison hides the specificity of each.[9] In short, between "peasants" and unwaged housewives there are both affinities and important differences. Each is subject to totally different pressures, and they respond in opposite directions to the same constraints. In order to appreciate the difference, let me consider housework as it is performed in the core.[10]

In core states the level of development of commodity production and the accompanying development of domestic markets has shaped the fundamental contours of nonwage labor. Until the most recent past, nonwage labor in these areas had predominantly been the force responsible for transforming commodities available on the formal market into forms necessary for the adequate maintenance and reproduction of the working class—that is, work with goods and services available almost exclusively in the formal economy.

Food preparation exemplifies the point. Unlike women in the periphery, U.S. working-class women are not expected to harvest their own food. Quite to the contrary, the history of working-class women has been marked by the rapid diminution of access to the means of food production (Dublin, 1979). Nevertheless, the majority of food consumption still requires, at the very minimum, an hour per meal to prepare, consume, and store against future use and this does not include time for shopping, which—far from being reduced—has in fact been vastly increased.[11]

Access to the least expensive goods and services is absolutely limited to those consumers who are willing to contribute unpaid efforts to their final consumable form. Gas is pumped by customers; low-cost dentistry is provided only to those who will put up with an assembly-line process rather than the more convenient appointment form; warehouse-like retail outlets require the customers to do their own sorting of the merchandise (even to the extent of having to match paired items during really "special" sales) and to transport it to a central point to complete the exchange.

Much of housework is labor that has to do with preserving the value of commodities. Cleaning, laundry, and the variety of other similar activities that take close to a full working day—whether or not one is also working for wages—fall within this description (Currie et al., 1980). Similarly, child-care arrangements outside the home via informal, nonwage labor are predominantly those that augment arrangements available via formal channels. The following descriptions drawn from interviews of working-class families in the Boston area exemplify the process:[12]

Mr. Henry works from 8 a.m. to 4 p.m. In addition, two evenings a week he is on call to work through the evening until 8 p.m. Mrs. Henry works a 4 p.m. to 11 p.m. shift. Because of their commuting time, there is an hour each day when they must use a childcare arrangement; also there is an occasional evening to be covered when Mr. Henry works overtime. To cover these hours, the Henrys exchange child care with one of their neighbors.

The Hunts' youngest son goes to a day-care center one morning each week and their older son attends public kindergarten every morning. Mr. Hunt works a 9 to 5 schedule and Mrs. Hunt works from 3 to 11. They need a babysitter for 2 hours (from 3 to 5) each day; otherwise their children are in the care of a parent.

Mr. Wyatt is due at work at 7 a.m., his wife at 8 a.m. Thus, Mrs. Wyatt is responsible for preparing Oliver for nursery school and Chris for first grade. Oliver is picked up by Mrs. Gray, who cares for him along with her own child until both can be dropped off at nursery school. Chris walks to a friend's house and waits there until school time. At noon, Oliver returns to the Gray's house, where he plays until Chris picks him up at 2:30. Chris and Oliver then walk to another neighbor's home, where they are cared for until 5 p.m. when their mother returns home from work.[13]

Far from the commodification process's eradicating it, household work has taken place in a context that absolutely assumes the constant availability of nonwage labor. The goods and services resulting from increasing commodification as well as their distribution and exchange are fundamentally shaped by the assumption that nonwage work is available.

A few examples will make the point. Rather than industry concentrating on the design and production of washers and dryers that could easily be operated by one or two attendants in a communal laundry, since the Second World War, the home appliance industry has produced appliances just large enough to accommodate the laundry of an average sized family. In short, these appliances are designed specifically under the assumption that the labor they necessitate will be available outside of a direct cost to capital.

Then came a ripple effect. With the appearance of these laundry appliances—appliances that required the nonwaged attention of a family member—a new kind of clothing industry exploded. Wash-and-wear became the goal of every manufacturer mass producing moderately priced clothing. But every "housewife" knows that the promise of wash-and-wear is only as good as the availability of someone to remove the garment from the dryer immediately and place it on a hanger. These appear to be mundane examples, but their very ordinariness is crucial for guaranteeing the control of the labor they necessitate.

Finally, the reorganization of production that has supposedly signaled the end of industrial society has itself vastly intensified labor carried on in the home (see, e.g., Bell, 1973). Let me return to the washing machine and dryer. Not only is more rather than less laundry carried on privately outside the wage, but standards of cleanliness have improved enormously. These standards represent more than just expected bits of ideologies promulgated by greedy appliance and detergent manufacturers; for, indeed, they necessarily reflect changes in the work place and in the expectations workers must meet on their jobs. An industrial worker may get away with a dirty shirt; a service employee of IBM must wear a white one, and a clean one every day.[14]

Further, the changes in production processes characteristic of advanced capitalism have drastically altered standards of proper parenting. A shift to production techniques that increasingly demand a degree of literacy and a relatively sophisticated ability to handle symbols has penetrated the home as much as the school. In addition, changes in labor control have required an internalized discipline (Frank, 1932). While the original threat of undereducated children in the United States was posed by a Sputnik, "Why can't Johnny read?" was in reality a question of the kind of labor force that would be available and the kind of responsibility that parents were required to take on. Any parent who failed in this responsibility was un-American (Gesell & Ilg, 1943).

To bring out the best in children required not only work early in the life of the child but virtually full-time labor. Learning began not at six or seven, as had been believed, but—according to contemporary "experts"—in the first days of infancy. Retardation was just around the corner for any child that did not have the full-time attention necessary to provide the constant stimulation that proper intellectual growth required. Further, and most important for the issue I am raising here, that stimulation could not be provided by anybody but those to whom the infant was biologically bonded—preferably, of course, the mother (Bowlby, 1966).[15]

Thus, an expansion of wage employment in nurseries and day-care centers to accommodate these newly discovered needs of children was absolutely ruled out. Rather, what was demanded was a vast increase and intensification of unwaged obligations of parents (Ellis & Petchesky, 1972).

In contrast to the picture painted by those who insist on the dualism of capitalism and patriarchy (e.g., Eisenstein, 1981; Hartmann & Markusen, 1980), it seems abundantly clear that domestic labor, rather than being some original state imported into capitalism by the need to reproduce a sexually ordered society, results in point of fact from the development of capitalism itself. That is to say, the devaluation of the work accomplished in the main by women is not explained on the grounds of women's subordination. Rather, women's subordination is explained—reimposed and guaranteed—on the grounds that domestic labor is re-created in a manner that calls forth a subordinated group who will accomplish it outside the formal control of capital. The locus of patriarchical control is not found in its pan-historical perseverance but in the contemporary organization of production. In that sense, women's subordination in the home is not the oldest of extant social relationships but among the newest.

Commodification and Varieties of Nonwage Labor

The Informal Sector

The principal feature of nonwaged housework in the core is that it decreases the share of subsistence borne by capital by increasing the value of commodities quite independent of the wage labor they embody. These nonwage labor activities referred to as "housework" are those that provide—for free—the conditions either absolutely required for the exchange value of the commodity (what if everyone refused to do home laundry?) or for the enhancement of the value already embodied in the commodity, such as in food preparation and storage, preserving household and personal items, and the rest of those activities so familiar to women.

As I conceive it, a criterion of housework is the extent to which it comes in direct contact with commodities. It completes the full circulation of commodities and thus has literally no value outside of commodity production. It could not even exist *as such* outside commodity production. This is not to say that unwaged reproductive labor could not be found in a variety of noncapitalist societies, but only that the set of social structural relations that guarantee its existence and continual reproduction (and thus its nature) would be totally different from those found within capitalist societies. Further, noncapitalist societies may indeed continue to oppress and exploit women, but that relationship of domination will necessarily be linked to social structures specific to those societies and their specific processes of accumulation.

There are, however, other forms of nonwage labor occurring within the capitalist world-system that should be distinguished from housework— namely, those that actually produce goods and services *relatively* independent of the formal sector, and those that are associated with the circulation of these goods and services outside a formal market system. Some of these activities are described vividly by Colin Leys.

> Smallholders provide cheap food crops, pastoralists provide cheap beef, petty traders provide cheap distribution, "subsistence" transporters provide cheap communications, the makers of shoes out of old tires and bicycle repairers and the charcoal burners and sellers provide cheap goods and services designed for the poverty life-style of those whose work makes the "formal sector" profitable, and which enables them to live on their wages (1973: 426).

But these are exotic examples of what have become very ordinary activities even in core countries. They are in fact so ordinary that *Business Week* recently devoted its cover story to the degree to which the "shadow economy" is edging out growth in the formal sector of core areas.[16] Quoting from economists and government officials, *Business Week* set the size of the "shadow economy" at 14% of the U.S. gross national product and noted that its growth rate is substantially faster than that of the formal sector.

The degree to which this shadow economy infiltrates the regular aboveground sector in core areas is illustrated by the following. The official statistics on construction in Germany show declines; nevertheless, sales of building materials are on the rise. Obviously, the materials are used for construction that never shows up in the official counts. In France the picture is the same: While the French construction industry is down, the cement business is flourishing. French officials estimate that if just the official statistics on construction are consulted, close to 50% of cement sales cannot be accounted for.[17]

These data indicate that in core areas, construction and rehabilitation of housing is beginning to mirror the pattern in the periphery, where housing is one of the chief products of the informal sector. In Rio de Janeiro's favellas, for example, four out of ten families live in houses that are built either by themselves or by family members (Perlman, 1976). Such petty commodity housing has a material impact on financial institutions and structures, on markets for materials, and on housing "retailers" (Turner, 1976).

Nonwage Labor and
Its Links to the Formal Economy

Just as housework is to be distinguished from labor conducted in the informal economy by the degree of contact with commodities generated in the "regular" economy, so too can a major distinction be drawn between different sectors within the informal economy itself.[18] That is to say, the degree to which capitalist industry supplies raw materials distinguishes, in important respects, different labor activities in the informal sector. According to one report, close to 80% of furniture producers, the majority of plastic shoemakers, and most of those working with metal products depend on the formal sector for their materials. Conversely, shoe repairers, sandal makers, and the majority of those working with glass and aluminum obtain their supply from discarded materials. The differential use of capital equipment in manufacturing and transport in the informal economy has also been documented. Informal commercial activities also have different degrees of dependence on the formal economy for their supplies (Gerry, 1974; 1978).

Yet we should not overdraw the similarity between housework and those activities in the informal sector that depend upon capital goods. While manufacturers of washing machines depend on labor supplied via the nonwage activity of housewives, capital equipment and goods employed as inputs in the informal sector have—at least theoretically—alternative uses in the formal sector. In short, while both housework and some labor activities in the informal sector are linked to capitalist firms through their input dependency, the natures of the links, I will argue below, are totally different.

Wage Levels and Forms of Nonwage Labor

Similarly, the way each of these activities—housework and labor organized via informal mechanisms rather than the wage—affects subsistence levels discloses an altogether different relationship to the dominant economy. The argument has been made that housework reduces subsistence costs to the individual family since it produces goods and services that, if purchased on the open market, would be a good deal more costly (Malos, 1978).[19] All that *may* be true. And in that sense housework performs a service relative to wage levels in much the same fashion as the informal market does for goods and services. Whether or not housework, however, actually functions to reduce the wages of individuals who have direct access to that labor is not the foundation of its systematic relationship to the formal economy. What housework does do, systematically, is allow the production of both goods and services that would have to embody a good deal more wage labor in the absence of housework.

The *low price* of commodities that depend for their exchange and preservation on nonwage labor is enjoyed by those households who have ample access to this labor *and* those that do not; but the wage levels of households that necessarily employ this nonwage labor are not a function of the services. It would be more accurate to say that the use value of the wages is a direct product of the accessibility of nonwage labor. Stretching a dollar is indeed work. Nevertheless, while—dollar for dollar—housework may improve the standard of living, it does not *directly* affect the level of the wage.

In contrast, the informal sector maintains low subsistence costs to capital by directly augmenting the wage. Informal economic activities actually generate income, and, to the extent that they are sufficiently widespread, any form of income is worth more because it can be spent in an informal market where prices are lower.

Hart (1973) divides legitimate informal income opportunities into five categories: (1) primary and secondary activities including farming, market gardening, building and associated activities, self-employed artisan work, shoemaking, tailoring, and manufacturing of beers and spirits; (2) tertiary enterprises with relatively large capital inputs, such as housing, transport, utilities, commodity speculation, and renter activities; (3) small-scale distribution, including the work of market operatives, petty traders, street hawkers, caterers in food and drink, bar attendants, carriers, commission agents, and dealers; (4) other services, such as those rendered by musicians, launderers, shoeshiners, barbers, night soil removers, photographers, vehicle repairers and other maintenance workers, brokers and middlemen, and purveyors of ritual services, magic, and medicine; and (5) private transfer payments, including gifts and similar flows of money and goods between persons, borrowing and begging.

Even though it describes activities in Ghana, Hart's list can easily accommodate comparable nonwage activities occurring in a variety of places, including core areas of the world-economy. However, when they do take place in the core, it is usually via the commodities that accompany or facilitate activities through more "normal" channels. People continue to do "normal" work but "off the books". In either case, though, like housework, rather than representing vestigial arrangements these nonwage sector activities are a function of the arrangements peculiar to advanced capitalism. Each takes on its particular character in relation to constraints imposed by the processes that compose the formal subordination of labor to capital. Nevertheless, that is where their similarity ends. Housework is called into being as a way of increasing the value of commodities independent of the labor they embody. Thus, rather than being a substitute for wage work, from the point of view of the household, housework comprises merely the necessary but unpaid activities that are required in order to guarantee day-to-day survival. On the other hand, informal sector activities are related to commodification in a totally different way. Rather than being the accompaniment of commodification, they arise when that process is halted. Nevertheless, the circumstances calling forth a halt in that process— disinvestment in the core or investment for export processing in the periphery—in all likelihood create totally different kinds of informal sector activities.

The Systemic Basis of Nonwage Labor

Labor Reserves and Unwaged Labor

Within classical Marxism the connection between nonwage labor sectors and wage relationships is relatively straightforward. Through a variety of mechanisms, the capacity of nonwage "traditional" economies to support populations outside the wage is systematically eroded. The traditional spheres must then give up the supplies of labor necessary for capitalist production at wage rates compatible with acceptable profit levels. During periods of contraction or rapid changes in production processes, traditional sectors reabsorb the surplus labor until it is called forth once more into the active army of the employed.

As important as this account has been, it omits any attempt to account for the existence of so-called traditional spheres beyond their role in mobilizing and resecuring the reserve army. Other than the limited response of giving up or reabsorbing labor supplies, the nonwage sectors are pictured as otherwise relatively impervious to the forces that call forth or expel that labor.[20]

The apparent, relative imperviousness to the development of capitalist production, it is argued, has been guaranteed by the state (Burawoy, 1976: 1053; Bernstein, 1979; Van Allen, 1972). While it is in the interest of individual firms to extract as much cheap labor as possible from so-called traditional sectors, the capitalist class as a class requires that some minimal protection be offered to these labor reservoirs. In the absence of such protection, the very social basis for cheap labor would be absolutely eroded, and this would have the effect of eventually driving up labor costs. Even in the periphery—not to mention core areas—a complex system of safeguards established by the state in collusion with organized labor maintains a high-wage sector of the working class immune from the competition from the mass of others engaged in nonwaged activities. The view presented in these accounts is that the protection afforded to some sectors of high-wage workers by the state is in the long-run interest of the capitalist class, even if individual members of that class do not immediately appreciate its effects.[21] The notion that the state is relatively autonomous is used to explain the apparently paradoxical relationship between the state and individual capitalist firms. But, relative autonomy notwithstanding, over the long run these long-run interests of the capital class must somehow be translated into short-run advantages for firms; otherwise the stability the state is said to afford would be constantly subject to undermining by the operation of those firms it is intended to protect.

The distance between long run and short run is closed by the increasing systemic—though, as well, contradictory—relationship between waged and unwaged labor forms. Quite independent of their role as labor reserves the social processes responsible for recreating nonwage labor have been fully incorporated into the "normal" market behavior of firms. While these non-waged activities are now crucial for firms, they also, on occasion, threaten the unlimited access to labor supplies. Thus, the contradiction. What capitalist production increasingly assumes on one hand, it necessarily undercuts on the other.

The Level of Paid Subsistence
and Varieties of Nonwage Labor

While there is little question that the state has played a decisive role in creating nonwage labor activities and relationships, the stability of these relationships is guaranteed, in the most part, because the labor theoretically unavailable for formalized employment is increasingly available for nonwage work—work that, in spite of its informality, transfers surplus to capitalist firms (Portes & Walton, 1981). How this transfer is accomplished, however, absolutely differentiates various forms of nonwage work and the sectors of capital that have different stakes in nonwage labor.

First, so-called housework, as I have argued, reduces overall subsistence costs by decreasing the amount of labor that finished commodities must embody before they are transformed into usable goods and services. But— and this is the crucial point—housework does not *necessarily* reduce the subsistence costs of the individual household in which it takes place. Two conditions would have to be met. First, the reduction in the necessary paid labor that housework allows would have to be translated into a reduction in prices. Whether or not this happens is largely open to question and is a matter settled by a wide variety of factors far beyond the simple availability of unpaid household labor. Further, the price reduction would have to be relatively more available to those with ample access to the unpaid labor than to those with relatively less. Secondly, the costs of accomplishing the housework would have to be significantly less than the costs of what the housework is a substitute for. Whether or not this is the case depends upon highly specific conditions—for example, the degree of segmentation of the labor force.[22]

Apart from its (more-or-less) individualized impact on the level of subsistence, however, housework functions systematically at the level of the general economy to reduce subsistence costs. That is to say, it does not necessarily reduce the wage needs of the household, but the employment needs of capital itself. The great explosion in the so-called service sector notwithstanding, the increased "leisure" of wives of high-waged workers— as well as the enforced leisure of all kinds of other women—is transformed into nonwaged work that makes redundant the labor not of high-waged husbands but of a less privileged labor force. Washing machines replace laundresses; clinics replace receptionists; warehouse-like retail establishments replace sales personnel; food preparation replaces cooks (Katzman, 1979).

In contrast, work in the informal sectors of production and marketing directly reduces subsistence costs that must be covered by the wage. Unlike housework, this form of production and distribution directly "frees" workers from the dependency on the wage. Moreover, rather than making redundant a marginal mass of workers, it takes up their available labor and engages it in a wide variety of pursuits that eventually have the effect of reducing the pressure on the wage component of their fellow-poor fully engaged in the formal wage sector.[23]

The "Relative Autonomy" of Unwaged Labor Forms

There is an important corollary to these distinctions. Housework can reduce capital's labor costs only to the extent that it is in direct contact with either the wage or some form of transfer payment. (Its existence assumes this contact; in fact, housework cannot easily exist without it.) Because of this distinctive feature, housework has relatively less capacity to develop an autonomous existence outside of the sway of either the wage or the state.

In contrast, informal-sector activities—those that actually produce and distribute goods and services outside of the formal market—have a very different relationship to the availability of the wage or transfer payments. Since informal-sector labor activities are not as substantially actualized by their contact with commodities and commodified services but by their relative distance from the formal sector, nonwage labor in the informal arena comes into existence with a fall in employment. *Doing dishes enhances the value of the wage; making sandals out of discarded materials is a substitute for wages.*

The privatization of labor that housework expresses allows for the reduction in paid labor, not necessarily that of those who have the direct use of that housework but of those who would otherwise provide the service in the paid labor force. Informal-sector production and distribution take up and use surplus labor supplies.

Wage Levels and Unwaged Labor Forms

I would offer a third distinction between unpaid household labor and unwaged informal-sector work. I know of no studies that empirically investigate this hypothesis, but it seems reasonable to expect that the proportion of the household consumption fund made up of informal-sector employment is inversely related to individual household wage levels. The higher the amount contributed by the wage, the lower the intensity of informal labor activities (Arrighi, 1973a; Quijano, 1974; Bienefeld, 1974). Conversely, I believe it would be found that the intensity of unwaged domestic labor is much less affected by wage levels. It is precisely this relative independence from wage levels that forces all but the most wealthy families into privatized household labor and extends the duration of this labor more or less to the same degree, whether or not there is the same amount of available time to accomplish it (Vanek, 1974; Cowan, 1976).

These distinctions amply demonstrate, I believe, that although they are subject to subordination to the forces associated with capitalist productive relations and certainly related to the levels of subsistence covered by the wage, unwaged household labor, on the one hand, and labor associated with the informal or subsistence sector, on the other, are the concrete results of entirely different processes occurring within the world-economy as a whole and thus actually express very different relationships to capital.

Households and the Composition of Consumption Funds

Nonwage Labor Decomposition and Reformation of Households

Finally I come to households. Because working-class subsistence and reproduction costs are provided by a combination of resources other than just the wage, it has been necessary to make distinctions between these resources before discussing their impact on the household.

Because subsistence is more than just the wage, a hallmark of contemporary household structures is their capacity to weave together a variety of labor forms. Household relationships guarantee that various forms of compensation will be joined to complete a consumption fund adequate for sustaining and replenishing the labor force. Since different forms of resources are susceptible to different kinds of pressures, however, household composition and dynamics will differ markedly depending upon which form predominates as the major contributor to the fund.

When we turn to the labor that takes place in the informal sector, it seems abundantly clear that, in contrast to housework, it is largely a response to changes in the formal sector—and relatively short-term changes at that. Nevertheless, those short-term changes have long-term effects.

Sources of Pressure on Nonwage Labor

Increasing oligopoly, over the long run, prevents expansion of the informal sector but probably has little effect on the degree to which unwaged labor takes place within the individual household. If anything, to the extent that oligopolist conditions coincide with embodying in new products services that had previously been available in the informal sector, the burdens of unpaid housework will actually increase (rather than decrease). All sorts of examples come to mind. We can return to household appliances. As they came to replace personal services made available by domestics and firms, unpaid housework increased. At least in this case we can see an inverse relationship between informal-sector activities and the intensification of housework. Shopping in the neighborhood store has been replaced by the huge chain store; what the corner grocer or alley peddler did for the housewife, she must now do for herself. The gas station attendant, whose job is a casual one for many young people, has been replaced by do-it-yourself gas pumping.

With the price rigidity that generally attends economic concentration in the formal sector, new *forms* of informal employment might emerge. Nevertheless, in the case of informal manufacturing and market activities, their very expansion often spells their demise. At a certain point in their growth, the size of their market justifies a takeover by the formal sector. For example, shoe manufacture in many peripheral areas has long been the province of an informal manufacturing sector, but there is every sign that this production will soon be taken over by fully capitalized firms (World Development, 1978).

In contrast, housework seldom develops an independent market; thus we cannot expect that it will be taken over by capital. True, there has been a growth in service-sector employment (teaching, medicine, retail services, and the like), but the very shape of these new services has in fact demanded not less unpaid work but just different kinds (Weinbaum & Bridges, 1976). Let me take medicine for one example. Over the last 50 years its growth has been phenomenal. But none of the growth has represented a diminution of unpaid household work connected with illness. Rather than taking place primarily in the home, however, this labor now means the long trip to the doctor's office or clinic, the lengthy wait in the reception room, the next drive to the pharmacy, and so on. The examples are as endless as is the work.

The Crisis of the Family

Though not as penetrable by the growth of formal markets—if anything, intensified by such growth—housework shares in another way the vulnerability of informal sector labor to the growth of wage labor.[24] The expansion of the labor force over the past 20 years in the United States has been accomplished in part with the historically unprecedented incorporation of "housewives" into the ranks of paid labor. There is no question that the attractiveness of this supply of labor has been its relatively low cost to capital. This cheapness was the effect of both an historical exclusion from the labor force—thus the sort of political powerlessness that results from (and indeed perpetuates) this exclusion—and the fact that housewives were perceived to have access to resources supplied by labor other than their own (Smith & Mellor, 1982). Yet precisely because their attractiveness to capital has been conditioned upon their status as nonwaged workers, the incorporation of housewives into the ranks of the employed paradoxically has had the effect of eroding the *institutional* basis for the larger than "normal" amounts of surplus their labor can transfer to capital. Though not disappearing with the growth of women's employment in the wage-labor force, the grounds for nonwage housework are substantially undercut.

Women increasingly demand release from a variety of traditional reproductive obligations. Such demands take the form of challenges to prior forms of sexuality, to traditional child-care practices, to the obligation to bring a pregnancy to term, and to the lack of appropriate community services. It is within this context that the so-called family crisis has emerged in core, industrialized areas of the world economy (Smith & Mellor, 1982).

The material basis for women's dependence on men is not exclusively a matter of their relatively low wages (although it is that as well), but that reproduction of the labor force on capitalist terms has called into being work that goes without wages. The capacity to carry out that work is a function of the degree to which it can come into contact with the wage. It is for this reason that, though increasing in absolute numbers over the past two decades, the household containing but one adult member is a relatively unstable form. That is to say, while increasing numbers of women are living alone with their children sometime during their lives, for individual women this period is a relatively fleeting one. A surprising proportion quickly form new household units that contain more than one adult member (Slesinger, 1980; Ross & Sawhill, 1975). Complaints about divorce notwithstanding, paired households continue to be the rule for all income levels for no reason other than that contemporary reproductive arrangements assume a quantity of so-called free time that is available only by pairing "leisure" hours (Currie et al, 1980).

Conclusion

Let me conclude by saying that, since it is clear the reproduction of the working class depends upon a variety of resources drawn from a variety of social relations, the degree to which households maintain themselves as such and the degree to which they are eroded is a function of a variety of pressures—not just those directly related to labor-force needs in the formal economy—although such pressures in the last analysis will be related to the capitalist/wage relationship. This is just to say that households in the world-economy have long since ceased to be merely passive reservoirs of labor supplies, if they were ever just that.

It has become increasingly clear that household units have a more complex relationship to productive activities than had earlier been recognized. Notions of neither a universalized gender subordination nor a unity of nonwage labor throughout the world-economy can unravel those complexities. Rather, they are unraveled when concrete investigations are conducted into the specific relationships that shape specific reproductive activities carried out under specific circumstances.

NOTES

1. Throughout this chapter I will refer to nonwage work as all those forms of labor that are organized outside of direct formal market control. This includes what usually falls under the heading of housework, petty commodity production, and petty distribution of goods and services. However, housework, as I will argue in what follows, is to be distinguished from nonwage subsistence production, distribution, and exchange.

2. I am not totally satisfied that the *key* to informal labor activities is that they are "off the books", although obviously the regulation of the state is an important—indeed crucial—aspect. For example, Robert Bach (1978) argues that current U.S. immigration law *requires* the state to turn a blind eye to migrant workers and thus actually creates their political weakness, which, in turn, supports their exploitation. But I am not entirely convinced that these workers are in the informal sector.

3. For a review of the various ways housework has been neglected as a serious area of study see Myra Marx Ferree (n.d.).

4. It should be also pointed out that the suspicion of an informal sector is one peculiar to the Third World. I will argue later that nonwaged activities in different areas of the global economy may reflect altogether different relationships to the accumulation process and thus cannot be identified with each other even when they are summed in the calculation of household consumption funds.

5. I found von Werlhof's paper stimulating, and in part this paper should be read as a dialogue with it. Nevertheless, what I am suggesting, contra von Werlhof, is that, unwaged housework is not to be identified with "peasant" labor.

6. There were some who questioned the persistence of nonwage sectors, but their emphasis was on agricultural production. Those that did consider industrial production alongside of the perseverance of reproductive labor carried out independent of wages treated that nonwage labor as more the exception that proved the rule. For example, consider Michael Burawoy's account: "As indicated in the distribution of family welfare benefits, even the industrial enterprise tends to treat the day-to-day maintenance of the labor force and the creation of a future one as though they constituted a single process (1976: 1052).

7. I am only too conscious of how limited this description is. I use it only to put into a context the development of U.S. social-scientific investigations of labor activities.

8. Rosa Luxemburg, in *The Accumulation of Capital* (1951), foresaw this development. However, I think it important to distinguish this process from that of so-called primitive or original accumulation. The recomposition of nonwage labor is an effect of the capital wage relation as well as one of its presuppositions. The same cannot be said of the social basis for original accumulation.

9. Where von Werlhof concentrates on the similarities between unwaged workers and between housework and other forms of nonwage labor, Portes and Walton (1981) go to the other extreme; they never even consider housework and certainly have little regard for women's special role in the informal sectors. For a discussion of women and development, though obviously from a point of view totally different than von Werlhof's, see Boserup (1970). For a discussion of the limitations of Boserup see Benería and Sen (1981).

10. When discussing peasants and housewives it should be clear that I am not discussing different people but different relationships; thus, a concrete individual may be both, just as a specific kind of work can be either waged or nonwaged and, in concrete cases of those who perform it, is both. Consider, for example, scrubbing floors in an office complex and performing the "same" work at home for oneself. Secondly, as I pointed out above, there is a distinction to be made, not only between housework and all other forms of nonwage work, but also between nonwage labor activities in the core and those carried on in peripheral areas. In what follows I will consider only the differences between housework and other nonwage labor activities in general.

11. It is particularly ironic that women's inferiority is said to be demonstrated by their constant shopping, when that shopping has been explicitly designed so that it necessarily requires more rather than fewer hours.

12. See *Monthly Labor Review*, October 1977, 50-55.

13. See *Monthly Labor Review*, October 1977, 50-55. It should be pointed out that these examples were generated by the authors of an article purporting to prove that substantial day care on a formal basis is *not* necessary. In short, what one might conclude are some fairly bizarre arrangements are in fact described as not only normal but entirely expected of those who engage in them. Leacock says that "industrialized countries already have forms for socializing domestic labor and child care. All manner of food preparation and dispensing services, cleaning services, and formal and informal child care arrangements are at hand. All that is required is to make them more healthy, accessible, and cheap by removing them from a profit-

making structure" (1981: 480). Of course, this is easier said than done. First, the fundamental organization of these "socialized" reproductive activities assumes the basic privatization of domestic labor and child care. Secondly, those actually working for wages in these sectors are predominantly female, and their wage levels are *considerably* lower than average in part because of the devaluation of women's work sustained by their privatized nonwaged activities. Thirdly, the cheapness of women's labor is becoming more rather than less important for capital; thus it is hardly likely that the social foundations of that cheapness will be eroded without a major struggle.

14. With but one exception that I know of, socialist-feminists treat housework as an ideological tool for the control of women. For the exception, see Weinbaum and Bridges (1976). I think it is important to note that increasing standards of living are more than just capitalist ploys, but are successes of the working class in improving their lot.

15. For a trenchant review of the bonding literature see Arney (1980).

16. *Business Week*, April 5, 1982, 64-70. *Business Week*'s examples are generally of work that is "off-the-books". I suspect that this is not really the kind of work that others would call "informal-sector activities". Further, work that is simply unregulated by the state but is otherwise no different from formal wage activity may be substantially different than that referred to within the general category of nonwaged.

17. *Business Week*, April 5, 1982, 64-70.

18. The nature of the links connecting the two sectors distinguishes different labor activities that take place in the informal arena. Thus, it is not entirely correct to talk about informal "economies", since it remains an open question whether or not the links between different sectors *within* the informal arena are stronger than those *between* that arena and the capitalized one. It is precisely the nature of these links that is most important when considering the manner in which the working class can reproduce itself.

19. In her article Malos sums up the lengthy debate on the value of housework.

20. Major exceptions to this treatment can be found in Meillassoux (1972), Arrighi, (1973b), and Burawoy (1976). But each of these continues to disregard the substantial link between the "traditional" sectors and the dominant economy.

21. There are several different views of this situation. For a general overview (but not including the one I present below) see Gordon (1972).

22. There is no doubt that housework increases the standard of living; it makes a dollar go farther. But it does not figure into the household consumption fund the way other labor forms do. On the other hand, it very much fits into the reduction in capitalist labor costs. Ironically, of course, the very group most affected by this reduction in labor is the group that then has little time to devote to the kind of housekeeping chores that substitute for paid labor. Nevertheless, because of the fact that commodity production assumes housework, it acts as a constraint on even those who can ill afford it.

23. There is probably a vast distinction between sectors of the informal arena that cater to the rich and those that cater to the poor. This is an important dimension to the links that join the two sectors—the informal and the formal—but the matter is beyond the scope of this chapter.

24. It is in this sense that the struggles against various South African apartheid laws that preserve the nonwaged subsistence activities of Black families, enforce the migration of workers without their families, and regulate women's sexual subordination—are all common struggles.

REFERENCES

Amin, Samir (1976). *Unequal Development: An Essay on the Social Formation of Peripheral Capitalism*. New York: Monthly Review Press.

Arizpe, Lourdes (1977). "Women in the Informal Labor Sector: The Case of Mexico City," in Wellesley Editorial Committee, ed., *Women and National Development*. Chicago: Univ. of Chicago Press, 24-37.

Arney, William (1980). "Falling in Love with your Child: The Politics of Parenting," *Feminist Studies*, VI, 3, Fall, 547-70.

Arrighi, Giovanni (1973a). "International Corporations, Labor Aristocracies, and Economic Development in Tropical Africa," in G. Arrighi & J. Saul, eds., *Essays on the Political Economy of Africa*. New York: Monthly Review Press, 105-51.

Arrighi, Giovanni (1973b). "Labor Supplies in Historical Perspective: A Study of the Proletarianization of the African Peasantry in Rhodesia," in G. Arrighi & J. Saul, eds., *Essays on the Political Economy of Africa*. New York: Monthly Review Press, 180-236.

Bach, Robert (1978). "Mexican Immigration and the American State," *International Migration Review*, XII, 4, Win., 536-48.

Baran, Paul A. & Sweezy, Paul M. (1966). *Monopoly Capital: An Essay on the American Economic Social Order*. New York: Modern Reader Paperbacks.

Bell, Daniel (1973). *The Coming of Post-Industrial Society*. New York: Basic Books.

Benería, Lourdes & Sen, Gita (1981). "Accumulation, Reproduction, and Women's Role in Economic Development," *Signs*, VII, 2, Win., 279-98.

Bernstein, Henry (1979). "African Peasantries: A Theoretical Framework," *Journal of Peasant Studies*, VI, 4, July, 421-43.

Bienefeld, Michael (1974). "Notes on the 'Theory of Wages' and on Unequal Exchange," Working Paper No. 19, Brighton: Institute of Development Studies at the Univ. of Sussex.

Boserup, Ester (1970). *Women's Role in Economic Development*. London: Allen & Unwin.

Bowlby, John (1966). *Maternal Care and Mental Health*. New York: Schocken.

Braverman, Harry (1977). *Labor and Monopoly Capital*. New York: Monthly Review Press.

Burawoy, Michael (1976). "The Functions and Reproduction of Migrant Labor: Comparative Material from Southern Africa and the United States," *American Journal of Sociology*, LXXXI, 5, Mar., 1050-87.

Burawoy, Michael (1978). "Toward a Marxist Theory of the Labor Process: Braverman and Beyond," *Politics and Society*, VIII, 3-4, 247-312.

Burawoy, Michael (1980). *Manufacturing Consent: Changes in the Labor Process Under Corporate Capitalism*. Berkeley: Univ. of California Press.

Burns, Scott (1977). *The Household Economy*. Boston: Beacon.

Bureau of the Census (1975). *Historical Statistics of the United States, Colonial Times to 1970*. U.S. Department of Commerce, Bureau of the Census, Series D. Washington: U.S. Government Printing Office, 142-51.

Cowan, Ruth (1976). "The 'Industrial Revolution' in the Home," *Technology and Culture*, XVII, I, Jan., 1-23.

Currie, Elliot, Dunn, Robert & Fogarty, David (1980). "The New Immiseration: Stagflation, Inequality and the Working Class," *Socialist Review*, No. 54, Nov.-Dec., 7-31.

de Janvry, Alain (1974). "The Political Economy of Rural Development in Latin America," Giannini Foundation Paper No. 2, Univ. of California at Berkeley, Dept. of Agricultural Economics.

Dublin, Thomas (1979). *Women at Work: The Transformation of Work and Community in Lowell, Massachusetts, 1826-1860*. New York: Columbia Univ. Press.

Edwards, Richard (1980). *Contested Terrain: The Transformation of the Workplace in America*. New York: Basic Books.

Eisenstein, Zillah (1981). *The Radical Future of Liberal Feminism*. New York: Longman.

Ellis, Katherine & Petchesky, Rosalind (1972). "Children of the Corporate Dream: An Analysis of Day Care as a Political Issue under Capitalism," *Socialist Revolution*, No. 2, Nov.-Dec., 9-28.

Emmanuel, Arghiri (1972). *Unequal Exchange: A Study of the Imperialism of Trade.* London: New Left Books.

Ferree, Myra Marx (n.d.). "Housework," unpubl. mimeo, Univ. of Connecticut.

Frank, André Gunder (1967). *Capitalism and Underdevelopment in Latin America.* New York: Monthly Review Press.

Frank, L. K. (1932). "Life Values for the Machine Age," in *Our Children: A Handbook for Parents.* New York: Viking.

Gerry, Chris (1974). *Petty Producers and the Urban Economy: A Case Study of Dakar.* Geneva: ILO.

Gerry, Chris (1978). "Petty Production and Capitalist Production in Dakar: The Crises of the Self-employed," *World Development,* VI, 9-10, Sept.-Oct., 1147-60.

Gesell, Arnold & Ilg, Frances (1943). *Infant and Child in the Culture of Today.* New York: Harper.

Gordon, David (1972). *Theories of Poverty and Unemployment.* Lexington, MA: D. C. Heath.

Hart, Keith (1973). "Informal Income Opportunities and Urban Employment in Ghana," *Journal of Modern African Studies,* XI, 1, Mar., 61-89.

Hartmann, Heidi & Markusen, Ann (1980). "Contemporary Marxist Theory and Practice: A Feminist Critique," *Review of Radical Political Economics,* XII, 2, Sum., 87-94.

Katzman, David (1979). *Seven Days a Week: Women and Domestic Service in Industrializing America.* New York: Oxford Univ. Press.

Laclau, Ernesto (1972). "Feudalism and Capitalism in Latin America," *New Left Review,* No. 67, May-June, 19-38.

Leacock, Eleanor (1981). "History, Development and the Division of Labor by Sex: Implications for Organization," *Signs,* VII, 2, Win., 474-91.

Leys, Colin (1973). "Interpreting African Underdevelopment: Reflections on the ILO Report on Employment, Incomes and Equality in Kenya," *African Affairs,* LXXII, Oct., 419-29.

Luxemburg, Rosa (1951). *The Accumulation of Capital.* London: Routledge & Kegan Paul.

Malos, Ellen (1978). "Housework and the Politics of Women's Liberation," *Socialist Revolution,* 41-72.

Meillassoux, Claude (1972). "From Reproduction to Production," *Economy and Society,* I, 1, Feb., 93-105.

Noble, David F. (1977). *American by Design: Science, Technology and the Rise of Corporate Capitalism.* New York: Knopf.

Perlman, Janice (1976). *The Myth of Marginality: Urban Poverty and Politics in Rio de Janeiro.* Berkeley: Univ. Of California Press.

Portes, Alejandro & Walton, John (1981). *Labor, Class, and the International System.* New York: Academic Press.

Quijano, Anibal (1974). "The Marginal Pole of the Economy and the Marginalized Labour Force," *Economy and Society,* III, 4, Nov., 393-428.

Ross, H. L. & Sawhill, I. V. (1975). *Time of Transition.* Washington: Urban Institute.

Slesinger, Doris P. (1980). "Rapid Changes in Household Composition among Low-Income Mothers," *Family Relations,* XXIX, 2, Apr., 221-28.

Smith, Joan & Mellor, Kirsten (1982). "Reproducing the Sexual Division of Labor," unpubl mimeo.

Stack, Carol (1975). *All Our Kin: Strategies for Survival in a Black Community.* New York: Peter Smith.

Turner, John (1976). *Housing by People: Toward Autonomy in Building Environments.* London: Marion Boyars.

Van Allen, Judith (1972). " 'Sitting on a Man': Colonialism and the Lost Political Institutions of Igbo Women," *Canadian Journal of African Studies,* VI, 2, 65-82.

Vanek, Joann (1974). "Time Spent in Housework," *Scientific American*, 5, 116-20.

Wallerstein, Immanuel (1981). "Cities in Socialist Theory and Capitalist Praxis," unpubl. paper prepared for the Research Committee on Urban and Regional Development, Tenth World Congress of Sociology, Mexico City, Aug. 16-21.

Weinbaum, Batya & Bridges, Amy (1976). "Monopoly Capital and the Structure of Consumption," *Monthly Review*, XXVIII, 3, July-Aug., 88-103.

Werlhof, Claudia von (1979). "Women's Work: The Blind Spot in the Critique of Political Economy," unpubl. paper presented at the seminar, "Underdevelopment and Subsistence Reproduction," July 7.

World Development (1978). Special Issue, VI, 9-10, Sept.-Oct.

6

HOUSEHOLDS, MODES OF LIVING, AND PRODUCTION SYSTEMS

Georg Stauth
Sociology of Development Research Center
University of Bielefeld

I. "Household"—Issues of Controversy

The household is by no means a unit that, all by itself, developed the dominant relations of production in capitalism. On the other hand, of course, it is not merely a sheltered, affection-based locus of recreation where the members of "organic" groups can seek relief from the rude world of big administrative and economic powers. Rather, the household represents both; it unites the ruins, if not to say the garbage, of both "worlds": the world of organic existence and the world of capitalist structures. It articulates the leftovers of what creates, favors, and protects life with what is left behind by the huge apparatuses of administrative and economic systems.

Capitalism means continuous commodification, yet within the "household" a set of "primordial", organic functions are maintained, restructured, and finally, one could say, "protected" from becoming commodified. It therefore appears that the household is an institution resisting the encroachment of the "realm of commodities".

On the other hand, the household is an institution in capitalism that appears to gain its importance purely through economic status as an institution providing for the formation of labor and involving money transactions. These money transactions, "imposed from the outside", obscure the productive nature of non-monetarized work relations (domestic labor/subsistence production), channeled "inside" and "between" households.[1] Thus, subsistence production is disguised in a monetarized "economy", so the household can appear as a unit reduced to an accounting system or to a "budget", through which "incomes" are shared among various individuals who, for whatever reason, have decided to pool them.

To my understanding, the household includes and articulates both the maintenance of necessary functions of "shelter", however restructured, and of organic existence, on the one hand, and the development of a system of (socially created and determined) economic transactions on the other.

This ambiguity of the household provokes a whole range of problems and issues of controversy, of which I will refer to only some.

What is Primordial about the Household?

Many views of the household are bound up with the dichotomy between the home and the family on the one hand, and the outside world on the other. And of course there is an underlying pattern of primordiality in this dichotomy: Home and family have always existed in history and have always viewed the world as the outside. Furthermore, the structural separation between production and reproduction in capitalism has been faithfully reflected by modern sociology in terms of (a more or less topographically defined) boundary between home and work.

The study of households has not gone into such dichotomies, since it defines "home" as an *economic* unit in itself, and as such the home is essentially linked to the rise of capitalism. The process by which home and family are transformed into household in capitalism, however, leaves untouched certain functions that were consanguineously and co-residentially determined prior to the emergence of capitalism. Such functions remain tied to the individual, who, in a state of self-objectification, exercises them. These functions (e.g., giving birth, preparing food, providing affection) can neither be dissolved by commodification nor sustained through institutions; they remain the "nearest things" of the individual. We could state then, that the household as a totality is not a primordial institution, but rather that it "inherits" certain primordial functions that are basic to its existence.

The *economic* function of the household lies in its function of securing and guaranteeing the reproduction of commodified labor. This function might have been performed by homes and families in former times, but if so, it was not their essential purpose. Historians and anthropologists stress that the coherence of house, "kin-group", and "domestic functions" does exist all through history and through regional boundaries; thus they find the "domestic economy" tied to these basic, primordial factors. But of course the type of coexistence, and the shape and the importance of these factors, vary strikingly over history and regions. Furthermore, a definition of the household based on these factors will not help us understand its *economic* (i.e., socially created) nature, its central place in defining the essential character of capitalism, and the central role it plays in the accumulation process.

The Proposed Definition

The problem of whether the household is transhistorical or modern leads us immediately to the problem of its definition; this is crucial if one wants to avoid the appliance of a transhistorical inventory.

The definition proposed here includes what has been said above: The household is the capitalist institution securing and guaranteeing reproduction of (commodified) labor. There is, of course, a transhistorical element in capitalism: the generation and regeneration of human beings, to whom—if it makes any sense—capitalism could be applied.[2] This element is not dissolvable through commodification, although it may continuously be reshaped; it remains the eternal "mirror of economy". There are various functions and various types of labor use grouped around this mirror of economy (Baudrillard, 1973), and it is exactly the institution of the household that protects these functions through the disposition of (non-commodified) labor. Elsewhere I referred to this set of functions and non-commodified labor processes as "subsistence production" (see the other chapters in this volume, as well as Arbeitsgruppe Bielefelder, 1981; Elwert & Wong, 1980; Bennholdt-Thomsen, 1981; and Schiel & Stauth, 1981).

We must, therefore, extend our definition of the household; it is the unit that reproduces capitalist labor by maintaining subsistence production. Previously, reproduction of labor in capitalism was characterized by sharing of income, but my argument here is that reproduction in capitalism involves a sharing of income *plus* subsistence production. So "household" here is defined as the unit that, in fact, integrates both.

The Household: Unit of Exploitation
or Unit of Resistance?

In the eighteenth century, it was "enlightened" opinion that militated in favour of the intimacy of the family circle, and that interpreted the family as a "natural society" and made of it the privileged haven of felicity. In contrast to this, since the beginning of the twentieth century, it has been innovative writers who have attacked the family, and conservative opinion which has defended it (Flandrin, 1979: 9-10).

Similar controversies, it seems, could arise when studying the position of households and their roles in the world's capitalism of today. Households, in contrast to families, are an economic necessity to capitalism, not just one of its naturally arising features. To attack or defend the household is therefore neither "progressive" nor "conservative". The whole issue, in fact, depends on how one interprets the various observations concerning the role of the household in the so-called "new social movements" in the core countries and the periphery. So to propose, as I do, the study of households as a point of departure for the study of the defensive measures that people take to survive and to oppose the destructive effects unleashed by the capitalist system is not necessarily to defend the household as progressive.

II. Households and the Economic World-System

There are proposals for studying households as though they were purely "economized" systems, that is, for studying only the "income-sharing" side of their existence (see the other chapters in this volume, as well as Hopkins & Wallerstein, 1979; Research Working Group on Households, 1982). It is indeed necessary to follow this approach to understand clearly the scope and range of the economic determination of the household to capitalism.

On this view, subsistence production is a source of income, like the other monetarized sources, whose equal (comparative) status is then established by "shadow prices". Thus, the household is conceptualized as "a set of practices that ensure the sharing of resources drawn from a multiplicity of labor forms" (Research Working Group on Households, 1982: 21). Looking, then, at households from a "world-systems perspective" would obviously suggest the study of their inherent structures, inter-household relations, and their external relations to other institutions of the world-system. An interregional context for this study has to be established, but it could produce an evaluation of changes of household structures in various contexts to show the effects of the mechanisms operating within the capitalist world-system. The key question would be, How is the household transformed in different phases of capitalist development and in different regions, taking into account the dimensions of ongoing minimization of differences between core countries and peripheral ones?

Households and the
Antinomies of Capitalism

In light of the pervasiveness of the capitalist mode of production, we can distinguish three basic antinomies that are structurally determined by the capitalist world-system.

(A) There is a conflicting relation between the unity and universality of the world-economy and the multiplicity and local specificity of political and cultural forms (unity versus variety).

(B) There is an antinomic relation between *individual*, market-oriented decision-making concerning production and the *social* determination of needs in terms of distribution of income. This antinomy becomes even more evident in the relation entailed between individual needs (however socially determined), and the average, socially necessary labor-time required to meet those needs. There is a similarity of needs worldwide, but the expenditure of labor-time necessary to meet them varies to an incredible extent.

(C) The antagonism between capital and labor brings with it a contradiction between objectified and "living" labor: As capital accumulates, the required labor input into the capitalist production process diminishes.

Most obviously, the antagonistic relation between capital and labor is important to the study of households; in fact, though, all three of these basic antinomies of the capitalist world-system are important.

(A¹) The state mediates between the world-economy and specific, local political and cultural forms by influencing the composition, quantity, and quality of income, thus influencing in turn the type and extent of both inter-household relations and relations of households to other economic institutions. The disparity and diversity of household structures, then, owe themselves in part to the policies of the state, especially, of course, of its social-policy sector.

(B¹) With the second antinomic relation comes a contradiciton between the individual control of production systems, on the one hand, and the growing universality of socially determined needs on the other. And with this come further conflicts: The more social determination, the less "capitalist" will be the nature of the socio-economic relations; the more generalization, the less individual control; the higher the sociality of needs, the less is their satisfaction.

(C¹) With the diminishing of labor input into the production process, brought (following the third antinomy) by an increase in the capital accumulated therein, comes a steady diminution of the importance of *wage* versus other sources of household income.

Based upon the bearing of each of the three antinomic relations of world-capitalism, the following statements can be advanced.

(1) Households need and postulate state action; thus they are the sites of the implementation of diverse policies.

(2) Households are the loci of resistance to the destructive trends undermining the balance and self-dynamics of the system. The household, then, is the economic unit of flexibility opposing the self-destructive dynamics of economic and administrative powers; it is the institution responsible for the "salvation" of the capitalist world-economy.

These statements suggest the following proposed research program.

Households and Incomes

In relation to how working-class households earn their life-time income, I propose to distinguish between three major categories:

(a) There are households whose group members live totally from subsistence economy *(subsistence-redoubt households)*; this type of production belongs only "geographically" to the capitalist world-economy.

(b) There are households that in a life-time perspective have basically one source of income: wage. This group produces as part of the world-economic division of labor; it lives from services in kind, stipends of administrations, and "commodities" bought in the market. The production *inside* the system provides for the means of reproduction *(life-time proletarian households)*.

(c) There are households that split their income in a life-time perspective between income deriving from wage—or market sale—(production inside the system) and from subsistence (production for direct consumption). This division of life-time income of a household leads to the consequence that the "employer" does not pay for the costs of reproduction of that labor (a good example for this group is that of migrant workers).

A further conclusion, which refers more explicitly to the status of subsistence production can now be drawn. The establishment of subsistence production as a source of income, in the purely economistic view of households, shows that the possible flexibility of the households relies fully on their capacity to combine subsistence production with "other" sources of income. Thus, even in a purely economistic perspective, I conclude the following:

(3) It is subsistence production that determines the status of households in the capitalist world-system (subsistence production being obviously a specific source of income).

Households and the Development of the Capitalist World-System

The comparative study of various regions and various phases of the development of the capitalist world-system might be based on the following hypotheses, which summarize the major trends:

(a) The three categories of households are, in a way, parallel to the regional subdivisions of center/semiperiphery. (Percentage differences could be used to define the status of regions in the center/periphery model.)

(b) The processes of "expansion" or "contraction" correlate with shifts from the "life-time proletariat" in the direction of "subsistence-redoubt households", and vice versa.

(c) "Part-life-time-proletarian households" have always been in the majority, and there are long-range tendencies suggesting that an increasing portion of the world population will be transformed into a *partially* protelarianized labor force.

From the study of these tendencies we could expect to draw conclusions that lead back to an understanding of the inherent mechanisms and tendencies of the capitalist world-system. The study of the household and its role in the capitalist world-system, in terms of the primarily economic categories set forth above (e.g., the subsistence-redoubt household), leads us to the following question: How does the *system* survive? The household, then, as a point of departure would be studied as the institution that, given the various antinomies of the system, the limited supply to be drawn from the system, and its various stages of boom and regression, is smoothing out the deficiencies of the system.

III. Subsistence Production, Households, and Accumulation

But instead of asking simply how, given its deficiencies, does the system survive, I pose a somewhat complementary question: Given the destructive forces of the "systematic" relations evolving in capitalism, how do and could people survive? This question then does call for the study of the operation, subsumption, and/or integration of the basic functions (and the necessary labor processes devoted to them) that secure survival. Perhaps the system survives only as long as it gives space to let these functions be executed.

The Basic Antinomies of Subsistence Production

The concept of subsistence production suggests that a "non-category"— production for immediate consumption (i.e., unpaid work for generative and regenerative production)—is important for categories like accumulation, surplus labor, and surplus product; this is a "non-category" because its "measurement" is a proper contradiction in itself. The objects of interest are the individual workers, be they male or female; therefore, the unit of analysis, is the unit of production and consumption for the immediate production of its members (i.e., the household).

The household, therefore, is tied to the interest of the worker, not only on the level of purely economic rationalization (combination of income-resources) determined through the system, but, furthermore and even more essentially, also as the institution that allows for the realization of the interest of the workers in keeping certain generative and regenerative functions under their control. These double interests of workers coincide with necessities of balance entailed in the system: The externality of subsistence production can always be used—both in stages of expansion and contraction—as a field of stabilization of the system.

There are various curious problems with this concept of subsistence production:

(a)   Subsistence production in history has never existed as a unique, pure category of social production; it has always been related to other types of social production (tributary, market production, or production for circulation between the units of reproduction).

(b)   Subsistence production entails a biological/anthropological bias; it seems that, throughout history, women played a major part in maintaining this type of production.

(c)   The fact that the measure of subsistence production has seldom been attempted suggests that until today societies have attributed a normative importance to subsistence production rather than a quantitative one.

The subsistence-perspective would rather stress the way *individual* workers produce the means of survival under specific conditions, determined by *production systems*. Thus, the systems are of interest in this perspective only: in their relation to the process of reproduction of the individual worker. And the study of systems as such remains of secondary interest.

Households and Subsistence Production

The given antinomies of subsistence production determine the set of analytical instruments and perspectives to be applied in the study of households. One would have to gather one's own data rather than use the material already available, and the data would be descriptive rather than quantitative. The type of analysis suggested would be *micro* analysis rather than *macro* analysis. Comparisons could then be drawn on the level of cases rather than on the level of (geographical) regions or (political) states. More general results could be drawn in combination with the type of studies described in Section II of this chapter. Three major areas of study then could be enumerated:

(a)   The destruction, integration, and recreation of various forms of subsistence production in relation to the development of various production systems require attention. The study of the relative importance of subsistence production as a source of "reproduction" of workers in households in relation to the worldwide, integrated production systems suggests a structural relation of subsistence production to the world-economy, rather than a geographical one.

(b) The biological bias of subsistence production (its "nature-bound" mechanisms deriving from its character as production "in kind" and its sexual bias as being predominantly attributed to women) suggests the study of the types of relations of production that are tied to this category inside the households and between households. The division of labor inside and between households calls for study here, mainly because these types of labor divisions are essentially *different* from the divisions set up by the big production systems of the economic world-system (although, of course, they are strongly interrelated).

(c) The "use-value" character of subsistence production, its qualitative rather than quantitative orientation, and its form as a basic necessity (i.e., as a pre-condition of all other social action), all point to its relative importance in establishing norms and social values. The study of households here could be based on the hypothesis that various sets of linkages between subsistence production and other forms of social production, in relation to the big production systems, lead to *different* forms of *social integration* from the perspective, first, of relations between households and, secondly, of relations between a set of households and a system of production.

Households and Production Systems

For the study of various *cases* in specific regions and phases of capitalist development, the subsistence-perspective can be based on the following concepts:

(a) All non-subsistence sources of reproduction in households derive from (work-)relations either to other households or to centers of accumulation (production systems).[3]

(b) There are different types of production systems (fluctuating in "time and space" that determine the "amount" of subsistence production; that is, different production systems require different types of reproduction.

(c) Given a high portion of subsistence production (as the main source of reproduction of a household), then the external economic relations are basically inter-household relations. However, given a low portion of subsistence production, the basic external economic relations may be those of the household to a production system.

(d) The capitalist integration of subsistence production (as represented by households) leads to the prevalence of non-conjunctural forms of social integration, and to their being of growing importance to the balance of social systems in capitalism. As an example of this, one can observe the restructuring of normative linkages between households under conditions of strong subsistence-oriented reproduction and parallel non-economic coercive forms of relations imposed by extractive reproduction systems; for instance, a low commodification of the labor force necessitates other forms of its social integration.

(e) Low commodification of the labor force, normative inter-household linkages, and the coercive control of labor and its living surroundings (however "poor" households may be under such conditions) all suggest the "feeling" of strong control by individuals and collectives of their reproduction and their living surroundings. Strong commodification and low subsistence inputs lead to the destruction of inter-household linkages and to the feeling of a loss of control over "the immediate means" of reproduction and the small world of living surroundings.

There is an essential, structural relation between households and production systems; that is, the economic side of the household—its sources of income—are structurally determined by production systems that do exist in a given local setting. On the other hand, the subsistence side of the household requires its own sociality; thus it creates its own social institutions, such as local markets, festivities, and neighborhood functions, which serve as "separate" institutions of inter-household returns. Households share relations that remain relations of consumption and production for the immediate reproduction of household members, even when different distributive functions are developed.

Thus, a new object of study emerges: Big economic and administrative systems, even from a pure economistic perspective, appear to oppose not only households but inter-household relations as well. So I would like to suggest that the implementation of economic and state mechanisms operating vis-à-vis inter-household relations should be also included in the study of households.

IV. Conclusion

"As a fundamental principal of all its acting industry suggests that any human and natural phenomenon is well suited to be treated as exploitative material, and thus to be subjected to the variations of value and furthermore to the vicissitudes of experience" (Klossowski, 1970: 30). It may well be, then, that *anything* may be suitable (and thus be treated) as a means for exploitation; however, *everything*, at the same time and all over the world, surely cannot be. The purely economic conceptualization of households and their study in the world-systems context would lead us to understand only how the system survives (how anything can be more and better exploited—specifically, how subsistence relations are increasingly exploited). Missed, however, would be how the people (together with and within that system) survive, only as long as they find human and natural phenomena that are actually *not* exploited.

The study, then, of the subsistence side of the household should further the understanding of changing income patterns and contribute to an understanding of how people, living and acting in concrete localities and "socialities" (however different and multiple they may be), react vis-à-vis the mechanisms imposed by the system.

NOTES

1. This is best expressed by Marx: "In wage labour. . .even surplus-labour, or unpaid labour, appears as paid" (Marx, 1967: 540).
2. Bataille points out: "There would be no potlach if its last aim would have been appropriation and not waste (*depense*) of useful wealth" (1975: 99f.).
3. By taking subsistence production as the "natural" economy of the household, I do not exclude the existence of a set of relations between households that remain tied to subsistence production. Actually the household is the unit that serves to integrate the necessary and basic functions of reproduction that resist capitalist commodification. These functions have their own social reality, and it is inter-household relations that remain tied to the social necessity of these functions.

REFERENCES

Arbeitsgruppe Bielefelder Entwicklungssoziologen (1981). *Subsistenzproduktion und Akkumulation*, Bielefelder Studien zur Entwicklungssoziologie, Bd. 5. Saarbrücken: Breitenbach.
Bataille, Georges (1975). "Die Aufhebung der Ökonomie: Der Begriff der Verausgabung," *Das theoretische Werk*, Bd. 1. München: Rogner und Bernhard, 33-236.
Baudrillard, Jean (1973). *Le Miroir de la production ou l'illusion critique du materialisme historique*. Paris: Casterman.
Bennholdt-Thomsen, Veronika (1981). "Subsistenzproduktion und erweiterte Reproduktion," in *Gesellschaft: Beitrage zur marxistischen Gesellschaftstheorie*, No. 14. Frankfurt: Suhrkamp, 30-51.
Elwert, Georg & Wong, Diana (1980). "Subsistence Production and Commodity Production in the Third World," *Review*, III, 3, Win., 501-22.
Flandrin, Jean (1979). *Families in Former Times: Kinship, Household and Sexuality*. Cambridge: Cambridge Univ. Press.
Hopkins, Terence K. & Wallerstein, Immanuel (1979). "Grundzuge der Entwicklung des modernen Weltsystems: Entwurf für ein Forschungsvorhaben," in D. Senghass, ed., *Kapitalitische Weltökonomie: Kontroversen über ihren Ursprung und ihre Entwicklungsdynamik*. Frankfurt: Suhrkamp.
Klossowski, Pierre (1970). *La monnaie vivante*. Paris: Minuit.
Marx, Karl (1967). *Capital*, Vol. I. New York: International Publishers.
Research Working Group on Households, Labor-Force Formation, and the World-Economy (1982). "Household Structures and the World-Economy," unpubl. working paper, Fernand Braudel Center, SUNY-Binghamton.
Schiel, Tilman & Stauth, Georg (1981). "Subsistenz-produktion und Unterentwicklung," *Peripherie: Zeitschrift für Politik und Ökonomie in die Dritte Welt*, 122-43.

7

DEVELOPMENT AND UNDERDEVELOPMENT OF HOUSEHOLD-BASED PRODUCTION IN EUROPE

Tilman Schiel

Sociology of Development Research Center
University of Bielefeld

Household, Family, and Enterprise:
On the Usefulness of Certain Concepts

As the reality of "socialism as it actually exists" demonstrates, even revolutionaries' thinking tends to be affected by concepts dominant in those social systems they try to overthrow (or believe they have already overthrown). The result is that the "new" society is in many respects only a continuation of the old one through other means. First of all we have to free our thinking of certain *historically* developed concepts that we have internalized as *eternal*. Looking at the conditions that allowed these concepts to emerge, and at the historical conditions under which they did not, *could not*, emerge, may help us overcome our biases in conceptualizing future possibilities, not simply by replicating the past, but instead by showing that other possibilities had existed, that capitalism was *not* unavoidable, and that therefore truly radical new alternatives can also be viable.

The concept of the "household as an income-pooling unit" (Wallerstein, 1981) is an example of a concept that can blur our analysis of the "real world" and our view of future necessities and possibilities, because its scope is too general. It is quite usually taken for granted that the household is

AUTHOR'S NOTE: This is a cooperative article; many of the ideas proposed in it have grown out of continuous discussion with the members of the SDRC at Bielefeld. But special thanks go to an "outsider", Heide Lindemann, an historian with whom I had many discussions about these topics, and who inspired the drafting of some parts of this chapter.

simply a unit for consumption: It uses the (pooled) incomes of its members, and redistributes these incomes to its members, but, as this conception would obviously have it, it does not *produce* incomes. These are generated elsewhere, outside the confines of the household; but where? Conventional economics (particularly the branch called "national accounting") provides us with a patent "solution" by the great division of the "national economy" into two basic types of complementary economic units: "households" and "enterprises".

The latter have by definition the privilege of being productive; the former, also by definition, are reduced to the role of pure consumers. A distinguished British economist, J. R. Hicks, states this with unmistakable clarity: He characterizes production as geared to the satisfaction of needs of *others* by the means of *exchange*, and concludes from this characterization that only *paid* services belong to the sphere of production. He excludes services (not to speak of material goods) within the family for the sake of "a precisely defined meaning" of the word "production" (Hicks, 1962: 30f).

This precise definition indeed is, as he concedes, not at all self-evident. The classical political economists would have had qualms about this definition because they were still dealing more consciously (and more honestly) with the fundamental inhumanity of capitalism: its tendency to acknowledge individuals as worthy humans only according to their economic utility *for capital*. Production therefore is accepted as productive only when it is production *for capital*; work is accepted as productive only when it takes place within the capitalist production of *value*, irrespective of the specific usefulness of the work, of its specific use value, and even of its importance for the maintenance of human life.

In the early period of *specifically* capitalist (i.e., industrial) production, this concept of productive labor was still too "revolutionary" to be accepted by everyone as "eternal truth". Even such a prominent analyst of the capitalist economy as Adam Smith had such qualms about accepting this definition of "productivity", especially concerning a whole range of "services". Also, he still had not lost sight of the importance of labor spent in productive activities *not* (or not yet) internalized into the confines of capitalist enterprise.

In his comments on various parts of Smith's work, Marx developed some interesting ideas about productive labor *not* as confined to the capitalist process of value-production (see Marx, 1956: 122ff.; Schiel & Stauth, 1981: 131f.). Productive labor in the view of capitalists, Marx argues, is only *relatively* productive labor, i.e., labor that is productive in relation to the means needed for its maintenance or reproduction. In short, labor is productive from the point of view of capital only when it produces *more* than would be necessary for the sustenance of the working people—when it produces a *surplus*.

It is obvious, though, that this productivity itself is based on other labor spent exactly for the simple reproduction of human beings to enable them first of all to provide capital with relatively productive labor for its own benefit. This form of reproductive labor is called "absolutely productive labor". Insofar as a "household" performs such labor, it also performs (although without acknowledgement by capital) "entrepreneurial" activities. The specific capitalist view of productive labor also led therefore to a biased view of the "household" as an (unproductive) unit of consumption: this can even be seen in the capitalist analysis of the family farm, where (at least implicitly) a fictive separation is made between "enterprise" and "household", the one being the "economic agent", the other the supplier of the work force only (see Marx, 1956: 328ff.).

Using the concept of absolutely productive labor we can state that most of the households nowadays clearly are still at the same time also enterprises, and that there exists virtually no household that has no entrepreneurial aspects at all. Beyond this general point, the specific relationships of the entrepreneurial element to the respective households under different relations of production (including the concomitant different exchange relations) deserve our attention, and this will be the main aim of this chapter. But before this historical sketch can be drawn, a look at the content of absolutely productive labor will be necessary so as to be clearer about the forms this labor takes.

Besides economic (in the everyday meaning of this term) or entrepreneurial tasks, we find certain other tasks performed within the social unit comprising household that constitute both the fundamental condition of all labor, and at the same time the literal origin of absolutely productive labor—the procreation of new life. This is quite a peculiar task, whose peculiarity can indeed be seen simply in the fact that here and only here a certain "division of labor" is unavoidable. Therefore one has to make a conceptual distinction between the unit performing this task and the unit performing the economic ones, although both units may be co-extensive (though they may not be [Chaytor, 1980: 28]).

The unit of procreation I will call, quite "conventionally", the "family", is the group performing the *generative* reproduction of human life. One can call this the "demographic aspect" of a quite complex social phenomenon. But even the "pure" descent view of kinship must refer to the wider social implications, because this function is at the same time the basic means for the "recruitment" of new members in any society, and because the family therefore also has an active part in forming the social structure. This fact was blurred for some time by the search for the "nuclear" family as a social universal. But the crucial element is not this quite often elusive and contested nuclear family; rather, the minimal nucleus of every family is crucial: The mother and her infant children are the true constituents of every society. (Analyses of recent hunter-gatherer societies give some probability to the suggestion that this has been the original social unit, with at least a certain degree of stability, below the organizational level of the band.)

Beyond this minimal nucleus we find a great variety of family forms that are quite "elastic" and form a relatively loose (and often fast-changing) periphery around this core structure of every family. The family therefore is *in itself* quite an unstable, rather "informal" group; certainly it is—qua family—not characterized by corporateness. This becomes still clearer when we consider Henry Maine's characterization of corporate groups. At least in "pre-genealogical" societies, each *family* "dies" after some decades of existence (greater kin-groups being the units that never die), but even in "civilized" society the family as a social group has no permanent existence except in name.

The family "alone" therefore has no permanence, unless material "glue" is provided by common property, (or better supra-individual property because "common" is associated in too many Marxist concepts with "original communism" and connected ideas such as egalitarianism). The management and utilization of such property provides the family with means for consumption (or for direct exchange against consumer goods), but this does not necessarily "work" on an egalitarian base of "familial communism"! Rather, the management of supra-individual property can give the "manager" a position superior (both in access to means and in status) to other members, usually legitimated exactly by the "responsibility" (which is often ideologically determined) of caring for the common interest without selfish motive.

But in light of the above, these features also give this social unit the characteristics of an "enterprise". Such a permanent household held together by property (understood, not in the legal sense, but as *effective* economic property) can therefore be characterized as a very specific combination of family and enterprise. The combination of the family with at least some autonomous means to produce goods for its members "creates" the household as a social unit. This unit provides for regenerative reproduction through production geared to the wants and needs of its members and to the requirements for their day-to-day reproduction. This common or supra-individual property therefore is the material base for corporate characteristics and stability, giving more permanence to these social groupings.

Nevertheless, despite this combination of family with a material base for corporateness, it is easy to see that, although the family is the precondition of the household, the two groupings are *not* identical: They are not one and the same unit labeled only by different names, and they are not just different aspects (demographic and socio-economic) of the same social entity. For example, a household in polygynous and other peasant societies can contain several minimal nuclei (in the sense given above) and even several more "complete" families. Moreover, and contrary to a current opinion (Wallerstein, 1981), a household can comprise members of different *classes*, as the (somewhat peculiar) cases of the Roman *familia* or the Greek *oikos* show, and as do more recent examples such as that of the American plantations. This Greek example even led to a very influential (but also potentially somewhat misleading) concept of the household, which can still be found in writings on economic history or on economic anthropology. This is inherent in the concept of a domestic economy (*Hauswirtschaft*, sometimes even *geschlossene Hauswirtschaft*) as an early evolutionary stage of economic development. But before we come to this I will try to summarize my concepts of "family", "household", and "enterprise", and at the same time give a sketch of the aim of this chapter.

The household, as it is commonly understood, comprises several elements that are not identical, although they condition each other. There are differences in the "tasks" or functions of these elements, which moreover are by no means co-extensive. The family is the unit of procreation or of *generative* reproduction, and maintains the continual "recruitment" or creation of *new* members of a society. The household, in the specified meaning proposed here, is the unit for *regenerative* reproduction, for the maintenance or recreation of the *existing* members of a society (Schiel, 1977). Both family and household are here performing *absolutely* productive labor, which can be further divided into labor spent in (a) reproductive production and (b) productive reproduction. (This distinction is obviously "inspired" by Marx's concept of productive consumption and consumptive production in the introduction to the *Grundrisse*.) The one characterizes production whose goal is to permit continuous reproduction, a production that is threatened by the quantitative and qualitative expansion of capitalism, but which is nevertheless, at least at a rudimentary level, indispensable if reproduction is to be maintained. Therefore it becomes "underdeveloped" by capitalist development, but never abolished, because this would also abolish the whole social system based on it. This contradictory, even antagonistic relation deserves our attention in the last part of this chapter (also Schiel & Stauth, 1981; Stauth, this volume).

The second form, productive reproduction, results in a very basic "product": the (future) producer him/herself, but not simply as an organized mass of living cells (biological reproduction). Equally important is this productive reproduction of the producer as a *social* being.[1]

Both family and household are performing *absolutely* productive labor, so that the combination of both elements constitutes an entity that in its primary aims is a *non*-commercial enterprise and is at the same time also the precondition of every commercial enterprise, irrespective of the latter's organization, which may well (and in fact this has quite often been the "normal" case) coincide entirely with the household. Furthermore, it is obvious that this is at the same time also the precondition of all *relatively* productive labor, or in blunt, "impolite" words, of *exploitation*.

The capitalist process (still continuing) of a separation between the household, as the sphere of "personal privacy" and the entreprise, as the sphere of "impersonal, commercial business", is the result of a peculiar historical development that deserves our attention because it provides a clue to the specificity of the capitalist economic system. The following sections therefore will try to outline the long-term processses of socio-economic development in precapitalist Western Europe. This period was characterized by a prevalence of the household, which regulated both generative reproduction within the family (and which therefore was prone to change in cases of both "endogenous" and "exogenous" demographic catastrophes [Kriedte, 1981]), according to the internal (as well as external) demand for labor power, and also production within the enterprise, which allowed the household to fulfill the tasks of regenerative reproduction.

In this perspective a specific result of capitalist development appears as the underdevelopment of the household, which thereby tends to be reduced to the "mere subjectivity" (to use the terminology of *Grundrisse*) of the family as the supplier of potential labor power only, i.e., without the means for its realization or objectification. These means for the objectification of labor power—the means for labor to become a reality—have a reified existence in capital as "mere objectivity". The enterprise then becomes identified with commercial activity; productivity becomes identified with relatively productive labor, to the same degree that the means for the objectification of labor become reified in their new mode of existence as capital—but capital not as a *thing*, rather as the reified expression of social relations.

The Specificity of
Internal Exchange in Feudalism

The following pages will sketch very briefly some peculiarities of the feudal mode of production that in the relevant debates are often neglected, misrepresented, or even denied (Schiel, 1981; Kriedte, 1981).

Since Adam Smith contrasted the urban, commercially minded economy as a "dynamic" motor with a "conservative, static, unimproving" (without cities, literally "uncivilized") countryside (Smith, 1970: Bk. III, Ch. 4, 502ff.; Kellenbenz, 1974: 45f.), the concept of a dualism between town and countryside has become and remained a commonplace (e.g., in "dualist" theories of "developing economies"). There too we can detect the origins of the notion that towns and town-based (or at least town-induced) commerce were extrafeudal, and that the town was a "dynamizing" "foreign body" within a "static-immobile" agrarian feudal economy.

In this tradition the town-country opposition was further developed within the context of a very simplistic evolutionist model. The sequence "domestic economy/urban economy/national economy" was associated with the quasi-identical sequence "natural economy/money economy/credit economy" by the so-called historical school of economics in nineteenth- and early twentieth-century Germany (connected with Hildebrandt and, to a lesser degree, Bücher et al.). Although this concept soon came under attack, its influence upon concepts of feudal economy is still felt.

Another economic historian, Rudolf Häpke, developed the more appropriate concept of the "market region" (a forerunner of Christaller's "central place" concept): One town, or several towns of different size (and different tasks in an emerging division of labor), form *together with*, and become "embedded" within, the surrounding countryside, constituting an "economic community". Decisive in this concept is that the market region emerges *before* the towns develop, and that the market region is the precondition for the emergence of the towns (Kellenbenz, 1974: 46f.). Although oriented to the development of the Low Countries, this concept can also contribute to a better understranding of the character of *commerical* activities *within* (i.e., as part) of the feudal economy.

It is worth noting in this context that in the very period that advocates of the "closed domestic economy" thesis (or the *oikos* theory in its most pointed version) offer as "proof" for the "natural economy" of early (agrarian) feudalism, the Carolingian rulers implemented a policy of *planned* institutionalization and development of *markets*. Their intention was to enhance the "public revenues" by *monetary* receipts from tolls and similar market dues. (Significantly, basic consumers goods were exempted from these duties, with the argument that the conditions of the poor should not be affected; this hints that market goods were also a necessary part of the subsistence of the "lower orders".) Although this policy of setting up market was not always successful, it raises doubts upon the "natural" character of this economy. (Nevertheless, these public incomes were a considerable part of Carolingian revenues; for this whole complex, see Schlesinger [1973].)

Such doubts are reinforced if one goes on to consider the fundamental conditions wrought by the natural, climatic, and other geographical idiosyncracies of Europe north of the Alps. In terms of its physical conditions, Europe is "one of the most varied regions in the world in its local agricultural conditions'' (Duby, 1972: 175f.). The different ways in which these local conditions were managed, and even turned to advantage, suggest convincingly that *every* economy ''above'' the level of hunting and gathering was dependent to a considerable degree on exchange beyond the locality. (This exchange, moreover, quite early on took on the form of markets; the leading authorities in European prehistory speak of a first European ''common market'' existing as early as the Bronze Age [Clark & Piggot, 1970: 295].) The different potentials and scarcities, ''asking'' to be leveled out by exchange, led to the existence of markets—not as casual phenomena, but as a necessary part of the *system*.

Here we can state an idiosyncracy of feudalism that distinguishes this economy from other forms of tributary peasant society: Feudal times not only saw a (mostly external) trade in luxuries for the ruling class, but also an essential *internal* trade in everyday necessities. This stemmed from an internal differentiation of production induced and reinforced by natural variations, and developing still further in response to demand resulting from exchange based on diversified production. This peculiarity also left its mark quite early on the household economy, because the enterprise—even when still ''embedded'' in the household as the prevailing and regulating social entity—took on a commercial character through this bias toward participation in market exchange. This tendency of the entrepreneurial part of the household to a partial commercialization gave it the potential for becoming independent from and even ''sovereign'' over the subsistence part.

But this tendency did not affect all households to the same degree; rather, it varied in different stages of the development of the feudal economy. In the early epoch the households of the nobility (which even on the scale of the demesne retained features of the household economy, albeit in combination with entrepreneurial aspects) naturally had a bigger commercial component than the peasant households. Changes in this combination took place, though without a separation of the two components into specialized types of households, as we will see. Some commercial ''trades'' that later became important can be traced immediately (without the ''detour'' of urban development) to this early household economy (Kriedte et al., 1977: 57, n. 45). (In a more abstract way, they can be traced to the ''Z goods'' discussed by de Vries [1972: 47ff.].) In the geographical periphery of Central Europe, therefore, commercial activities ''conserved'' their *origins* in both noble and peasant entrepreneurship for a long time (Kellenbenz, 1962).

Recalling the concept of ''proto-industrialization'' (and from the perspective of *longue durée*, and also with an eye to the pre-conditions of the later developments) one can see early feudalism as the period of ''proto-urbanization''; in this light, one can see market regions forming in this period through the entrepreneurial activities just described as they took place in the context of the household economy. This, in turn, prompted the (re-)emergence, or at least the recovery of the towns, which now had new, different functions and forms. The reurbanization during "developed" feudalism was therefore part and parcel of the feudal system, and not at all the overthrowing of a "natural" system by the new money economy. Especially in its more developed form, the feudal system would have been doomed to utter failure without markets (and without towns), for it was based not only on natural conditions "asking for" such economic institutions, but moreover on social constellations requiring them.

The socio-economic system was based on the dominance of a class of warriors who could secure their monopoly of armed power, and therewith their superiority over the mass of peasants, only by their superiority in armament, which they had gained since the time of the great migrations. It is obvious that the feudal nobility therefore was dependent on products that could not be produced (or not in sufficient quality and quantity) within the domanial economy. Production in arsenals run by the state was also not viable, because the state was to a great extent "privatized" during the early phase, and the warrior class (for reasons that cannot be offered here) had to be formed by knights who equipped themselves.

But, as we have suggested above, the peasant economy was never based on autarchical peasant holdings either. The peasant household was always dependent on external resources and inputs, which gave the peasant enterprise its commercial component; in short, the "peasant family household was incomplete" (Hilton, 1978: 6, 10f.). "Natural economy" (as criticized likewise by an economist like Eli Heckscher and an historian like Marc Bloch) was a fiction. Moreover, it tended to be a bad fiction, often taking the form of a romantic-reactionary ideology based on the rustic, jovial landlord who lives amidst his loyal peasants enjoying a simple country life clad in clothes spun by his loving wife, content with the fruits of his estate. Indeed, in this view, money "naturally" enters the stage from the start as an element of decomposition and decay, in the classical guise of the "eternal jew", the "alien usurer and haggler" who contaminates this touching bucolic idyll. (Small wonder that the concept of "natural economy of feudalism" was so attractive to German historians of the nineteenth century!)

Developments Preceding and Preparing
the Crisis of the Fourteenth Century

By now it should be clear that the evolution of feudalism becomes intelligible only when viewed as resulting from a combination of effects (as a synergetic process par excellence), namely of both rural and urban developments. Both types of development, as I have outlined, result from a specific combination of subsistence and commercial activities within the enterprise formed by the household economy, which stimulated the interaction of what in modern terms can be called a "subsistence sector" and a "market sector" of the feudal economy. This suggests that most concepts of modern theories of development are more appropriate to the European past than to the Third World present. (But who will wonder when one considers the general Eurocentric bias of our sciences? Yet it begins to be clear that the world from which our concepts are drawn is a "world we have lost", and so there is little consolation for the Third World in these apparent parallels.)

The armament "industry" of the Middle Ages, as just described, provides a good illustration of the interaction of the subsistence and market sectors of the feudal economy. Moreover, the industry offers a representative example of links between the rural and urban sectors. The production of armaments required a rising specialization and division of labor based on the organization of guilds. This, in turn, led to the formation of market regions and then to the growth of towns, such as Solingen. "Urban" growth, though, did not diminish the importance of rural industries in the surrounding districts, and even favored neighboring regions that provided wood and other natural resources.

But the dependence on marketed goods was also enhanced by the social imperative of splendor and generous life-style. In short, the demand for luxury goods provided by long-distance trade and (increasingly) by town-based artisanal production reached considerable dimensions. Prepared by the formation of market regions (and by the survival of some urban centers), the towns, as centers of artisanal, commercial activities supplementing and completing rural production, could make their rapid re-entry into the European economy. This re-entry was favored, moreover, by the policies of the princes who wanted to concentrate commercial activities in the towns, where they could exert more control over the tolls, dues, and other "fiscal" revenues than was allowed by production for the market conducted as a sideline on the demesnes or by the peasants (who sometimes had to pay parts of their rent in handicraft products suitable for commercial activities of the landlords).

This development of a "market economy" based in the towns produced "economies of scale" and also "external economies", for instance, the concentration of artisans' shops in a small area, or generally the concentration of population favoring a greater division of labor and creating an internal pool of "effective demand" for commercial goods. It also had "backward linkage" effects upon the agrarian economy of the rural nobility, whose economic base tended to become less and less sufficient because of a rising demand for weaponry and luxuries. As a counter-strategy the nobility tried to increase their revenues by making full (and more!) use of its "public" incomes from banal rights (*banalités, Banngerechtsame*), and also by augmenting their resources by a transformation of the demesne economy as the "heart" of noble wealth.

The "classical" form of the demesne economy, which used labor rent—labor power, that is, "free of charge"—lost ground to other forms of rent such as product and money rent (Weber's "*Rentengrundherrschaft*"). (This was true at least in most of the relevant areas; exceptions will be left out for the sake of simplicity.) This came about mainly through internal colonization (*Landesausbau*) with incentives for peasants to bring new lands under plow and thus to form new peasant households on the "inner Americas" (Wallerstein, 1974). These colonists were attracted by favorable conditions: At first, land was quite abundant and labor quite scarce. Partly because of the attraction of the growing towns, the lords had to compete for new settlers, whose position was thereby strengthened so that their status became quite similar to that of urban dwellers. (For parallels between *Rodungsfreiheit* and *Stadtfreiheit* see Dilcher [1973: 18]; for general parallels between the legal situations in new settlements and towns, see Kroeschell [1972: 210ff.])

Nevertheless, inherent in these originally favorable conditions was a self-defeating tendency for the peasants. The towns and the princes tried legally to monopolize commercial production in the urban sphere; in addition, the landlords tried to raise the agricultural production of their peasants by concentrating their labor on commercially productive activities. Except for some branches, where conditions forced the peasant household economy to combine with other activities (e.g., mining and metalworking), the sideline production of "Z goods" by the peasants was impeded, although it could never be totally suppressed and (as we will see) would have a most remarkable comeback later. But the landlords' "policy" of creating new peasant households also served to soften the restrictions against marrying and forming a family, precisely because new labor power was needed. Marriages of new settlers were encouraged and the relevant dues reduced. The generally good conditions for new settlers also stimulated marriages and generative reproduction. The long-term effects thereby set in motion helped reverse the conditions for the peasantry. With the cultivation of more and more virgin land, and with the rise in the population stimulated by the aforementioned developments, "internal colonization" approached a crisis. At this point, the lords no longer had to compete for peasant labor; instead, the peasants had to compete for now scarce holdings. Under these new conditions the lords in turn could raise the rate of exploitation.

Paradoxical and irrational as this may seem, this again reinforced the population trend. Because the expanding exploitation also meant that the peasants had to supply both more surplus labor and more labor for their own enterprise in order to intensify their production, the peasants reacted by raising their production of additional labor power, that is, by expanding generative reproduction (Boserup, 1965). These demographic processes continued to the point of catastrophe: Marginal soils were cultivated even though they were unsuitable, and as the pastures were thereby reduced, the balance between cultivation and animal husbandry broke down. These soils, unfit to begin with, were soon devastated, resulting in a rapid decline in agricultural productivity.

We must add one further comment to this outline of demographic trends and the confusions sometimes triggered by the debates between the Neo-Malthusians (Postan, Le Roy Ladurie, et al.) and their opponents (Brenner, Bois, et al.). Implicitly, the short sketch above hints that the demographic development and the resulting crisis does not fit perfectly into the Malthusian model. The growth in population was not simply a reaction to improved conditions that continued until it reached an upper ceiling; on the contrary, the *decline* in the social conditions initially reinforced the growth in a catastrophic way! (This, at least, is strongly suggested by Third World parallels.) The population explosion was not simply a consequence of improved conditions, but an adjustment of the peasantry to deteriorating conditions. The only strategy to counter this deterioration that the peasants themselves could control was to enlarge the labor pool allowing for an intensification of production both to satisfy the pesants' own needs and to meet the demands of the exploiters to satisfy *their* needs.

Another qualification must be made: Ester Boserup, an outspoken anti-Malthusian, has argued (1965: passim) that a relative overpopulation in agrarian societies is no disadvantage but, rather, a *necessary* condition of developing new methods and techniques of intensified agriculture, since these innovations require higher labor intensity. Jan de Vries (1972) has applied this thesis to the European case in a most interesting way. If non-agrarian productive activities of peasant household economy (production of "Z goods") are taken into account, such a population trend can, through specialization, lead to improved productivity both in agriculture and manufacture by the transformation of "Z goods" into "M goods" (manufactured goods); but we shall come back to this later. Note, though, that Boserup's argument is supported by the timing of the first introduction of certain agricultural improvements, such as crop rotation and other methods to shorten the fallow period, marling, and the application of lime, although the fruits of these improvements were to be harvested only later (White, 1972; Duby, 1974).

Agrarian Crisis and Urban Crisis

The decline in productivity that took place before these various potentials for improvement could become effective was an important *endogenous* cause for the famines in the second decade of the fourteenth century and for the concomitant epidemic diseases such as dysentery, which was especially devastating in the countryside. (Towns, still relatively small and containing a minority of overall population, could use their wealth to level out deficits of grain by imports.) The depopulation of the countryside now contributed strongly to the decline of feudal rents, both quantitatively and qualitatively. (Where labor rent was still important, this decline reduced the labor force available for production on the demesne below a critical level [Kriedte, 1981].)

This was also true in the special case of England during the preceding period, where there was no gradual dissolution of the "old" domained economy as took place on the continent. Instead, as Postan and others have shown, special conjunctural developments and favorable conditions for commercial grain production led to a re-enserfment—a *real* "second serfdom". But depopulation rang the death knell for the classical demesne economy as a combination of subsistence and commercial activities within a big *oikos*-like "household-enterprise". On the continent, this knell had already sounded with the transformation of the rural economy by the policy of "internal colonization" described above. The lord himself withdrew from the sphere of production (except where he became an "agrarian entrepreneur" of a more modern type), and he was content with surplus-appropriation as an activity *external* to the productive process. The demesne was no longer the organizational center regulating production; this function was shifted to the village community, again with parallels to the town in the sense of an association based on communal solidarity (but not in the modern sense, for it was still impregnated by the medieval "*ordo*" or hierarchy [Dilcher, 1973: 22]). The processes of production came to be controlled and organized by the peasants themselves by means of cooperative, communal associations, such as the German *Markgenossenschaft*. (Moreover, such institutions as the *Flurzwang* became common; these institutions are no mere relics of "primitive communism", but adaptations to these new organizational tasks [Kroeschell, 1972: 218f.; de Vries, 1972: 46.)

Agrarian production could recover from this catastrophe and reach a new equilibrium, because this very depopulation allowed marginal soils to be taken out of cultivation, thus resulting in a rise in the productivity of labor. By the same process the conditions for the extension of animal husbandry were also improved, because more land was given back to pastoral use. Given the lower population, the supply of land reached sufficiency again.

But this new, still somewhat precarious equilibrium was now destabilized from the "demand side". The series of plagues starting in the middle of the fourteenth century naturally (because of the much higher population density and more frequent communication and contacts with the "outer world") hit harder in the towns, harder than in the countryside. This in turn affected feudal rent because the depopulation of the towns led to a sharp reduction in demand for basic foodstuffs, the main products of the agrarian economy. The lords could no longer sell their grain and the other fruits of product rent and (as far as it still existed) labor rent, and this accelerated transition from old forms of rent to money rent. (Even in England, now finally commutations to money rent were taking place.) This transferred to the peasants the burden of finding the money to pay the lords for the sale of their goods under unfavorable conditions. The peasants were therefore pushed into the market, not at all by their own choice.

However, exactly because the peasants' base was still their household economy, they were more flexible than the lords, because they could meet the daily needs of their social unit through subsistence production and adjust the commercial part of their enterprise to new conditions with less pain. But their ability to react and adapt to changes in the structures of demand and supply and their readiness to improve and innovate is also proof enough that no "natural economy" tottered into a sophisticated world of early capitalism (Croot & Parker, 1978). In fact, it shows that the peasant had long since achieved a good understanding of an economy in which market exchange played an essential part.

Both the manner in which the peasant household participated in the market (as always by combining subsistence and commercial activities within the household enterprise) and the money rent of the nobility remained feudal in content, despite the changed forms. The dependence of the peasants had certainly become relaxed, and they were now quite independent in their economic decisions and organization. A degree of dependence remained, however, and formed the base for continued exploitation by the lords. For instance, they still asked the lord's consent when they wanted to marry or wanted to take over a holding (these were always occasions for payments to the lord, who thereby enhanced his income), and they still did not have complete freedom to move at will (although this, too, could be "bought" from the lord).

Restrictions on movement, however, were partly countered by other developments, as the situation following the Black Death shows: Heavy losses among the urban population left a high demand for new inhabitants, which stimulated the migration of peasants into the towns. This demand enhanced the bargaining power of the peasants, and to a certain degree provided some compensation for continued feudal dependence. The great number of holdings still vacant enabled the more prosperous peasants to enlarge their enterprise under favorable conditions. This could be of considerable advantage for these peasants, when their geographic situation enabled them to take up the production of goods with a higher income elasticity of demand than grain and other basic foodstuffs. In a time when the general scarcity of manpower led to a considerable rise in the incomes even of unskilled day laborers, the market for meat, cheese, butter, and other products of a pastoral and/or dairy economy was expanding and created excellent conditions for at least a part of the peasantry in favored situations.

At the same time, there developed a greater degree of choice between different occupational possibilities and ways to make a living, not only in the sphere of peasant production, but also in that of paid labor. But the new situation also involved a degree of differentiation within the peasantry (and even more between the peasants and the non-peasant "lower orders"). This tended to undermine the solidarity that had come with the emergence of communal and other associations during the transformation of the old seignorial demesne economy and the resulting strengthening of the peasantry. The base on which peasant resistance could flourish became threatened by this differentation, and the possibilities of uniting with non-peasant groups were weak, especially after these non-peasant (or often sub-peasant) groups were brought into the countryside by a further development—the decline of the towns.

The crisis (or better: both sides of this crisis) of the fourteenth century not only led to the completion of the transformation of the manorial economy (and with that the end of "classical" rural feudal production, whose importance has been contested anyway). It also marked the beginning of the decline of the urban economy that had developed as a complement to agrarian production, and at the same time at the cost of non-agrarian rural production. The medieval symbiosis of town and country was "naturally" also subject to a transformation, and the town by no means emerged as the great winner, as the theory of the exogenous dissolution of feudalism might imply. The town, after all, was part of this symbiosis (and of feudalism); moreover, the dissolution of feudalism from within took place mainly in the countryside, where the events just mentioned set in motion decisive changes.

The towns did not make up their heavy losses without detrimental results in the *long* run too. The countryside won back economic grounds, and not only in agriculture. The combination of the different elements in the household economy encouraged expansion of other commercial activities too, such as the transformed production of Z goods. (For the decline of town economy and the development of rural commercial production, see Hilton [1978: 18] and Kriedte et al. [1977: 36ff., 57ff.].) In England, but on the continent too, the more "enterprising" members of the landed nobility often improved their incomes by making full use of the natural advantages connected with great landed property.

In sheep rearing districts, water power was used quite early on for the *commercial* production of textiles by means of the fulling mill and gig mill. (Kellenbenz, 1974: 48f.). (It was somewhat rare, however, for textile production to be combined with sheep rearing on the same estate [Thirsk, 1961: 71f].) Together with mineral deposits and wood (charcoal, later also sea-coal), water power was also necessary for such "classical" rural industries as metal-working, and mining. Glass production was another rural commercial enterprise.

Triggered by losses in manpower and the ensuing rise in wages, and reinforced by the "reaction" of the countryside to these crises, the relative decline of the towns deprived them of the monopoly position that formerly they had nearly achieved in the commercial sector during the high medieval epoch. Now, urban products became too expensive, and the guilds were too inflexible (concerning technical innovations as well); in short, urban production could not respond positively to new developments on the demand side that would have required a switch to cheaper mass production. But none of these disadvantages existed in the countryside (Kriedte et al., 1977; for North America and Japan, see Jones, 1968).

Late Feudalism and
Proto-Industrialization

For the sake of simplicity and historical priority, this section concentrates on English developments (but for an interesting account of the contribution of the countryside to the commercial production of France, see Meuvret (1974). Because development there was so typical, there is a wealth of literature about various aspects of the English case, but I will concentrate mainly on one seminal article (Thirsk, 1961), with supplementary consultation of Kellenbenz (1974) and Jones (1968). As other works make clear, parallel developments can be found on the continent (Kriedte et al., 1977) and even in North America and Japan (Jones, 1968).

The new—or renewed—flowering of commercial economy in the countryside had, as we have seen, a whole series of interconnected causes. The transformed structure of agrarian feudalism led on the one hand to a diminishing "effective demand", and to a changing pattern of demand (weaponry, "exclusive" luxuries, etc., were no longer the "best-sellers"), of the "traditional" feudal nobility. On the other hand it created a new potential for "mass demand" by the "new" landed nobility—a potential that was especially favorable to rural commercial production (based on estates that were smaller but more economically utilized and better managed, and greater in number than those of the "old" nobility). Effective demand for rural commercial M goods and, at least for several decades, for paid labor, was also enlarged by those peasants who had the opportunity to take advantage of this changed situation.

On the other hand, the guild-based production of the towns was handicapped by the loss of manpower. Moreover, guild-based production was too much geared to the old patterns of demand of the traditional nobility and too inflexible to change fast enough from this pattern of "high quality/low quantity/high prices" to the new one of cheaper (and "fashionable") mass production. This was in good measure due to rigidity in the use of productive techniques inherent in guild production. Moreover, as we pointed out, the new techniques depended on energy sources that were more likely to be found in suitable form in certain rural districts, rather than near the old towns. In these districts therefore we find the starting points for cheaper mass production. Some other advantages for cheap production in rural areas connected with the peculiarity of the peasant household economy will be outlined soon.

Moreover, within agricultural production, the sagging prices for goods such as grain, with a low income elasticity of demand, favored a successful establishment of commercial production of non-agrarian goods in the countryside; as we said, agrarian production naturally shifted to goods with a high income elasticity of demand (e.g., meat and dairy products). All forms of animal husbandry (which had fallen below a reasonable level during the former period of population growth and which therefore were likely to recover ground in any event) now had a buoyant conjuncture.

This was significant for rural industries, not only because the improvement in rural incomes brought a shift of demand to manufactured goods according to Engel's law, but also because animal husbandry was less labor-intensive than grain cultivation or plow agriculture in general. Labor power was thus set free for a development "with unlimited supply of labor". (For the similarities and differences in versions of this famous concept in development economics, see Kriedte et al. [1977].) Peasants (or, in larger agricultural household enterprises, the servants and farmhands as well) had time left for sideline activities after their agricultural-pastoral activities. With the further possibility of raising agricultural productivity, through the abandonment of the production of Z goods within the peasant household and their purchase as M goods with the returns from increased labor input into the agricultural activities proper, clear possibilities for a rural division of labor appear.

The English case illustrates this: Grain production is concentrated in regions especially suited for it, where there are no rural industries, save for some activities directly connected with grain production, like malting and milling. The rise in productivity can be explained by the shift to better suited soils, but also by the abandonment of Z goods production, which was in turn taken up by rural industries in other regions characterized by animal husbandry in combination with non-agrarian commercial sideline activities of the rural households. For this latter combination one can roughly discern two different patterns: sheep raising and a fattening/dairy husbandry.

Sheep raising was mostly an activity for landlords; this is hardly surprising because extensive grazing lands were needed for flocks large enough to be profitable. But there were interesting exceptions in non-enclosed areas, which also were, of course, the poorest ones. In some less fertile regions we find a pattern of small landholders grazing sheep on moors and other commons, while also engaging in complementary commercial production, plus a bit of subsistence agriculture. But the most extensive sheep raising took place on the estates of the new nobility, where, because it required little labor, it was most profitable.

Although the processing of the *wool* remained for a long time within the household economy, further processing of the *cloth* was quite early done with the aid of water-powered mills (i.e., with an energy-source also connected with landed estates). The processing of wool within the household economy fit in quite well with estate economies, because it could be given out either to dependent servants to ''keep them busy'' during slack times or to small peasants in the vicinity of an estate. A certain type of ''big enterprise'' was therefore found in this wool-centered economy, both at the ''base'' and in the finishing stage, but in the intermediate stages it was combined with peasant household enterprises. So, separating these three steps, we have (1) raw material/big enterprise; (2) intermediate product/small household enterprise; (3) finishing big enterprise (but manned by a labor force provided again by small households); further internal differentiation within all stages was there from the beginning. Here a putting-out system developed in which a nobleman or rich yeoman frequently took the central place.

The fattening/dairy complex was marked by quite different patterns, because it was also viable on smaller holdings, especially after the introduction of new fodder plants and stabled cattle raising. So we find this form in areas with partible inheritance or ''borough English'' (*Minoratsrecht* or *Ultimogenitur*), which is a kind of disguised partible inheritance often allowing elder children to receive parts of the land during the lifetime of the father by way of donation. Here, even on poor soils, small holdings can continue successfully for a long time, in spite of the partition of the plots, so long as the commons are not enclosed.

But the pattern of inheritance here also quite often led to a very dense population even if the soil was poor, because the expectation of acquiring a plot kept people in the region (indeed, where large areas were used as commons, migrants were attracted from other regions, especially in such cases as the one outlined below.) The dense population, combined with the relatively small demand for labor power (at least in fattening husbandry) and the tendency of the plots to become much smaller, obviously favors the establishment of household-based commercial production of Z goods. This becomes still more obvious if we look again at the process of differentiation within the peasantry mentioned above.

A "lower middle" peasant could do best by concentrating on dairy production, which was also more labor-intensive, by abandoning sideline Z goods production when there was a market for those products (i.e., both his dairy products and the M goods he substituted for Z goods) within reasonable distance. But by thus raising his specialized production he became a superior competitor for the smaller peasants on the verge of marginality. This had the double effect of enlarging both the demand for M goods and potential labor force for rural commercial production of just these goods. And this development has another advantage: As providers of market goods, the dairy producers had connections to urban markets and merchants. They could raise funds to start businesses in the countryside, or at least they could step in as middlemen. The same connections also worked the other way, smoothing the way from the urban merchants to the small producers.

This short sketch will suffice to show how this type of agrarian production was enmeshed with the market economy, the non-elimination of the household economy being the very keystone. It should be kept in mind that in the example outlined, this crucial condition could be maintained only so long as the commons remained in existence. But more generally one can characterize the development of rural commercial production in the late pre-capitalist period in this way: The combination of agricultural production (both subsistence and marketed production) with commercial production has a tradition reaching back far into the medieval economy, and this complex was adaptable even to great changes in the overall conditions.

For instance, it outlived urban production because of a whole range of advantages: First of all, labor power was much cheaper in the countryside than in towns, because there the reproduction was at least partly based on subsistence production of food, which had to be bought by urban laborers. Later, this labor power became "free" labor, though more to its disadvantage than otherwise. Rural labor was free from guild restrictions, either from the start (e.g., in the case of mining) or through the influence of a big noble "protector". (This freedom was not at all incompatible with a rather servile standing vis-à-vis the nobles, as East Elbian examples demonstrate!) Nevertheless this freedom also prepared the ground for another freedom appropriate to capitalist development, just as the whole development outlined above prepared the ground for real capitalist production (Jones, 1968: 71).

All this meant that production based on this labor had a high measure of flexibility and adaptability to, for instance, the development of new forces of production, i.e., the introduction of new techniques (but also forms of utilization of labor "adapted" to these new techniques); this flexibility further extended to the quality of products (cheap products for "popular" use by using substitutes for raw material, higher outputs meeting rising demand for these cheap goods, sensitivity to changes in fashion, and so on). In this *rural* context therefore further developments, such as greater manufactories and the first industrial plants, emerge too, and here—not in the towns—did the self-made men, innovators, and daring entrepreneurs flourish (often with a nobleman as protector and financier in the background).

Commercialization of the economy therefore was not at all a progress achieved by big enterprises; it was not coincident with the growth of large-scale production as we are wont (in whose interest?) to think. To the contrary, for a long time this development was based on a *shrinking* of a certain type of enterprise, namely the subsistence part of the household economy, which had to be leveled out (with only partial and declining success) by the commercial part of this small-scale enterprise. Labor from the household was increasingly "shifted" to the commercial sector from the subsistence sector because of the insufficient size and quality of the plots and other unfavorable conditions.

Capitalism Was a Progressive Stage in History—Was It (Not)?

After this short review of the development of household-based commercial production with all its obvious advantages, the reader may well wonder why this wonderful arrangement of labor and commerce was eventually abandoned, with all those well-known costs both in monetary and in human capital. Indeed I have asked myself this question, arriving at some provisional ideas and possible answers, which I will discuss in this last section.

A part, perhaps a small one only, of the answer perhaps can be found in the example given above of the reproduction of *cheap* labor depending for its viability on the further existence of the commons. I began to ask myself whether the enclosures were really such an advantage for *proto*-capitalist development as is assumed in the well-known argument that the enclosures set free "underemployed" labor ready to be employed in an economically "rational" fashion in cotton mills and the like. We shall address the question of "readiness" below, but first another problem presents itself: Did these late enclosures create a "pull" factor, as just mentioned, in the sense that investments drew on and profitably absorbed this new labor pool or, rather, a "push" factor?

First, we must recall that these late enclosures (which were quite different, both in character and effects from the earlier enclosures, which were clearly *pre*-capitalist) *destroyed* the base for the reproduction of a labor force on which a quite successful commercial economy was based. So instead of creating opportunities for "capital" in general, the enclosures created at first some obstacles. Instead of being in the general interest of commerce, these enclosures rather seem self-interested, in the sense that they favored *one part* of the ruling classes only, namely the nobility/gentry (which still held the decisive political positions) and the larger agricultural entrepreneurs. Indeed, for a great part of commercial interests they created this problem: The base for the old cheap labor waned away, and there emerged the urgent *need* to find other ways of utilizing, for their commercial undertakings, labor power that had been forced into radical change. "Capital" was perhaps simply *forced* thereby to transform itself into capital proper!

A *new* type of commercial enterprise, one that would break away from its feudal past, had to be developed, and for this, a new type of labor power had to be *created*. This was not done by the enclosures that (like earlier enclosures) by themselves "produced" only a mass of wretched humans; the formation of a "ready", appropriate labor army with the proper docility and discipline first had to be achieved by (proto-)capital. This was by no means an easy task, and its success depended on a new form of *dependency by integration*. The emerging enterprise could no longer count on subsistence-based labor, and so it had to switch to labor power based on market integration (i.e., *internalized* into the "world of commodities"). But to be useful for this, the labor had to be "qualified" for this new type of economy. The last decaying forms of the household economy, suffering under rapidly deteriorating conditions, together with the emergence of "organic" manufactories and other big enterprises were decisive elements in "primitive accumulation" and constituted the nursery for a labor power appropriate for the true capitalist mode of production.

This labor power had to be appropriate, not only in quantity but, moreover, in quality, because it now depended for its minimal existence on market inputs. This again meant the enlargement of "effective demand", but in the long run it also meant subjection to the manipulation of capital (now the supplier of even the most basic inputs) via the law of value, because only by market integration is the reproduction of labor power subjected to this law. For this law determines the value of a commodity according to the amount of *socially average* necessary labor it contains. This "social average" now is a consequence of *specific* capitalist production, which first reduces *qualitatively* skilled, complex labor by technical means to simple average labor, and secondly reduces the necessary amount of labor on the *societal* scale to an *average quantity*.

By this same law the value of labor power can be determined only by the amount of socially average necessary labor entering into its reproduction, which in turn means only by the amount of *commodities* themselves produced as reifications of socially average necessary labor. Only when the reproduction of labor power is integrated as much as possible into the "world of commodities" (Marx) can capital *directly* manipulate and *control*, by its own law, the value of labor power through the reduction of the socially average necessary amount of labor devoted to the reproduction of labor power itself. But before this economically impersonal "iron law" could have effects, there had to be much "pump priming" by comparatively high *aggregate* investments. Where now did these come from?

The same measures that forced the commercial interests to re-adapt to a radically changing situation also provided much of the capital needed for this pump-priming. A market-integrated labor power had, at exactly the beginning of this development, to be kept cheap by lowering the reproduction *costs* (i.e., the costs for the commodities used for this reproduction), which were first of all also costs for (variable) capital. This now made the production of carbohydrates (cultivation of grain, potatoes, and so on) more profitable again because, with the new situation of masses of expropriated people, these became Giffen goods. This rising demand made farming, now also on a capitalist base (with industrial capital goods and expropriated, baseless labor power), an attractive business.

This development, in combination with the very enclosures that uprooted the old commercial labor force, also made land a scarce and much demanded commodity that was dearly paid for (Bairoch, 1973: 492ff.). Small proprietors, whose land was too small-scale to be competitive after capital penetration of the agricultural production, could nevertheless now sell their highly valued plots quite easily at attractive prices. These prices, given the prevailing small economies of scale and low overhead costs for industrial enterprises (unlike those for agriculture), quite often provided them with a sufficient starting capital (Bairoch, 1973). But this by no means answers all the questions raised.

After all, household-based commercial production combined with the putting-out system had formed a well-developed system (still capable of further development) that allowed a sophisticated division of labor with a related raise in productivity, and also met the need for efficient distribution of commercial goods (Marglin, 1976). Therefore "technical" arguments do not convincingly show the superiority or progress of true capitalist production over the formerly prevailing system as outlined. A further *economic* argument was given above, namely that the loss of an own-subsistence base—though in the starting phase it also led to problems for the applier of the new totally dispossessed labor power—in the long run also formed a vast pool of effective demand.

What was formerly produced by own means now came within the scope of capitalist production. By the reduction of the household to the function of the family, its former entrepreneurial activities became conquered by, and incorporated into the domain of capitalist enterprise. "Goods and services" transformed into commodities thus (becoming part of "production" in the "precisely defined meaning" of Hicks) have a double advantage for capitalism:

(1) This transformation increases the domestic market, i.e., the possibilities of realizing surplus value.
(2) It sets "free" (in a sense that Illich [1980] argues was illusory) domestic labor, which is then at least partly available for capitalist production (moreover, this forms a very elastic labor supply). The "rest" is left behind in the shadow unilluminated by the bright theories of economic analysis—"shadow work", as Illich has called it.

The separation of "household" and "enterprise", de-forming the household into the "pure" family and monopolizing "production" for capital, enlarged the *economic* domain of the latter by reducing the *social* autonomy of the former in the fashion of a zero-sum game. With this final (in what may turn out to be a literal sense) development of the household, the differentiation and the (formerly only imperfect) separation between production and reproduction becomes an antagonism (Schiel, 1977).

This brings us closer to finding a more sufficient answer to the question raised above. What if the whole process was not (or at least not by itself) simply a matter of economic calculus plus technical progress? What if quite other—namely political and social—reasons of control and domination played an equally important role? The picture then begins to show some other features. The approach attempted here of viewing these developments instead as a systematic underdevelopment of the household leads to exactly these conclusions.

According to this approach, this process was an enforced measure of splitting up the household into its two components: the first was a now separate unit (the enterprise) monopolizing the productive activities as far as possible, and the second tended more and more to be reduced family, whose main task for production is *demographic*. By this reduction, *reproduction as a whole* becomes subject to capitalist dominance and control. (Transfer payments as a necessary "household income" point clearly to this.) Without its own entrepreneurial means, the household can be held at ransom by capital and by the state. The underdevelopment of the household to the family (or, in other words, the reduction of production to reproduction) resulted in a "de-reification"—in a family stripped, *abstracted*, from its material base.

The social reason for this creation of a new and total form of dependence in the economic world (which is the counterpart of formal freedom in the political world) can again be seen by glancing back at the very transition to the capitalist economy. Even the completion of the *formal* subsumption of labor under capital was not sufficient to establish the capitalist mode upon this base. The worker had to be controlled tightly and directly (with no possibility for escape) by a paramount, impersonal force—the machine, which was no longer controlled by the worker but, rather, imposed its rhythm on the attached labor power. This was the technical aspect of the necessity for *real* subsumption of labor under capital—capital, not only as a *legal* relation of (non-)property, but as a special use-value fit for tightly controlled exploitation.

For as long as the "objective" complement to labor (the means of production) was only formally (juridically) a monopoly of the propertied classes (as was land in feudalism), it was at the most also *formal* capital only; in practice, it was treated by the workers (just like land in feudalism) as *their* property (Kriedte et al., 1977: 118f., 274; Marglin, 1976: passim). The means of production therefore had to be appropriated in reality by the "capitalist" for them to really become capitalist; first of all they had to become real capital, i.e., economically effective as capital. (Poulantzas [1973: 29] argues that juridical ownership of the means of production is in itself insufficient for their transformation into capital; this must be accomplished through real economic ownership.) So the other side of real subsumption of labor under (real) capital is this: the real appropriation of capital by the complete *alienation* (in the fundamental sense) of the means of production from the working households in the technically suitable form of mega-machinery.

Therefore, even *after* its formal subsumption, the household used the means of production *as if* they were its property, and still behaved in an "undisciplined" way (and still had enough autonomy to use furtively, in part of its available time, the means of production, employing some of the pooled labor for its very own ends); so it had to be underdeveloped into the family. This "primitive" alienation had to be achieved, and this state had to be perpetuated in an irreversible process! This permitted the "taming of" the willful "capriciousness" and "immature irrationality" mentioned in contemporary so-called philanthropic writings intended to improve the proletarians in their nascent state as household-based workers. In other words, the very base of the socio-economic system had to be "civilized", in the strict sense of the word. The abstracted family no longer belonged to the *societas* alone, but mainly to the *civitas*—the sphere "higher" than private interests and therefore of "common, general concern". (Consider the interest and care that the family attracts in the programs of rightist parties!)

Despite its appearance as a "sphere of privacy", the family has thus become a *public* affair, a matter of public concern and interference (radically different from the Roman *familia* or other households). It has become "nationalized" and "socialized" for the sake of the general interest—of the capitalist class—so that it can achieve, at the societal level and in a controlled way, the reproduction of an *appropriate* labor force! For this reason, "public compulsory schooling" has taken away a part of the preparatory measures from the family (thus showing also that "public" interest intervenes in the "privacy" of reproduction).

One element in the reproduction of labor power must especially be kept within the boundaries of the "nationalized" family: the housewife. One result of the successful "taming" of the household through its de-privatization has been the subsumption of the content of housewives' work under the reproductive exigencies of capital, where it then becomes identical with contribution to the reproduction of that most singular (and, for capital, important) commodity—labor power. Through the expropriation of the household, capital achieved permanent disposal over this commodity while relieving itself of any immediate responsibility for it, responsibility that was shunted back onto the household and, particularly, the housewife. This commodity could by no means be (re)produced in a capitalist manner without the loss of capital's very own base. But through the "nationalization" of the family via the state, capital can maintain effective control over the production without having to attempt to take over labor power directly (which would be impossible). Such an attempt would result in a backward step to slavery, a form where the reproduction of labor power and the family is virtually the private property of every single "master". This indeed would require high investments in labor, since the whole worker is bought instead of just his or her labor power, and there are concomitant risks of the possible total loss or at least "devaluation" of those investments in conjunctural downswings and, respectively, of rising costs in upswings.

The capitalist transformation of the household, via nationalization, into the family as the collective property of capital in general is therefore more advantageous, because capital can avoid investments in labor that carry all the risks of deterioration and cyclical fluctuations, and that make conjunctural adjustments and adaptability inherently difficult.

"Social security", transfer payments in the form of government subsidies, public relief, and the like, have at once several advantages for capital.

First of all, the family is by these means established as the collective property of the "nation", because it thus becomes vitally dependent on the state or generally on "public" institutions. This dependence on social security and the like eventually *deforms* the consciousness of those who are dependent, leading them to feel that it is impossible (or at least too dangerous) to fight against this very institution, the state, which "guarantees" their survival. In positive words, these people tend to identify themselves with the state, or at least tend to see a convergence of their interests with those of the state, because they really do in a vital sense depend on this institution. (This has already been seen and appreciated by such outstanding, and admittedly brilliant, reactionaries as Carl Schmitt and Ernst Forsthoff.)

Social security, as an enforced saving by the workers, also provides capital with substantial funds for investment. Moreover, this enforced saving has another important function for capital, namely the "public management" of the *socially necessary* product/labor by the ideal general capitalist (necessary for guaranteeing the reproduction of labor power in the long run, beyond the scope and possibilities of *single* persons or families, which tend to consider only the *individually*, or at the most the *absolutely, necessary* product/labor; for these differences see Schiel [1976: Ch. 2, p. 1]). This "public administration" of *social* funds for reproduction also gives some guarantee that the socially necessary product/labor also has the specific capitalist form (necessary for the effectiveness of the law of value) of being at the same time congealed *socially average necessary* labor!

"Direct" wages therefore tend to become reduced to payments for the absolutely necessary product (absolutely necessary labor being also provided by the household directly, as absolutely productive labor); they reflect the *value* of the absolutely necessary labor power. This can also be seen in the tendency nowadays for a worker's family to be able to afford a "decent" living (i.e., a life above the level of bare necessities), often only through the additional wage labor of the housewife, by which the result of the pooled *labor* of the family again tends to be reduced to absolutely productive labor. It would be worth investigating whether in capitalist core countries the pattern of a family living on one wage income is changing into one in which both husband and wife have to earn wages to have just the sufficient income for day-to-day living.

The household as an income-pooling (i.e., consuming) unit therefore is *not* a normal phenomenon; it is, rather, an anomalous result of underdevelopment of the most serious kind. It has by now, as Illich's work shows, even become a monstrosity. Alienated from material means for self-realization, the household is subject to manipulation from all sides and for all purposes. The antagonism already described as emerging from the attempted radical separation of production (enterprise) and reproduction (abstract family) paralyzes resistance to this underdevelopment, for it is at the roots of a contradiction within the modern labor movement. Whereas the new forms of production (enforced mass cooperation, great agglomerations of workers, and soon, providing contacts) to some extent at least compensated a portion of the workers (the *wage* laborers "privileged" by acknowledgement as being "productive") for the loss of their former autonomy by creating new potentials for organized politics, at the same time, the other part (the sphere of reproduction) lost political power, and was declared to be the "private" therefore "unpolitical" "realm of leisure," "recreation", and even of "true creativity". (But why, then, whole ministries for such "non-politics"?)

This is also a remarkable result of the capitalist fetishism of production. It is not capitalist production as the process of *objectification* of labor power (i.e., of the reification of *subjectivity*!), which is justly felt as a process of alienation, that is seen by the wage-earning worker as his self-realization, but his *leisure* time. Therefore he "naturally" enjoys the labor that is located in the leisure sphere, outside the boundaries of capitalist production, as part of *his* self-realization. But this self-realization of the male wage earner means that he does not see how this implies for the housewife an alienation of *her* work, which is seen (and enjoyed) by him as part and parcel of *his* leisure (Evers & Schiel, 1979: 323ff.). Because this really is a necessary part of his *re-creation,* his reproduction within this sphere does not appear to him as production. Because he "accepts" the capitalist view of productive labor, he demands work from others, especially his wife and children, without acknowledgment of this work as *labor.*

Subsistence reproduction is first alienated from the *objective* means of self-realization, and then declared the sphere for self-fulfillment—what a cynical dirty joke! For it is precisely in this de-reified household that, to a great extent, the former measures of autonomy and effective resistance were lost. What once was the heart of resistance by the "lower orders" has been transformed, even in the eyes of many a workers'-movement activist, into the "tranquil realm" where he finds his deserved recreation. But new forms of political opposition at least give him some hope that this illusion will fade away and make room for a political revaluation of the sphere "left out" of "politics".

At last, now, an attempt can be made to answer the question heading this last part of this chapter: In view of my last points, it seems quite doubtful that capitalism is really at such a "progressive" stage in history as even many Marxists still believe. At bottom it contained—also as a condition of its very existence—process of underdevelopment described above. Compared with former stages, then, capitalism also has an element of regression and disadvantage for the household. Is the solution therefore to go back?

The sketch of the performances of household economy and putting-out system as forming in combination an efficient system of production and distribution may suggest such a step.

But rejection of the *economistic* justification of capitalism as "progressive" does not on the other hand automatically justify the populist (narodnist) or neo-populist (traceable in the environmentalist movement) romanticisms that look to a mystified "past" in search of our future. It shows, rather, that industrialization at all costs was *not* the only viable alternative for development. It shows that commodity production and general commercialization of an economy was not automatically identical with capitalist development, especially not with the specific capitalist use of wage labor. Therefore it also shows implicitly that transcending capitalism does not necessarily mean going back to the stone age (as a sticker to be found on some Mercedes cars tries to suggest), that is, back to an exchangeless, "natural economy" nor to an "Asiatic depotism" of a "distributing dictatorship". Many alternatives lie in between, but a viable one must first of all reconstitute a new unity of production and reproduction for a more autonomous creation of life.

For we have seen that reproduction—far from being opposed to production, as the view of the household as a unit of "pure" consumption might suggest—is a *necessary* part, the *conditio sine qua non*, of production. Likewise, we have seen that subsistence production (although not identical with reproduction, which indeed can take on a dangerous form of market-dependent reproduction) is in much the same way the base of surplus production. Once we have seen through the assumption that reproduction is the opposite of production, and that subsistence production is the opposite of surplus production, we can also revise the way we envisage socialism. Instead of seeing it as a modification of "pure" commodity production plus redistribution by the state (a combination that can also be found as a characteristic feature of capitalism), it should be seen as a "rebirth" of subsistence production on a qualitatively new level. Subsistence production should be a base of surplus production indeed, but this "surplus" will become re-transformed into an enlarged socially necessary product, or into a qualitative improvement of expanded social reproduction. Socialist subsistence production will then become the basis of surplus production, which in turn will serve the satisfaction of *wishes* beyond the necessary wants and needs of the whole population.

NOTE

1. The need to include socialization within the family as a part of *generative* reproduction was brought to my attention by Ilse Lenz of the Free University of Berlin.

REFERENCES

Bairoch, Paul (1973). "Agriculture and Industrial Revolution," in C. Cipolla, ed., *The Fontana Economic History of Europe*, Vol. III, *The Industrial Revolution*. London: Fontana, 452-506.

Boserup, Ester (1965). *The Conditions of Agricultural Growth: The Economics of Agrarian Change under Population Pressure*. Chicago: Aldine.

Chaytor, Miranda (1980). "Household and Kinship: Ryton in the late 16th and early 17th Centuries," *History Workshop Journal*, Issue 10, Aug. 25-60.

Clark, J. G. D. & Piggot, St. (1970). *Prehistoric Societies*. Harmondsworth, England: Penguin.

Croot, Patricia & Parker, David (1978). "Agrarian Class Structure and Economic Development," *Past and Present*, No. 78, Feb., 47-55.

de Vries, Jan (1972). "The Labour/Leisure Trade-off," *Peasant Studies Newsletter*, I, 3, Mar., 45-65.

Dilcher, G. (1973). "Rechtshistorische Aspekte des Stadtbegriffs," in H. Jankuhn, W. Schlesinger & H. Steuer, eds., *Vor- und Frühformen der Europäischen Stadt im Mittelalter*. Göttingen: Vandenhoeck & Ruprecht, 12-32.

Duby, Georges (1972). "Medieval Agriculture, 500-1500," in C. Cipolla, ed., *The Fontana Economic History of Europe*, Vol. I, *The Middle Ages*. London: Fontana, 175-220.

Duby, Georges (1974). *The Early Growth of the European Economy*. Ithaca, NY: Cornell Univ. Press.

Earle, Peter, ed. (1974). *Essays in European Economic History, 1500-1800*. Oxford: Clarendon.

Evers, Hans-Dieter & Schiel, Tilman (1979). "Expropriation der unmittelbaren Produzenten oder Ausdehnung der Subsistenzproduktion," in Arbeitsgruppe Beilefelder Entwicklungssoziologen, ed., *Subsistenzproduktion und Akkumulation*, Bielefelder Studien zur Entwicklungssoziologie, Vol. V. Saarbrücken: Breitenbach, 279-332.

Hicks, J. R. (1962). *Einführung in die Volkswirtschaftslehre*. Reinbek: Rowohlt.

Hilton, Rodney (1978). "A Crisis of Feudalism," *Past and Present*, No. 80, Aug., 3-19.

Illich, Ivan (1980). "Shadow Work," unpubl. ms., Cuernavaca.

Jones, E. L. (1968). "Agricultural Origins of Industry," *Past and Present*, No. 40, July, 58-71.

Kellenbenz, Hermann (1962). "Bauerliche Unternehmertatigkeit im Bereich der Nord- und Ostsee vom Hochmittelalter bis zum Ausgang der neuren Zeit," *Vierteljahresschrift für Sozial- und Wirtschaftsgeschichte*, Band 49, 1-40.

Kellenbenz, Hermann (1974). "Rural Industries in the West from the End of the Middle Ages to the 18th Century," in P. Earle, ed., *Essays in European Economic History, 1500-1800*. Oxford: Clarendon, 45-88.

Kriedte, Peter (1981). "Spätmittelalterliche Agrarkrise oder Krise des Feudalismus?" *Geschichte und Gesellschaft*, VII, 1, 42-67.

Kriedte, Peter, Medick, Hans & Schlumbohm, Jurgen (1977). *Industrialisierung vor der Industrialisierung*. Göttingen: Vandenhoeck & Ruprecht.

Kroeschell, Karl (1972). *Deutsche Rechtgeschichte*, Band 1 (bis 1250). Reinbek: Rowohlt.

Marglin, S. A. (1976). "What Do Bosses Do? The Origins and Functions of Hierarchy in Capitalist Production," in A. Gorz, ed., *The Division of Labour*. Sussex: Harrester, 13-54.

Marx, Karl (1956). *Theorien über den Mehr wert*, I, in *Marx-Engels Werke*, Bd. 26. Berlin: Dietz.

Meuvret, Jean (1974). "Monetary Circulation and the Use of Coinage in Sixteenth- and Seventeenth-Century France," in P. Earle, ed., *Essays in European Economic History, 1500-1800*. Oxford: Clarendon, 89-99.

Poulantzas, Nicos (1973). "On Social Classes," *New Left Review*, No. 78, Mar.-Apr., 3-26.

Schiel, Tilman (1976). "Soziale Stratifikation in Vorklassengesellschaften: Über die Herausbildung der Grundbedingungen des Auftretens von Klassen," unpubl. M.A. thesis, Heidelberg.

Schiel, Tilman (1977). "Reproduktion und soziale Asymmetrie," unpubl. mimeo, Bielefeld.
Schiel, Tilman (1981). "Capitalist and Postcolonial Modes of Production," unpubl. Ph.D. diss., Bielefeld.
Schiel, Tilman & Stauth, Georg (1981). "Subsistenzproduktion und Unterentwicklung," *Peripherie: Zeitschrift für Politik und Ökonomie in die Dritte Welt*, No. 5/6, Sum./Aut., 122-43.
Schlesinger, Walter (1973). "Der Markt als Fruhform der deutschen Stadt," in H. Jankuhn, W. Schlesinger & H. Steuer, eds., *Vor- und Frühformen der Europäischen Stadt im Mittelalter*. Göttingen: Vandenhoeck & Ruprecht, 262-93.
Smith, Adam (1970). *The Wealth of Nations*. Harmondsworth, England: Penguin.
Thirsk, Joan (1961). "Industries in the Countryside," in F. J. Fisher, ed., *Essays in the Economic and Social History of Tudor and Stuart England*. Cambridge: Cambridge Univ. Press.
Wallerstein, Immanuel (1974). *The Modern World-System, I: Capitalist Agriculture and the Origins of the European World-Economy, 1600-1750*. New York: Academic Press.
Wallerstein, Immanuel (1981). "How to Conceive our Intellectual Task: Memo to the Research Working Group on Households, Labor-Force Formation, and the World-Economy," unpubl. memo, Fernand Braudel Center, SUNY-Binghamton.
White, Lynn, Jr. (1972). "The Expansion of Technology, 500-1500," in C. Cipolla, ed., *The Fontana Economic History of Europe*, Vol. I, *The Middle Ages*. London: Fontana, 143-74.

8

THE PROLETARIAN IS DEAD; LONG LIVE THE HOUSEWIFE?

Claudia von Werlhof

Sociology of Development Research Center
University of Bielefeld

If We Have Understood Housework, Then We Have Understood the Economy

Housework is a phenomenon that is most difficult to understand, but if we have understood housework, then we have understood everything. But this requires (and this requirement is still unfulfilled) that we do not view housework too narrowly or use it in a restricted sense, and that we relate it and indeed apply it to nothing less than the whole economy—in fact, to the world economy. Only then will the explosive character and the significance of the so-called women's question become recognizable in its generality. The women's question is the most general—and not the most special—of all social questions, because all others are contained in it; because it, in contrast to all the questions to date, leaves no one out. This claim reflects not conceit, or arrogance; on the contrary, it reflects something inherent in the functioning of our society itself. For our society itself has created an historically unique (to date) situation, namely the situation that the women are always "the ones below". But only from below, hence at the bottom of the cask, can the whole be seen as the whole. Nothing is more important—actually nothing is more vitally necessary—than to support this tendency of analysis "from below".

The Connection between the World Economic Crisis and War Danger: War Economy

The reasons that a really general theory of society and corresponding policy are necessary are nothing less than the currently beginning world economic crisis and the danger of war that is threatening us. I wonder more and more why this time no connection is being seen between crisis and war. In any case, the topic has not been raised up to now, not even in the rather broad peace movement in the Federal Republic of Germany, which is strange, because this connection has otherwise always been the subject matter of discussion. But today people are concerned only with moral or military-technological arguments. Why don't people simply ask, "How come there now is suddenly a danger of war? The east-west conflict is actually nothing new!" Or, "What does it mean, we must tighten our belts? What has happened to the economic miracle for which we sweated a whole life long? What have you done with that?" These simple and fundamental questions on war and crisis are simply missing, at least in the public discussion. Why?

The answer is at first very simple: If there is a worldwide economic crisis, then it means that everywhere economic changes will take place. But can these be implemented without the application of violence?

Recently a German politician himself used the term "war economy", and it is a kind of war economy towards which we are proceeding. I do not know what he meant by that, but I think that surely there is some objective background for this statement. To me it appears that changes in the world-economy are proceeding at full speed and are beginning to be noticeable more and more clearly also in the Western industrial nations. What is involved is not merely a cyclical crisis or a moderate structural change, but the beginning of a totally new phase of capitalist development, and nobody knows how it will look. It is characterized by the fact (which is exactly what is of primary importance) that it more or less does away with "free" wage labor. With this development, simultaneously, democracy, human rights, equality, freedom, and brotherhood are also called into question, not to speak of emancipation.

From the countries that were the first and the quickest to set out for this change we hear daily of the brutal consequences: first Chile, then Great Britain, then the United States. Pinochet, Thatcher, and Reagan are applying the new medicine, the drastic treatment of the Chicago Boys of Milton Friedman. The goal of this economic policy is to accelerate the process of adaptation of the national economies to the world-economy. But the Third World is already more "advanced" in this respect, especially since the costs of production could be brought down through the re-location of some parts of the industrial production from the First World into the Third World.

Now this strategy is also used in our own countries. But this lowering of costs is achieved above all through the use of the cheapest so-called unqualified, young, and mostly female workers, which the Third World offers in abundance. The use of this labor power by the Multinationals (i.e., by "our" capital) does not, however, take place in the form of free wage labor. Exactly the opposite is the case: What is involved here is an unfree, "femalized" form of wage labor, which means no job permanency, lowest wages, longest working hours, most monotonous work, no trade unions, no rise in qualification, no promotion, no rights, and no social security. It is plainly the militarily organized labor in the barracks of the so-called world-market factories and free production zones (Fröbel et al., 1980). The first people who succeed in introducing such conditions of work in our countries also would be the first to become competitive again and would make profit, for crisis means nothing but fall in the profits of enterprises. All this means that free wage labor, being too costly, must be done away with as far as possible, that there will be dismissals, that industries will be rationalized, that firms will be shut down, and that free wage laborers will be sent back to the industrial reserve army or be forced to accept conditions of work that are prevalent in the world-market factories.

The "Pillar" of Capitalist Production, the Proletarian, Is Disappearing

I think we are witnessing the historical moment in which the "pillar" of capitalist production, the free wage laborer or the proletarian, is disappearing, never to be seen again. We are talking of just that worker who, since the nineteenth century, has furnished the "classical" figure of the exploited victim of capital and is hence subjectively called upon to revolutionize society, at least so far as the opinion of the leftists is concerned. But the nonleftists too have dwelt essentially on this worker, although they did not call him "proletarian" when they talked of him, but rather as being part of the "middle class", the "silent majority", and so on. For the proletarian or the free wage laborer is not only the factory worker, but basically anyone who earns his livelihood mainly through a wage (or salary), including the white-collar worker and the government officer, too. This type of wage laborer constituted a majority in our countries; he was the base of society, of democracy; he was the voter; he was the "free, equal, and brotherly" citizen; for him were meant the civil and human rights; he was the allegedly equal and grown-up contract partner of the entrepreneur; he was protected by law against arbitrary action and violence, enjoyed social security, and was a permanent, if not life-long, employee in a factory or office; he was freely organized in a trade union; and he received a wage that was sufficient for him and his family at an average standard of living: the citizen, the "human being", the member of society, the free individual.

The "Vision of the Future" Is Vanishing, Leading to General Perplexity

All theories of progress and modernization, leftist, rightist, and centrist, agreed in the belief that this type of *homo faber* should be spread and would spread; the free wage laborer represents the "vision of the future" for all those who are not yet wage laborers and actually for the whole rest of mankind. That is the so-called proletarianization thesis, a favorite thesis of the leftists. The others refer to the object of this vision as "the expansion of the middle class", but actually mean the same thing. Also so-called women's emancipation is related to the expectation that women will become exactly such equal, quasi sex-neutral wage laborers, and the socialist countries claim to be emancipated or to have emancipated women, because many more women do wage labor there than here. Compared to that the so-called Third World fared the worst, for it had not "yet" progressed that much, was lagging behind, and was underdeveloped, precisely because it had so few wage laborers. And now this very wage laborer is to disappear?

Many people still cling to the belief that the present would turn out to be a merely temporary phase of cyclical unemployment, and that after some time . . . etc. But I think they are also perceiving slowly that that is not the case, and Oskar Vetter, our trade union chief, seems to have realized what is happening. The continuous erosion of the social achievements of the working class movement is now directly reaching, as he expressed it, the core, "the substance", the preserves (he was talking of the restrictions imposed on continued wage payment during illness). The result is total helplessness. Whereas no one can imagine a society and economy without the free wage laborer, especially not in capitalism, it is the capitalists themselves who are causing his disappearance. How is that possible? How can it go on like this? And what about the capture of power—the age-old dream of the leftists? What about the "dictatorship of the proletariat" or the running of the government by the middle class?

It cannot have been a mere illusion! Indeed it can: Already Marx discovered that equality and freedom can be only an illusion, from which only those suffer to whom these "equal rights" with capital have been suggested formally. So actually one should not be surprised if one day the equal and free proletarian, the hero of world history, is thrown mercilessly into the dustbin of that very history.

The Proletarian as Minority Phenomenon and the Discovery of the Informal Sector

The moment has come when some of those few who until now did not consider the proletarian as a kind of *non-plus-ultra* of human development could rub their hands and say with malicious pleasure, "Well, didn't we always say . . . " if it were not to stick in their throats. For the "farewell to the proletariat", as Mr. Gorz calls it (1980), does not mean a welcome to those who are not proletarians. Exactly the opposite is the case, and I do not share the really unfounded optimism of Mr. Gorz nor that of some other members of the so-called Alternative Movement, who think that now, with the abolition of wage slavery, slavery itself will be abolished. Wage will be abolished; that is right.

Nevertheless, one should attach some importance to the experiences and thoughts of those who are not free wage laborers but who know something about them—an importance that is now becoming relevant also for those who ignored these workers. For the proletarian wage laborer is a minority phenomenon during a particular phase of capitalism and is limited to a few areas of the earth. Today only a small percentage of the world population belongs to this category and it has never been more. The "proto-type" of the free wage laborer—the male, white, over-21, urban, industrial worker, is even rarer.

Eighty to 90% of the world population consists of women, peasants, craftsmen, petty traders, and wage laborers whom one cannot call "free" or "proletarian". Actually this fact has always deserved the attention now gradually being paid to it. This can be noticed not only in the debate on women's work, the Third World discussion, and the revived discussion on agriculture and peasants (i.e., in discussions on all those who are in principle not free wage laborers). What is promising to become the latest "hit" in the debate is the "informal sector", in which, of course, there is also wage labor, although this wage labor is, in contrst to that found in the "formal sector" of the economy, just not "normal". It is exactly this informal sector into which the former proletarians are pushed: into part-time work, contract work, seasonal and migrant laborers' work, illegal work, "borrowed" work,[1] as well as unpaid work like the "work for one's own" (Weizsäcker, 1979), "shadow work" (Illich, 1980), subsistence work, and, mostly "forgotten", housework—i.e., generally speaking, into (wage) labor that is not "free".

In the debate on this sector so far, people deliberately close their eyes to the fact that there is nothing new about this sector at all. What is new is only that it is now becoming the "alternative" for the ex-proletarians, which is why interest is being taken in it. But this interest is, as it always has been, one-sided (von Werlhof, 1978); the problem of the informal sector has been approached from the wrong end—from a standpoint that ennobles the proletarian and free wage labor and relegates other contributors and forms of labor to a secondary status.

What Sort of a Mode of Production Is Capitalism?

At least for now, in view of the regression (or progression?) in the area of free wage labor, one must ask oneself, as women have been asking for a long time, what sort of a mode of production capitalism actually is. This question sounds very strange, for on this question there was and there still is agreement between the protagonists in the debate also among those who characterize capitalism as an industrial system or the industrial society. Actually this is a sort of tacit agreement that begins already at the non-scientific level. They all say that capitalism has originated in and spread out of Europe through the achievements of Europeans, that it is a progressive mode of production, and that it functions through the interplay or contradiction between wage labor, i.e. free wage labor and capital, the results of which are progress, growth, incomes, profits, and accumulation; in the political sphere the results are the purported ideals of equality, freedom, and brotherhood—in short, of democracy. This capitalism with its political form of the democratic state is put forward as the ''vision of the future'' for the rest of the world.

This understanding of capitalism is for me nothing else but the glorification of the ''white man'' as the creator of culture, civilization, and humanity—the white man as the human being par excellence (von Werlhof, 1981). It is time now to free ourselves from a view of this conception as a positive one, for as such it has nothing to do with reality, being ahistorical, racist, Eurocentric, imperialistic or colonialistic, and of course sexist.

Not without reason did this conception begin to take shape exactly when the conquest of the world began; the first conquerors were the participants in the Crusades and the seafarers. This world, today called the ''Third World'', has up to now always been the object of totally undemocratic and uncultivated methods of robbery, plunder, rape, and mutilation. Simultaneous with the subjugation of the world took place the subjugation of women, known in Europe as the so-called witch-hunt, which went on for centuries and claimed millions of victims, as it is said so abstractly. Only on this foundation, which we have blotted out of our consciousness, did the Western world ''rise'' to the position of the First World and create for its justification humanism and enlightenment.

That is not all, for ''violence as the precondition of freedom'' has not only been that solitary act—even if it did last for centuries,—in the phase of ''primitive accumulation'', as Marx called it!

It was not so, and today we push even that out of our consciousness by asserting that our ideals would spread everywhere and finally cover the whole world. Today, as ever, our freedom rests on the unfreedom of others, our equality on the inequality of others, our non-violence on the violence against others, our wealth on their poverty, our democracy on dictatorship elsewhere; and that to an ever increasing extent.

Evidently our mode of production is not capable of producing anything new; it can only acquire already existing and produced things and "transform" them, that is, destroy them. For not only has the economic miracle vanished; one may also be permitted to ask what the result of hundreds of years of plundering the whole world actually is. Where has the whole wealth gone? What remains is "a hole in the ground", as Johan Galtung once said. Our interest in suppressing this fact is not different in science from what it is in politics. With almost unimaginable tenacity people uphold in ever new variants the thesis that capitalism has actually been realized only in Europe and the United States, that what one finds elsewhere are pro-, post-, or non-capitalist modes of production, or peripheral capitalist or deformed capitalist modes of production. In this way the blame is laid at the door of the victims. For the concomitant conditions of such modes of production are correspondingly characterized as traditional, backward, primitive, archaic, not yet developed, and the like. The people living under such conditions are considered to be—in contrast to us, naturally—stupid, lazy, apathetic, obstructive, conservative, narrow-minded, ignorant, and passive, but also emotional, dangerous, cheeky, bestial, clichés are well known. They are used for us in the same way as for the Third World.

Whether they are admired or hated—both come to the same thing—it is believed that only the so-called integration of these people and these conditions in the capitalist system can develop them to a certain extent from animal to man and promote them out of "nature" into society. Whether priest, development expert, entrepreneur, minister, or husband, none of them would like to be reminded that he is just that: priest, etc., only *because* the "partners"—as they are called today—are heathens, underdeveloped, exploited, subjugated, or women.

So the heathen, the backward and exploited, and the housewife *must* remain what they are. Indeed, their roles must be filled so that the priest, the developer, and the proletarian can become what they are.

So the "integration" of the former people into the roles of the latter is out of the question. Anyway, does one need to be *made* into a human being through this integration under the aegis of the state? People do not *become* human beings; they already are.

The "Pillar" of Accumulation and the "Vision of the Future" Are the Third World and the Housewife

But let us come back to the economy in its narrow sense. At least women must have noticed already where my argument leads: I am proceeding towards the significance of housework and all that is connected with it— yesterday, today, and tomorrow. What I want to say is that the work of women is rather comparable to the work in the Third World.

Just now I have tried to describe what we generally mean by capitalism, accumulation, growth, etc., and to delineate that class which excludes 80%

to 90% of the world population—the free, white, male wage laborer here, and the unfree, colored, female non-wage laborer there, along with the old people and the children. Now I ask you, is capitalism so incapable that it still has not succeeded in integrating these masses in its system of exploitation? Is it even in the process of abolishing itself by abolishing free wage labor? That would be rather improbable.

The solution of the puzzle is very simple: Everything is just the opposite of what it appears to be. Not the 10% free wage laborers, but the 90% unfree non-wage laborers are the pillar of accumulation and growth, the truly exploited, the real "producers", the "norm", and represent the general condition in which human beings find themselves under capitalism. And now this all is also threatening the proletariat to their great horror. For, against all protestations to the contrary, human beings under capitalism find themselves in unfreedom, inequality, unbrotherliness, surrounded by violence, misery, and oppression, without rights, without powers, unorganized, without wage, without property, insecure, starving, and shivering with cold—but working.

It is really not true that the "unemployed" do not work. They are without wage, without income, and must therefore work much more than the "employed" in order just to survive. They do everything, really everything that is possible in order to get a minimum income. Since one single activity yields too little, they must perform several simultaneously: They are simultaneously small peasants and seasonal agricultural laborers, petty traders and petty service people, producers and sellers of self-produced commodities, prostitutes and part-time wage laborers, contract- and home-workers;[2] in short, they all occupy all the roles that will gradually come to constitute the norm in our countries, too. The Third World is coming to us. It reveals to us the "vision of the future" and the real character of our mode of production. More explicitly, here, too, our economy will become "femalized", "feminized", "marginalized", "naturalized", or "housewifized"; only one thing will it not become—proletarianized.

Housework as the Model of Work

Now the catchword has been said: "the housewife". My thesis is that the principles of organization of housework will determine our future and not, as assumed until now, the princples of organization of proletarian wage labor. The housewife is the exact opposite of the proletarian. Let us first take this in the sense of contrast between white and black. In principle, every woman can be included, for under capitalism all women are housewives, whether they want to be or not. I am therefore by no means interested in the glorification of the housewife or as is otherwise usual, of the proletarian. Theorctically it could be very nice to be a housewife, for no one else has the opportunity to perform so manifold and different activities. Have a look at the biographies of women and you will be astonished. What I am pleading for is to perceive housewives from a different perspective. Let us first put on the spectacles of the contrast between the proletarian and the "pure" housewife, both rare, nevertheless typical, prototypical inventions of capitalism (Bock & Duden, 1977; Kittler, 1980). This economic couple is a very rare phenomenon, not only in all other parts of the world, but actually also in our countries, at least as far as one means thereby a life-long union. At the moment it is in the process of becoming extinct. In spite of this it has become the ideal type, which all people of the world should and must strive after, even if they never achieve it. It is the Western white middle-class nuclear family, which is today propagated again (it was propagated for the first time in the nineteenth century) through a huge propaganda campaign—even in the slums of Calcutta where no one really has a chance of realizing this noble ideal.

We have already talked of the definition of the proletarian or free wage laborer. The corresponding woman is the life-long, full-time housewife. The word "life-long" already hints at the fact that she is actually in a prison. (The "house"-wife as "apartment"-wife.) The life of the full-time housewife may be a little gilded, but that does not change its basic character. And nobody can change it through pure voluntarism, neither the wife nor the husband. Both may also be quite satisfied with this situation, for they perhaps do not know of any alternative and, above all, they do not have any. Moreoever, their relative economic security depends on their living together. They are a sort of Siamese twins of our economy.

The proletarian is apparently free, equal, fraternal, and so on. The housewife is the reverse of that: She is in reality unfree in a double sense:

(1) She is not free to choose or change the place and type of work or her particular job freely; she is bound to the apartment, the husband, and the children.
(2) She is also not free from all means of production, so one cannot say that she merely possesses her labor-power, which in a certain sense is the case with the proletarian.

She has something no man has, which is treated in our society like a means of production: her child-bearing capacity. Moreoever, she "has" the husband as "bread-winner".

In addition to this two-fold lack of freedom, she is not equal. Formally, of course, there is now equality of rights, but even where these rights are practiced, they have mostly harmful effects for women (e.g., in divorce law), simply because women are in fact unequal as long as they are housewives. Equality of rights for women is—analogous to the pretense of equality between proletarians and capitalists, i.e., like the alleged class-neutrality—only the illusion of alleged sex-neutrality in capitalism. Women, of course, are now considered full citizens; they have been granted voting rights and other rights, but the specific areas of law have been clearly split according to sex (e.g., marriage law). Thus rape in marriage is not a punishable offense. To tolerate rape belongs, so to speak, to the one-sided marital obligations of the wife.

In addition, the inequality is primarily a social inequality. It is based on the fact that the husband has "the queen of the commodities" (Marx): money in his pocket. The wife, however, is not paid for her work. The husband must give her only "board and lodging", which he must also do for a slave. Also, working hours, conditions of work, holidays, and leisure all are not settled by contract for the housewife; the marriage contract is not comparable to the employment contract. There is no right to strike, no fraternal or sisterly organization of housewifes; they are individualized and atomized. They do not enjoy social security on the basis of their work as housewives, nor are they protected by law from the despotism and violence of their husbands (hence, the houses for battered women). In the home no one watches over the observance of human rights; here they are a "private affair" and allegedly do not concern the public, even when physical safety is not guaranteed.

The wife should serve the husband and, above all, obey him; he can even sue her for this service and obedience. In short, the housewife is an unpaid worker who is at the disposal of the husband round the clock, all through her life; even more, she is at his disposal with her whole person, with everything she has, including her sexuality and child-bearing capacity, her psyche and feelings; she is at the same time slave and serf who is compelled to do all the work that the husband and the children "need", including expressing love even when she does not feel any. Here one works out of love and love becomes work (Bock & Duden, 1977). It may not always be an intolerable situation, but it is often bad enough; above all, there is no possibility of preventing its becoming one. This absolute contrast means, for example, that one need not look at the Third World in order to find that typical absence of human rights and of homogeneously "free" conditions of work and life.

I believe that the extremely different conditions of work of the free wage laborer and the housewife constitute the two poles of a continuum of capitalist conditions of work and relations of production, between which reality lies—leaning sometimes more towards free wage labor, sometimes more towards unfree, unpaid housework. All kinds of conditions of work existing in the world lie between these two poles, including those one usually places in a third, pre- or non-capitalist sphere.

Slave-work today, unfree forms of wage labor, home-industry, peasant production and the like all lie on this continuum of capitalist production, which is today becoming more and more like a slide inclining towards housework. For all have one thing in common: dependence on the market and, generally, on money or, more exactly, on a wage. All people in the world are in principle dependent on a wage, because they no longer have or control any means of production worth mentioning, such as land, tools, and know-how, on which they could survive. Also, conditions that seem to correspond to pre-capitalist societies lie in that continuum. In capitalism they are all united in the work of the housewife: forced labor, serfdom, slavery, and unfree wage labor.

That is why all other work can be understood only from below, from the point of view of housework, and not the other way round, from the point of view of wage labor. Basically housework, not wage labor, is the "model" of work in capitalism. All people in capitalism are of course potentially wage laborers, but in reality they are rather "housewives", industrial reserve army, relative surplus population, i.e., relative in ratio to the existing wage labor.

Only very few housewives are "pure" housewives. Almost everyone—both women and men—are for some time of their life or from time to time also wage laborers, or they sell homemade products out of home (above all, in the Third World). But never does the female wage laborer or the unfree male wage laborer resemble the free wage laborer. All conditions of femalized or directly female wage labor point rather towards the housework-like character of this work, so that it can be better understood as paid housework rather than as "nearly" free wage labor. (Understood in this sense, wages for housework is nothing new and also not a "revolutionary" demand.) The wage labor of women is organized and treated as an extension of their housework and, moreover, for this reason correspondingly badly paid. Women are therefore unequal to men outside the home, just as they are in the home. That is the reason all women are housewives and are always treated as if they are. This sexism also provides the model for racism: A colored wage laborer is just never a free wage laborer, and is not treated as one even when he or she is one. That is why there is also no race neutrality in capitalism.

Sexual Division, Hierarchization, and Devaluation of Labor

What we have here is a "sexual" division of all labor, and not just the "normal" sexual division between housework and wage labor. The sexual division exists also within wage labor and is worldwide, and it extends much beyond what is determined by biology. This division of societal work means at the same time a hierarchization between the sexes similar to that between the races and "classes", a hierarchization that is unique and unheard of in history. It means, as Ivan Illich says, an unprecedented "degradation" of work on the basis of a similarly unprecedented "degradation of women." Such a devaluation of especially women's work and, with it, of women's life and the female sex, and such a rigid subordination of women— standardized throughout the world and effective in all spheres of life, and also proceeding from that of men, were unknown in all the pre-capitalist forms of sexual division of labor, including the exploitative ones. It is important to know this, because in our countries both women and men believe that they are now better off than their earlier counterparts just as many people in the Third World still believe in the progress that the white man has allegedly brought to them.

They believe this because they are also victims of the suppression of history. Three hundred years of witch-hunt, running parallel to the colonization of the world, were necessary to snatch away from the women (as from the colored people) their power, their economy, and their knowledge, to erase from their brains and feelings what was still left of the consciousness thereof, and—continued in the upbringing at home—to socialize them anew, from their birth onwards, from generation to generation, from day to day, i.e., to force them into what they are today: housewives and "the underdeveloped". The housewife—and with her the "underdeveloped"—are the artificial products, the result of an unimaginably violent development on which our whole economy, our law, our state, our science, art, and politics have been built—the family, private property, and all the modern institutions.

This "model" is a worldwide export hit, not only today. The treatment of the colonies, the enforcement of an international division of labor following the pattern of the sexual division (namely the division into white wage laborers here and colored, "femalized" non-wage laborers there) was also practiced, tried out, and forced through by fire and sword. The Third World was the "witch" in those days, and is the "general-housewife", "the world-housewife" today, and this includes Third World men. The relation between husband and wife is repeated in the relation between the First World and the Third World.

Child-Bearing Capacity and
Female Versus Male Capacity for Work

The dissimilarity of the conditions of work and the division and hierarchization between working people leave the main question open, namely that of the content of the activities thus divided. Here the black/white contrast does not suffice for our analysis, nor does the simple below/above contrast.

The question about the content of the work is tantamount to the question about the "Why?" of the division, about its economic significance for the system.

At this point, at the latest, the souls part company. We know that women's work is, corresponding to its payment, considered to be worthless, unproductive, even parasitic, socially not necessary, viewed as a "natural process" and not even as work. The proof of this treatment lies in the following figures (UN): Taking the world as a whole we see that women perform two-thirds of the total work, but they receive only one-tenth of the world income and control only one-hundredth of the means of production in the world.

Obviously, the opinion about the whole Third World's contribution to the total work in relation to that of the First World (like that of agriculture in relation to that of industry) is similar to the opinion on women's work.

The work of the housewife consists in executing, producing, and preparing what should be free of charge for "the society"—what is excluded from the responsibility of the enterprises. This is work that the husband does not do and/or that cannot be purchased by a wage, because it is too lowly or because it cannot be had for money (e.g., the provision of "genuine" emotional care). According to feminists, the wife looks after the physical, psychological, and social production and reproduction of the husband as wage labor force and also after that of the next generation of wage laborers and housewives. In addition, she takes over some extra out-of-home duties; the housewife has to do double work.

The all-round duties of the housewife have as purpose the production of human labor power, the production of living human beings. It is production of human beings in contrast to the production of things. The housewife is "specialized" on human beings, the wage laborer on things. That is the "secret" why housework as a "model" of organized work will not disappear along with (free) wage labor, and that is the decisive qualitative difference between the two. Woman is in the truest sense of the word the soil on which the wage laborer stands. He is defined as human being, she as "nature".

The "true essence", so to speak, of this division and its starting point is nothing but the natural monopoly of women, namely their child-bearing capacity. In no mode of production throughout history is the child-bearing capacity, the prerequisite of production of human beings, so central as in ours, because the famous surplus value, the sole purpose of capitalist production, can be extracted only from living human beings. The more human beings, the more surplus value is in principle possible. It is no accident that the so-called population law of capitalism is considered to be nothing less than the ''general law of capitalist accumulation'' (Marx). It is this law that turns women into child-bearing machines and is responsible for the so-called population explosion.

Machines cannot produce any surplus, they can only imitate human labor. For capital accumulation and profit, human beings are irreplaceable, simply because they are living. Capital by itself is dead. Only its vampire-like sucking of fresh blood makes it appear living. That is why the producers of human beings are also for the entrepreneurs basically much more important than the producers of things; they are the prerequisites of the latter; without them nothing will work. (That is why everybody becomes nervous when women do not want to bear children, refuse to do housework and serve men, do not marry, do not ''obey'', and so on.)

The more labor power is pushed aside or made redundant by technology, the more the system has to put human labor to use in other spheres and, if possible, on a mass scale. This is the question never discussed by those who believe in the ''being alive'' of capital and/or those who can identify only wage work as work. The question today is how that unwaged work, including the work of masses of ex-proletarians, should be organized and controlled (without conjuring up the ''danger of socialism''). The historicial examples of such an organization of unwaged work on a mass scale can be seen in housework, in agriculture, and in the Third World in general.

The production of human beings in a society like ours is, however, not only the most important, permanently necessary, and the most difficult task; it is also particularly frustrating, because human beings are constantly humiliated, robbed, and exploited. That is why women have developed a specifically feminine capacity for work; they *had* to develop it. It gets its orientation from the fertility of their bodies. Creating new life (through childbirth) is the principle that women apply also to all other activities— earlier for the common benefit of all people, today for the benefit of the system.

Everything that women do must bear fruit and it must be gratis, like the air we breathe. This applies not only to birthing and rearing children, but also to the sundry housework and wage labor, the bestowal of additional emotional care on colleagues, the friendliness, the submissiveness, the being-always-at-others'-disposal, the healing-all-wounds, the being-sexually-usable, the putting-everything-again-in-order, the feeling-oneself-responsible, the sacrificing-oneself, the frugality and unpretentiousness, the renunciation in favor of others, the putting-up-with-everything, the helping-out-in-all-matters, the withdrawing-oneself, the being-invisible and the being-always-there, the passive being-available and the active ''pulling-the-cart-out-of-the-mud'', the having-phantasy and the being-emotional, the endurance and the discipline of a soldier. All these duties and qualities make up the feminine work capacity. It is complete, it is the most general and the most comprehensive work capacity imaginable, because it draws in and mobilizes the whole person. And its production "did not cost anything"; no formal training is necessary for it; nor is it conceivable. The "un-qualifiedness" of women is in reality a super-qualification. On its free-of-cost production and appropriation rests not only wage labor, but the whole accumulation.

Not the generalization of wage labor, but the generalization of housework is therefore the dream of all capitalists. There is no cheaper, more produc-tive or more fruitful human labor, and one can also enforce it without the whip. I believe that the restructuring of our economy will involve the ef-fort to re-educate the men and force upon them, as far as possible, the feminine work capacity. For the wage laborer does too little and knows too little. He can do only what he is paid for and what has been agreed upon by contract. He does not do a bit more than that and he has absolutely no idea of how human beings are reproduced. He functions like a robot, as an appendage of the machine, de-emotionalized; he avoids and sabotages every effort to press still more life out of him. He works for too short a time and is exhausted too quickly. He has no reason to take initiative and no motiviation for work, he cannot be mobilized for all purposes, as a per-son, as a whole human being. The masculine work capacity is much too inflexible and "unfruitful", it is short of blood. That is why it is used so rarely.

"Femalization" of the Proletarian and New Forms of the Socio-Sexual Division of Labor

The import of fresh "guest-workers"—who, because of their use-value-orientation and peasant background (see Shanin, 1980), approximate more closely the feminine work capacity—has its reason in these facts. Just as in the reverse case, cheap, young, female labor power is utilized through the transfer of industries to the Third World. That, and not our wage labor, provides the model of the future: the world-housewife or the worldwide "industrial reserve army", the "marginal mass" or the "relative surplus population". The more and more frequently formulated threats against this "surplus population" are therefore not only directed against the Third World, but equally against us. Those who cannot be used as wage laborers are everywhere considered to be the cause of the crisis, while they are in reality nothing but the necessary result and also the necessary condition of our mode of production.

What to do with the increasing number of "redundant people" is the most decisive question today. All forms of work that the non-wage laborers had to develop, and which are nowadays being induced from above, are interesting for us, because we shall also experience them soon. The Alternative Scene has already begun with it, be it on the farm, in the workshop, or at the home as houseman. The state has also begun with it, e.g., the F.R.G. through the campaign "women are able to do more", by propagating the idea of honorary social work and participation of the citizens in community work in general, and through the back-to-the-family and "mothers save the nation" program of the Christian Democractic Party.

And the enterprises have begun with it, through the dismissal of free wage laborers, and more and more frequent use of unfree, "housewifized", "naturalized" wage laborers, of illegal, "black", "borrowed", imported, and part-time workers, among them many women, until the men are also prepared to get down from the high horse of the proletarian, the equal and the free, and to accept conditions of work similar to those of women and in the Third World, and to agree to be in principle and now also in reality nothing more than "land", a natural resource, an object of capital.

This the enterprises will do only if they get and retain guaranteed control over women. So there is a danger that men will join in and let themselves be corrupted, just as they once let themselves be compensated with the housewife for the introduction of (by no means popular) wage labor, at the cost of women. Will they repeat the mistake? They can see what it has led to, and it has not led to the happiness of men in any case.

This shift is the beginning of "the change" (according to Franz Josef Strauss). It does not proclaim a new, different capitalism, nor even socialism; it proclaims the perfectly logical continuation of the existing system, the no longer embellished breaking out of its latent nature. Equality and freedom are luxuries that a war economy cannot even pretend to afford.

The so-called world-market factories in the Third World and production by contract (Bennholdt-Thomsen, 1980) in the cities and villages there give us a foretaste of our future: part-time and unfree wage labor in the factories, organized as in the barracks of the army, plus collective forced labor in the countryside, regulated not through wages but through credits, and all that on the foundation of the individual prison of the patriarchal nuclear family: The sexual division of labor survives the abolition of free wage labor and will even be reinforced.

An alternative is possible only if we, men and women, succeed in getting back forever not simply the wage, but much more—namely the means of production: our bodies and our children, our houses and our land, our knowledge and our creativity, and the results of our labor. We want all this without continuing to depend on "central powers" like puppets, so that we can work for our own, autonomous existence. However, for that not only do we need no proletarians, but also no housewives.

NOTES

1. "Borrowed work" refers to work performed for producer companies by laborers who are hired for particular jobs on a daily, monthly, or weekly basis from other companies whose sole business is to hire out these laborers.

2. Home-workers are those who work at home for a company; the parts they produce are assembled later in a factory, or sold directly in the market through middlemen.

REFERENCES

Bennholdt-Thomsen, Veronika (1980). "Investition in die Armen: Zur Entwicklungspolitik der Weltbank," in V. Bennholdt-Thomsen et al., eds., *Lateinamerika: Analysen und Berichte*, Bd. 4. Berlin: Olle & Wolter, 74-96.

Bock, Gisela & Duden, Barbara (1977). "Arbeit aus Liebe—Liebe als Arbeit: Zur Entstehung der Hausarbeit im Kapitalismus," in Dokumentationsgruppe der Berliner Sommeruniversitat für Frauen 1976, ed., *Frauen und Wissenschaft*. Berlin: Courage, 118-99.

Fröbel, Folker, Heinrichs, Jürgen & Kreye, Otto (1980). *The New International Division of Labour*. Cambridge: Cambridge Univ. Press.

Gorz, André (1980). *Abschied vom Proletariat*. Frankfurt: Europäische V.-A.

Illich, Ivan (1980). "Shadow Work," unpubl. ms., Cuernavaca.

James, Selma (1975). "Sex, Race and Working Class Power," in *Sex, Race and Class*. London: Falling Wall, 9-19.

Kittler, Gertraude (1980). *Hausarbeit: Zur Geschichte der "Natur"-ressource*. München: Frauenoffensive.

Shanin, Theodore (1980). "Die Bauern kommen: Migranten die arbeiten, Bauern, die reisen, und Marxisten, die schreiben," in Blaschke & Greussin, eds., *Dritte Welt*. Frankfurt: Sundikat, 72-85.

Weizsäcker, Ernst Ulrich & Weizsäcker, Christine (1979). "Recht auf Eigenarbeit stattPPflicht zum Wachstum," *Scheidewege*, II, 9, 221-34

Werlhof, Claudia von (1978). "Frauenarbeit: Der blinde Fleck in der Kritik der Politischen Ökonomie," *Beiträge zur feministischen Theorie und Praxis*, I. München: Frauenoffensive, 18-32.

Werlhof, Claudia von (1981). "Frauen und Dritte Welt als 'Natur' des Kapitals: Oder Ökonomie auf die Füsse gestellt," in H. Dauber & V. Simpfendorfer, eds., *Eigener Haushalt und bewohnter Erdkreis*. Wuppertal: Peter Hammer, 187-215.

II

Households, the State, and Accumulation Processes

9

BEYOND THE PEASANT TO PROLETARIAN DEBATE
African Household Formation in South Africa

William G. Martin

Fernand Braudel Center
State University of New York—Binghampton

Proletarianization in the
Capitalist World-Economy: Why Households?

It is widely accepted that capitalist development necessitates the alienation of land and labor. Indeed, is not wage labor the *sine qua non* of capitalism? Yet in this century of late capitalism a large proportion—one might guess well over a majority—of the world's population remains outside a fully established wage-labor/capital relationship. For the large rural and "marginal" urban populations of Asia, Latin America, and Africa wage labor often constitutes only a small proportion of their life's expenditure of labor time, and may contribute an even smaller proportion of socially necessary costs of reproduction on a life-time basis. Why should wage labor fail to entrench itself in the Third World? And why—or how is it possible that—wages should be so low?

It is amazing that the answers to these questions by the majority of both liberal modernizationists and Marxists should be located in the same sphere:

AUTHOR'S NOTE: This is a condensed version of a paper delivered to the Bielefeld Colloquium. Comments by Giovanni Arrighi, Torry Dickinson, and Zenebeworke Tadesse were particularly helpful and are gratefully acknowledged. Discussions on global household comparisons during sessions of the Fernand Braudel Center's Research Working Group on Households, Labor-Force Formation, and the World-Economy were also of much assistance. This essay draws on material from a larger project entitled "South Africa and the World-Economy in the Long Twentieth Century".

"traditional" society. For if both Parsons and Engels were and are cited in support of the historically universal movement towards the proletarian family (nuclear, non-productive, and wage-dependent), was not the absence of this development in the Third World to be found in the lack of capitalist penetration? The formula was quite simple: no wage labor, no capitalism. What is not modern is traditional.

To be sure, quite elegant theories to account for this situation have been developed. Leaving aside defenses of modernization theory, the seminal work in this area stressed the advantages to capital of preserving pre-capitalist modes of production, whereby the availability of cheap labor and surplus product is posited upon the contribution of pre-capitalist communities to the generational costs of reproducing labor.[1] The classic perception of proletarianization is thus stood on its head: No longer did capital relentlessly drive towards the full alienation of land and labor. Primitive accumulation becomes an endless process. How does one account for this paradoxical state of affairs? What had changed in the process of capitalist development to lead to such an anomalous outcome?

As other chapters in this volume indicate, the model of proletarianization derived from advanced capitalist areas has itself been seriously challenged in the last ten years. Work in "women's studies" has, for example, clearly demonstrated that contributions to the reproduction of labor from non-wage, "productive" activities form a significant proportion of the cost of reproducing the labor force. To equate wages with the socially necessary cost of the reproduction of labor is thus increasingly untenable for much of the working class in core areas during the "long" twentieth century. In a similar manner, the bounded singularity of the wage-labor/capital relationship in regard to the cost of reproducing the labor force has also been severely challenged; the existence of sharing obligations and transfers of goods and services between families is increasingly evident.

If our notion of the historical achievement of proletarianization in core areas is in doubt, does this not resolve our problem of the arrested rate of proletarianization in the periphery? Could not one argue that the secular trend of proletarianization is simply proceeding at a slower rate? The problem with this simple formulation is that the proclamation of the process supporting low wages and a low level of proletarianization in the periphery has been directly tied to a residual definition of the "traditional" or the "pre-capitalist": analyses of pre-capitalist or traditional areas are conceptually based on the negative referent of the achievements of advanced capitalist or modern areas, referents themselves under question. And, where the capitalist mode of production is claimed to be dominant, the argument is clear: Forces within the capitalist mode of production direct, through the exchange relation, the course of future developments.[2] The extent to which this recreates a dualist version of capitalist development (analogous to the modernizationists' beloved traditional/modern split) is left to the reader to decide.

Such a confusing and unsatisfactory state of affairs may yet find some resolution if we return to an investigation of the relationships between labor production, the relations and processes of production, and, especially, the manner of the integration of inequalities in these spheres. Seen in this light, an understanding of the development of the processes of proletarianization may be approached by differentiating emergent household complexes' interdependent, yet contradictory, relationship to capitalist production processes and markets. By moving forward along these lines it is possible to avoid the problems that inherently arise from a focus upon either isolated individuals on the one hand, or whole domestic communities on the other. Finally, it is hoped that by removing the vast majority of the population under study from a "pre-capitalist" limbo, and by elucidating previously hidden and substantive contradictions between households and capital, we may in future work locate the struggles accompanying the transformation of rural areas in their deserved place: a substantive phase of class struggle within the global relationship between capital and labor.

The Changing Constellation of Households in South Africa during the "Long" Twentieth Century

If we are to understand the course of proletarianization in southern and especially South Africa, it is first necessary to grasp the changing historical path of capitalist penetration. In this regard, the emergence of high levels of industrial production in the mid-twentieth century has misled many analysts: It is widely assumed that capitalist development in South Africa may be depicted as a secular movement, via primitive accumulation, towards ever-increasing levels of the capital/wage-labor relationship. One subsequently finds in much work the employment of an abstract and unilinear model of national capitalist development and its full conceptual battery: surplus-value, reserve army of labor, latent/floating/relative/absolute surplus population, and so forth. If we pay closer attention to the historical emergence of capitalist production and markets and their location in the global process of capitalist development, a quite different picture emerges.

The character of the destruction of pre-capitalist modes of production in Africa depended on several factors: the existing organization of pre-capitalist communities, the types of capitalist production processes promoted by colonial powers and their agents, and the course of struggle between these two sets of contending forces. In the case of southern Africa these factors varied significantly over both time and space (see, e.g., Wolpe &

Legassick, 1976; and Morris, 1976). Seen from the angle of the expanding world-economy there were three major waves of incorporation: Portuguese trading expansion in the fifteenth and sixteenth centuries; Dutch settlement in the Cape area beginning in 1652; and the British-led extension of control in the region, which began after the Napoleonic Wars and continued through the nineteenth and early twentieth centuries. Insofar as each of these waves of incorporation implanted different production processes and corresponded to a different organization of the international division of labor (between core and peripheral production processes) and the interstate system (as revealed by relations of hegemony), the political and economic reorganization of the areas being incorporated took markedly different forms. Seen from the angle of the pre-capitalist peoples confronted by colonial intrusions, an even greater variety of the organization of domestic communities existed: Political structures ranged from acephalous communities to large kingdoms, while the economic foundation of social life spanned from the hunters of the Kalahari to the preponderant agricultural and pastoral communities that formed the base of the large politcal confederations of the interior of the region.

The final and decisive phase of the incorporation of southern Africa into the capitalist world-economy took place between 1870 and 1920. It was of course during this period that colonial power was entrenched and extended throughout the region; central to this process was the development of diamond, coal, and especially gold mining. If large-scale mining set one boundary of the contours of the development of South Africa, the existence of settlers from a previous phase of incorporation was to delimit capitalist development just as forcefully. Both large mining interests and agricultural interests, however, sought the provisioning of "cheap" labor, and required no less than the forceful elimination of pre-capitalist modes of production and the promotion of a flexible household structure tied to the process of capitalist development. The rapid growth of the Witwatersrand area as a center of accumulation gave this movement a massive push, compressing it into a relatively short period of approximately fifty years.

In examining the decline of indigenous modes of production during this period, it is essential to observe the relations of production and reproduction that constitute the matrix of their operation and survival. Now while the voluminous literature on the late nineteenth-century penetration of exchange value, labor migration, "peasant" production, and so forth attests to the depth of capitalist penetration (Bunday, 1979; Palmer & Parsons, 1977), the truly crucial transformations must be sought in the transformation of the hierarchical and politically organized relations that had assured the continued reproduction of these communities on their own terms. One needs to ask, for example, the following kinds of questions: When was the male elders' control over the relations of reproduction lost? At what point were the relations organizing agricultural production substantively determined from outside the community? Most important, when did the ability of the domestic community to reproduce itself (including here, as one must, the social and political relations so crucial to the *pre-capitalist* organization of production) come to be terminated?

An answer to these stark, and admittedly simplistic, questions would affirm that an end to the functioning of pre-capitalist modes of production in most of our area occurred by the late nineteenth century. What is important here, however, is not exact dating, but rather an examination of the historical character—only now becoming clear as the result of ongoing historical research—of the emergence of households as pre-capitalist communities were dissolved. For what becomes evident is that there were distinctive and contradictory types of households that corresponded to the peripheral character of the market and production processes. Moreoever, as the character of peripheral capitalist development changed, so too did the nature of relationship between households, the labor force, capital, and the state.

One of the best descriptions of this process is by William Beinart, whose research on Pondoland provides one of the fullest descriptions of the process of incorporation. (Pondoland is an area of the Transkei and was one of the last sections of South Africa to be incorporated into the capitalist world-economy.) Initial contact with the expanding Cape market in the late nineteenth century led to an increase in surplus pastoral and agricultural production in order to provide for the purchase of blankets, beads, metalware, and agricultural implements; the massive loss of cattle due to rinderpest at the turn of the century promoted labor migration. Early migrancy thus took place against the background of sufficient land holdings but insufficient stock to work the land; earnings from wage labor by young males were intially reinvested in the rural economy, and it appears that per capita production may well have increased during the early stages of migration (Beinart, 1980). Equally notable, however, was the changing organization of production and reproduction.

In the last few decades of the nineteenth century, new implements such as hoes, picks and ploughs, and the adoption of ox draught enabled cultivation to be expanded in the area. Grain, always an element in the diet, gradually became more important for subsistence and export, once transport links to nearby towns and military concentrations had been developed. As hunting and raiding declined, the homestead, rather than communal groups organized by chiefs, increasingly became the basic unit of production. A good part of the surplus of every homestead was now directed through the traders to the colonial economy rather than to the chiefs (Beinart, 1980: 82-83).

The dissolution of lineage and settlement group control over the operation of production and reproduction similarly accelerated with migration:

> In the pre-colonial period, property was controlled by the homestead head although his powers were limited by the necessity of consultation with his brothers, sons and even elder womenfolk, and by the specific rights that different houses had to certain types of property. The homestead head was responsible for obtaining cattle by marrying off daughters or borrowing from wealthier men, and for seeing that the bridewealth of each male member of the household was paid. By the first decades of this century, cattle diseases and the commercialization of stock exchange had made it difficult for many homestead heads to fulfull this role. Younger men were increasingly responsible for replacing stock and for earning their own bridewealth (Beinart, 1980: 86).

Those who had previously regulated the community's access to land, livestock, and women—male elders and especially chiefs—were faced in these circumstances with mixed opportunities: They could utilize their privileged position to increase their own surplus production and income, yet even as they did so control over subordinate homesteads and the young slipped from their hands. Indeed, many chiefs did manage in the early stages of migration to garner an uneuqal share of the fruits of these new sources of surplus. Yet, as homestead reproduction became increasingly dependent upon the exchange of labor and commodities through the capitalist market, these political and social ligaments became increasingly redundant. The most direct route to continued assertion of chiefly power under these conditions was to re-locate or to buttress authority via the dominant political authority: the colonial power or its local agents. As Beinart notes,

> Many of the chiefly homesteads, which had been the wealthiest in the pre-colonial period, were able to retain their position in the early decades of the twentieth century. They were often among the largest stockowners, and herds could be passed from generation to generation. They were in the best position to expand rural production because of their access to the largest fields and the largest families, and they had the capital to invest in implements. Some chiefs still claimed stock from commoners on the grounds of old tributary rights, and some ran courts and kept fines although their judicial powers were not at first recognized by the administration. Additional income came in the shape of payments from immigrants, and from the allotment of plots. Most chiefs were Government headmen and received a salary, ranging from £6—or about two months' wages on the gold mines—to £60, except in the case of the Paramounts. While there were still calls on the chiefs to redistribute some of their resources, their position was now dependent in the last resort on the support of the Government rather than the support of the people (1980: 86).

It is evident that under these conditions any notion of the survival or continued functioning of a pre-capitalist mode of production becomes difficult to maintain even during the early period of labor migration; not only had the orientation and relations of production become locked into the capitalist market and production processes, but the very political and social organization of the community had become dependent on political authority from without. A central part of the process of the emergence of an economy set apart from community political rule was a movement towards a household unit particularly suited to, and adept at, managing the new productive relationships entailed with migration and surplus production. The example of the Mpondo people's incorporation has been cited at length because it constitutes one of the more detailed cases we have of such a transformation. How typical, one may ask, was this of other areas in South Africa?

It would appear that in the late nineteenth and early twentieth centuries that process of severing the pre-capitalist community along the lines that have been suggested necessarily accompanied the emergence of production for exchange and labor service. Distinctive types of households nevertheless emerged during this process, depending upon the nature of the link to the capitalist world-economy, the particular political character of the reorganization of pre-capitalist areas, and the economic resources that remained available given the penetration of a money economy. In the opening decades of this century the mix of these general characteristics suggests that at least three separate possibilities existed: cash-cropping households, labor-exporting households, and tenant households on settler farms (either share-cropping or labor-service). Each of these variations was formed by a predominant relationship with the growing peripheral economy, and each required a specific set of practices to assure both household production and reproduction.

As colonial control was extended and tightened during the course of the nineteenth century a prime response by African cultivators to the need to generate income for tax demands and basic consumer and agricultural goods was to increase agricultural output for the market. Mission stations were particularly active as loci of such production, which is hardly surprising as they offered access to land (often purchased with African funds), the new tools of production, and an environment free of the force of pre-colonial communal organization. Comments by two missionaries at an 1865 Commission on Native Affairs illustrate the changes in their districts:

> When I came to this country, 34 years ago, the wooden spade was used in agriculture; now the hoe and the plough are used, and the wooden spade has disappeared. Then the chief agriculturalists were women, now a great part of the agricultural labour is performed by the men. Burdens were then borne

on the heads of the women, now many of the people possess waggons for the transport of their goods. Then the hides of cattle and the hides of sheep were the clothing of the people; now the manufactures of the wool of the sheep and the cotton plant have been substituted.

And,

> I am not a very old man, yet I remember the time when the gardens of the natives were much smaller than they now are. I can well recollect the time when among the Kafirs, all field labour except fencing, was performed by the women. Now, however, the male part of the Kafir population, either universally or very generally, take a great share in such works. I can well call to mind the time when, with only one or two exceptions, there were no waggons [sic] in Kaffraria, but those belonging to Europeans: now, however, native waggons are so plentiful as to be quite a nuisance. I have vividly before me the days when no Red Kafir would degrade his cattle by putting them under the yoke; now, however, the veriest calf is made to work for its grass by these painted gentlemen (Bundy, 1980: 55).[3]

As these comments suggest, self-sustaining cash-crop production ideally required not only access to fertile land, cattle, and favorable prices for both agricultural inputs and products, but also new techniques of production and a specific organization of the household, with resident adults and child labor of both sexes. Threats to any one of these elements could curtail the viability of the cash-cropping household. Insofar as these elements obtained, and were indeed promoted by British merchants, traders, and missionaries (all of whom proclaimed throughout the nineteenth century the benefits of taxation, trade, and a peaceful peasantry under cash-crop production), the growth of an even larger "peasantry" seemed to be assured. Even the initial opening up of the mining fields further stimulated cash-crop production as intensive African agricultural production remained the only substantive source of surplus production in a sea of Boer pastoralists.

Yet the history of South African agriculture is written with the decline of such independent households in the late nineteenth century and their broad-scale elimination in the opening decades of the twentieth century. A variety of events such as natural disasters (e.g., rinderpest and East Coast Fever, which actually eliminated up to 90% of many cattle herds) and the Anglo-Boer War are often noted as causes; the penetration of cheap American cereals and an adverse movement of prices further beat on the door of survival. Yet African cultivators had recovered from such calamities before; it would have been specious to presume *a priori* that other means of agricultural production would offer goods as cheaply. Certainly in other parts of Africa during this period African cash-crop production, even in agricultural depressions, often showed far greater resiliency than settler production.[4] The curtailment of independent African production was instead to be integrally related to the development of alternative peripheral production processes in the form of both commerical settler agriculture and mining.

Without developed credit, transport, and political apparatuses, settler farms in the interior of South Africa during most of the nineteenth century were largely restricted to pastoral activities. Under these conditions sharecropping arrangements with the conquered African cultivators, who possessed the means of production (cattle, plows, labor), formed a highly advantageous system for settler farms, absentee landlords, and land speculators. Even under these conditions sharecropping could be "a highly commercialized relation" (Keegan, 1981). With the arrival of the mining complexes in the late nineteenth century, and especially in the opening decades of the twentieth century, many Boer farmers turned directly to commercial production, a process facilitated by government credit, the railway and road system, and the market associated with the mines. By the second decade of the twentieth century, South African agriculture had become fully integrated with the international market, both in terms of price structure and export-oriented production. From the wealthier Boer farmers' point of view (there was, it should be noted, increasing stratification among white settlers) African cultivation became a distinct threat: It locked up land and, more important, labor resources, as well as representing a prime source of market competition. In the areas under their most direct control, the Boer elite thus sought to eliminate indiscriminate sharecropping and to locate under their control both labor and the means of production (cattle, plows, labor, seed, and the like). This process was most visibly promoted by the 1913 Natives Land Act, which outlawed sharecropping tenancies and uncontrolled squatting on absentee-owned land. The act also legally limited African land rights to a mere 13% of the land area of the country. As one commission report described the working of the system and its variations,

> In large parts of the country the farmer depends on the squatter for his normal labour. The conditions under which such labour is available vary. Generally speaking, young native boys work on the farm and a certain quota of adult male labour must be supplied. The women-folk are also liable for domestic tasks. In exchange for this, the head of the kraal obtains ground on which he builds his huts, land on which he produces his grain for food, and drink and grazing for his animals (Inter-Departmental Committee, 1930: 11).

Like those of independent cash-crop production, these relations of production required a particular type of household structure, as the above citation suggests: Adult male labor was required for production on both the landlord's land and the tenant's allotment, while younger household members were the predominant suppliers of labor to the landlord's house, cattle, and lands.[5] Indeed, the reproduction of the relationship between landlord and tenant rested upon the ability of male elders to control adolescent labor in exchange for land and grazing rights. Where this had earlier been assured through elder and chiefly control over rights to land, cattle, and marriage, the transition to labor tenancy increasingly displaced the regulation of these resources into settler hands. (When control over the young later became of central importance, government commissions would recommend the re-establishment of chiefs on free land on settler farms, to no avail.) And, as commercialization deepened and more land was given over to crop production, landlords and their political bodies restricted to an even greater extent African access to land and cattle. As long as few opportunities existed outside agriculture, however, labor tenancy would remain a predominant form of the relations of production on commerical farms.

The demand for restricting independent African cultivation came not only from white farmers but also from mining companies, which remained the largest and best-organized recruiters of African labor. Unlike settler farms, mines with few exceptions required only male adult labor—a central requirement as we have seen of independent African cultivation and even labor tenancy relations. As the Pondoland example suggests, the reproduction of the mining labor force required a household unit that could juggle the absence of its most productive male members with the cultivation of the land. Given the necessity of a cash income, male labor from throughout southern African traveled to the mines, especially in times of economic distress. By the early twentieth century large areas had emerged as perennial suppliers of migrant labor to the mines. As male migrant labor became entrenched and households increasingly isolated, household production typically rested on a transition to labor-saving crops (as for example in the transition to cassava in southern Mozambique and maize monoculture in areas of South Africa), the increasing importance of female and child labor, and the supply and replacement of agricultural implements and cattle through migrant earnings. As long as access to land was assured, the system of combining migrant income with household production could be reproduced. In many areas such as Lesotho and Mozambique this combination continues to exist today, even in the face of an increasing shortage of land.

If the African household as a unit of cash-crop production declined markedly in the opening decades of the twentieth century as settler farms and mining sought to restructure the labor force, the interwar period saw even these latter systems threatened. At first glance this appears curious, for it is widely acknowledged that labor tenancy in this period dominated the relations of production on commercial farms. The percentage of South African Blacks in the mining labor force rose quickly in this period as well, as agricultural depression, over-population, and land shortages increasingly compelled labor migration from the reserves in order to replace declining household production.[6] It was, however, the very conditions and signs of the success of imposing labor migration, coupled with the emergence of new production processes, that led to their decline.

The household consumption fund of both tenant households and labor-exporting households rested upon contributions from production organized by the household itself and returns from the provisioning of labor power to landlords or mining capital. As returns from labor tenancy or household production declined ever further, the subordinate members of the household increasingly found urban wage labor a viable alternative. Commercial farmers, mining capital, and government officials all recognized the changes such a movement represented, and sought to counterbalance the growth of urban African households even as industrialization increased during the interwar period. As General Smuts outlined the problem before a meeting of municipal authorities in 1937,

> I need not point out to you, ladies and gentlemen, that this [influx of natives into urban areas] has become a movement of enormous dimensions and, unless controlled, it may lead to revolutionary social and economic changes in South Africa. ... In fact, the figure shows that in the last 15 years, from 1921 to 1936, the native population in our urban areas has practically doubled, from 587,000 to 1,150,000 (Native Affairs Commission, 1939: 29).

As the permanence of the Black urban population increased, it became evident that the loss of labor to the mines and especially the agricultural community would eventually be a severe problem. As the 1937-1938 Report of the Native Affairs Commission noted,

> The exodus of a family to the town is a direct loss of workers to the major industries [meaning mining and commercial agriculture] and an additional burden on the permanent native urban population struggling to survive'' (National Affairs Commission, 1939: 6).

The exodus of the young was particularly revealing: "It is reliably estimated that some 78 per cent of the lads under eighteen years of age who seek work in the Rand have come from the rural districts and have no parents living in the municipal areas (National Affairs Commission, 1939: 6). On settler farms this development was particularly crucial, leaving as it did elder members of the settlement who were often subsequently turned off the land to be placed in the reserves:

> The old people who are leaving the farms find it difficult to gain accommodation elsewhere; and the ingenuity of the Native Affairs Department is continually exercised to restrain the eviction (until they can be suitably accommodated on native land) of the elders of families whose young men have broken their contracts and deserted their farming work for the more alluring prospects of some distant city (National Affairs Commission, 1939: 6).

As even a cursory reading of official reports and legislative actions shows, a state and employers' offensive to regulate the labor supply among urban, rural, and mining sectors in this period sought to segregate sources of supply and thus sustain distinct relations of production and reproduction for each sector. The structuring of mining and agricultural capital for export production in a period of world-economic depression, while manufacturing was protected by tariffs, only increased contradictions within and across these sectors, adding an additional imperative to state intervention. (This was in fact a critical variable in the trajectory of these production processes and state policy in this period, but this is too large a topic to be developed here.) As one report stated,

> Native labour competition between primary and secondary industries can only be carried on at the expense of the former. The secondary industries are in a better position to compete, since they are aided by the privileged position which they enjoy at the expense of the primary industries, and by the fact that they do not export their products. A balanced economy demands that the basic industries of the country should not be undermined by the draining away of their labour to the privileged industries of the town (Native Affairs Commission, 1939: 7).

Access to urban areas and to higher wages than were available in mining and agriculture was to be restricted: Labor tenant contracts were to be enforced to ensure that younger household members remained on the land, and the reserves were to be developed so that the wage subsidy represented by household production could be maintained. And indeed an impressive array of legislation was passed during the interwar period to obtain these ends. Despite these measures, the inexorable march to urban areas continued and accelerated rapidly during and after the Second World War.

To trace the implementation of the formal character of *apartheid* as it relates to the crisis or urban wage-labor reproduction in the era following the Second World War is another task altogether. A few pertinent observations regarding this process must serve to indicate the resolution of the interwar conflicts.

Urban wage labor was an integral component of the industrialization of South Africa in the interwar period, which required a stable urban labor force. Higher wage levels attracted, as we have seen, migrants from both African reserves and settler farms. These wage levels were not, however, sufficient to cover the necessary costs of reproduction of the emerging urban household. As one government report noted in 1942,

> In Johannessburg a man earns on an average of £4 2s. 6d. per month and his family barely subsists on a joint income of £5 6s. 8d. to which his wife, children and a lodger have contributed; in order to house, feed and clothe them decently under existing conditions, not less than £7 10s. 0d. is needed (Inter-Departmental Committee, 1942: 29).[7]

Wages could be higher in urban areas while well-being was not, a distinction drawn quite clearly as early as 1930:

> They ["natives who have become urban dwellers"] are in many respects much worse off than the other two [Reserve or tenant] groups. They have neither the home and lands of the tribal native, nor have they the advantage of a system which supplies them with housing, food, fuel, and drink in exchange for three to six months labour a year (Inter-Departmental Committee, 1930: 12).

What we now call "informal sector" activity often represented a major contribution to household income under these conditions.

Nor did conditions improve in succeeding decades. Poverty, malnutrition, lack of housing, price increases, and the like were rampant in urban African areas, as was urban unrest (e.g., in the form of strikes and squatter movements) in the years immediately after the war. It is not difficult to see that the massive government intervention in the area of African housing, wages, migration, and so on under *apartheid* in the post-1948 period was directly related to the crisis in the conditions of the reproduction of the Black urban labor force.

The consolidation in the post-Second World War period of a large, Black urban working class posed severe problems for those production processes in mining and agriculture that depended on wage structures much lower than urban manufacturing wages. Mining capital's solution was to move back to its original sources of supply outside the boundaries of South Africa (Wallerstein, Martin & Dickinson, 1982: 449), areas where the labor-exporting household was still intact and relatively untouched by contiguous areas of urban or settler employment. The tightening of borders with surrounding African countries was crucial in this respect in order to prevent the inflow of population from these areas. To the extent that this permanent out-migration had operated to alleviate rural over-population in relation to land and cattle resources, rural conditions in surrounding labor-exporting countries would further decline. For commercial agriculture, a combination of a movement towards wage-labor in order to obtain the land used by tenants, strictly enforced contracts, the use even of prison labor, and foreign migrant labor (especially in border areas) formed the broad outlines of labor-force patterns. The vastly increased repressive power of the *apartheid* state was obviously of import in most of these areas. The South African state also set forth the clear boundaries of such foreign labor:

> The following is the policy laid down by the Minister of Native Affairs: "Extra-Union Natives should under no circumstances be allowed to bring their wives and children to the Union. Wherever possible wives and children should be directed to return to their countries [or] repatriated" (Owen, 1962: 17).

If we thus survey the African labor force in the post-war period, three distinct labor-force patterns emerge: a very low-paid mining labor force drawn largely from outside South Africa: a low-paid rural tenant labor force whose existence—as that of white agriculture in general— was assured through the state; and an urban labor force struggling under harsh conditions and hemmed in eventually by *apartheid*. As this suggests, the existence of any substantive levels of household production in the African reserves dropped off rapidly in the post-war period (Simkins, 1981).

Reprise

The historical development of households in relation to capital accumulation in South Africa as outlined above leads to the following observations.

(1) The incorporation of southern Africa into the world-economy entailed the destruction of existing pre-capitalist modes of production. The orientation and subsequent integration of African agricultural production into the capitalist market led not only to the utilization and replacement of much of the material forces of production and consumption goods via market exchange, but also to an altered set of relations of production in the form of the emergence of a new sexual division of labor increasingly organized by household units rather than pre-capitalist communities.

(2) The substantive form by which peripheral production processes were established and the trajectory of household formation and reproduction were integrally related. Production for the export market and core production processes could be organized by several different production units; contradictions between these divergent units of production and their respective labor and market requirements were matched by differing matrices of African household production and reproduction. And the rise of South Africa

to a semiperipheral position in the world-economy (the class and world-economic determinants of this process being taken as a given) demonstrates that what was possible in a peripheral area was not able to be continued as core industrial production processes were implanted.

(3) It follows that although "cheap labor" and "labor migration" were and are eminent indicators of the South African labor force, these terms gain meaning only via their location in the above processes of household and production process formation. Cheap labor and migration may rest upon and sustain a particular type of household unit (as in Mozambique, Lesotho, Swaziland, and the early twentieth-century African reserves); they may represent as well the destruction of an area of cash-crop production; cheap labor may even be located in relation to the development of a particular type of urban working-class household. And in no instance are these terms understandable at the level of the individual.

(4) This broadened understanding of the meaning of "cheap labor" and "migration" similarly applies to class formation and struggle. Landlord/tenant disputes, mass resistance to the alienation of land and labor, boycotts of traders, popular struggles against chiefs, and so forth need to be investigated in light of the peripheral character of capital accumulation and household formation. Male action on the Rand for example, seems to be matched in the 1920's by actions by women in rural areas—women being the main cultivators—in response to the impact of dipping regulations, rising prices in traders' stores, shortages of land, and the like. In this regard, the changing character of political authority and its relation to household structures is crucial. As we have seen, chiefs in many areas and periods were clearly agents of the colonial and settlers' state, not pre-capitalist remnants; landlords in other areas embodied the role of the political authorities, while the development of a strong South African state during and after the interwar period located class struggle, especially in urban areas, directly against the centralized state structure. The displacement of the political referent of a large proportion of the laboring population in South Africa after the Second World War to contiguous states also deserves much more attention than it has hitherto received.

5. In moving forward along these lines particular attention needs to be paid to the division of production relations by age and gender. We have tried to indicate, on the basis of the scant information available, that several sets of production/reproduction relations could be assured only by the location of women and the young in a particular place with these relationships. Thus, even given the preference by manufacturing and mining capital for male labor (even urban domestic servants were male in the first half of this century), women and the young were necessary to the reproduction of the labor force and rural production. This leads, as suggested above to divergent forms of class struggle by sex and age.

The above observations regarding household formation in South Africa suggest several more general implications. As I have tried to suggest, the employment of the concept of the household enables one to trace previously hidden relationships and contradictions between the labor force, class formation, capital accumulation, and political authority—relationships that tend to be obscured by reliance upon conceptual terms such as "articulating modes of production" and "migration of indivuals", or on amorphous classes such as "peasantries".

One is also able to distinguish between contradictory forms of commodity production through the location on the one hand of the limitations imposed by the in/flexibility of specific household structures, and the needs of competing production processes for labor and material inputs from households on the other. In the case of the former, the examination of the household's division of labor by sex and age across its labor activities is crucial and demonstrates that the meaning of such terms as "domestic labor" or "subsistence production" may change quite radically as one shifts between peripheral production processes and, especially, to core production processes. In the case of the latter, the contradictory labor forces required by core, as opposed to peripheral, production processes directs attention towards the divergent pattern of households across the temporal and spatial boundaries of the world-economy.

Unified by the global yet uneven process of capital accumulation, households in different zones of the world-economy—or as we have seen in an area that changes its location in the world-economy over time—can hardly be expected to exhibit qualitatively equal relationships to capital. And insofar as political authority is differentially located and centralized among core and peripheral states, whose boundaries do not correspond to the loci of control and organization of capital accumulation, the division of households by dissimilar sets of production and political relations demonstrates a primary source of the diffusion of proletarian struggle against capital.

NOTES

1. Southern Africa has been a particularly important area of this research. See, for example, Harold Wolpe (1972) and Meillassoux (1981).

2. As Meillassoux argues, there exists an "impossibility of introducing progress within the domestic sector," and "the subsistence economy belongs therefore to capitalism's *sphere of circulation* to the extent that it provides it with labour-power and commodities but remains outside the capitalist *sphere of production*" (1981: 128, 95).

3. These commentators undoubtedly underestimate the role of women in the early colonial period.

4. Take, for example, Uganda during the early 1920's, when the colonial state found African cultivators more competitive than settler production and supported Africans against the settler population.

5. Stanley Trapido's work on the development of this system remains the best source of information (1978). A research project being carried out by the African Studies Institute (University of the Witwatersrand) promises to re-write the rural history of the Transvaal and Orange Free State; see, as one example of their work, Matsetela (1980).

6. The extent to which rural African household production declined in reserve areas remains a matter of some debate. Most historians and government commissions report a quick decline in the interwar period; this view has recently been challenged by Simkins (1981).

7. The estimates of necessary costs rarely include any provision for entertainment and the re-provisioning of essential household goods.

REFERENCES

Beinart, William (1980). "Labour Migrancy and Rural Production: Pondoland, c. 1900-1950," in P. Mayer, ed., *Black Villagers*. Capetown: Oxford Univ. Press, 81-108.

Bundy, Colin (1979). *The Rise and Decline of the South African Peasantry*. Berkeley: Univ. of California Press.

Inter-Departmental Committee on the Labour Resources of the Union (1930). *Report*. Pretoria.

Inter-Departmental Committee on the Social Health and Economic Conditions of Urban Natives (1942). *Report*. Pretoria.

Keegan, Tim (1981). "The Sharecropping Economy, African Class Formation, and the 1913 Natives' Land Act in the Highveld Maize Belt of South Africa," unpubl. paper delivered at the History Workshop, Feb. 5-9, Univ. of Witwatersrand.

Martin, William G. (forthcoming). "The Incorporation of Southern Africa into the World-Economy." unpubl. Ph.D. diss., Department of Sociology, SUNY-Binghamton.

Matsetela, Ted (1980). "Aspects of Sharecropping and Proletarianization in the Northern Orange Free State, 1890-1920: The Life Story of Emelia Pooe," unpubl. paper presented at the South African Conference, Jan. 2-5, Univ. of London, Centre of International and Area Studies.

Meillassoux, Claude (1981). *Maidens, Meal and Money*. Cambridge: Cambridge Univ. Press.

Morris, Mike (1976). "The Development of Capitalism in South African Agriculture," *Economy and Society*, V, 3, 292-343.

Native Affairs Commission for the Years 1937-1938 (1939). *Report*. Pretoria, U.G. No. 54/39.

Owen, Ken (1962). "Foreign Africans: Summary of the Report of the Froneman Committee." Johannesburg: South African Institute of Race Relations.

Palmer, Robert & Parsons, Neil (1977). *The Roots of Rural Poverty*. Berkeley: Univ. of California Press.

Simkins, Charles (1981). "Agricultural Production in the African Reserves of South Africa, 1918-1969," *Journal of Southern African Studies*, VII, 2, Apr., 256-83.

Trapido, Stanley (1978). "Landlord and Tenant in a Colonial Economy: The Transvaal, 1880-1910," *Journal of Southern African Studies*, V, 1, Oct., 26-58.

Wallerstein, Immanuel, Martin, William G. & Dickinson, Torry (1982). "Household Structures and Production Processes: Preliminary Theses and Findings," *Review*, V, 3, Win., 437-58.

Wolpe, Harold (1972). "Capitalism and Cheap Labour-Power in South Africa: From Segregation to Apartheid," *Economy and Society*, I, 4, Nov., 425-56.

Wolfe, Harold & Legassick, Martin (1976). "The Bantustans and Capital Accumulation in South Africa," *Review of African Political Economy*, No. 7, Sept.-Dec., 87-107.

10

HOUSEHOLD ECONOMY AND FINANCIAL CAPITAL
The Case of Passbook Savings in Brazil

Eva Machado Barbosa

Sociology of Development Research Center
University of Bielefeld

In this chapter I assume that households must be seen as playing an important role in the capitalist world-economy, not only for the reproduction of the labor force, but also for direct reproduction, that is to say for the accumulation of capital itself (Research Working Group, 1982). One aspect of that role is shown here through an analysis of the Brazilian Savings and Loan System (SBPE), which reveals an important connection between the household economy and national or international types of financial capital.

Specifically, I want to discuss the way in which the wage income of Brazilian households has been tapped by Brazilian financial institutions, thus funneling needed resources from the former to the latter.

Historical Background

Capital markets that channel small savings in liquid form and transform them into long-term capital for investments play a cental role in the accumulation of capital. The virtual absence of such markets in Latin America until the 1960's was a main obstacle to the rapid development of capitalism in this area. The efforts of U.S. foreign policy to maintain political stability in Latin America after the Cuban Revolution were based, however, on the doctrine that the fulfillment of this task would be possible only through the economic development (i.e., development of capitalism) of these countries. Therefore, in order to finance the development of capitalism in Latin America, it was urgently necessary to establish an efficient capital market in the area.[1]

The development of capital markets in Latin America was directly implemented by the U.S. Agency for International Development (AID) with the cooperation of several institutions like the Bank for International Development (BID), the World Bank, U.S. universities, and leagues of U.S. savings and loan associations (see U.S. House of Representativs, 1972; U.S. AID/Institute of Financial Education, 1977). One central element of this process was the organization of savings and loan systems, which were to be used to finance real estate investments in order, it was claimed, to solve one of the most explosive problems in Latin America: the housing question. In this task the AID and the BID developed an informal cooperation: While the BID was responsible for low-income housing programs, AID concentrated on the organization of financial institutions for middle-income programs. The first Interamerican Conference on Savings and Loan (in Lima, 1963) was organized by these two institutions, which also helped to create the Interamerican Union of Savings and Loan in November 1964. Savings and loan systems have been created in the following countries: Peru, 1958; Chile, 1960; Dominican Republic, 1962; Equador and Argentina, 1963; El Salvador, Bolivia, and Panama, 1964; Venezuela, 1965; Brazil, 1966; Nicaragua, 1967; Costa Rica, 1969; Paraguay and Colombia, 1972; and Honduras, 1973 (see U.S. AID/Institute of Financial Education, 1977).

As in the Brazilian case, which will be briefly presented below, the organization of savings and loan systems in Latin America has not solved the grave housing problem in the region; rather, it has served more to create the necessary financial institutions for the development of financial capital and for the promotion of industrial capital in the building sector through real estate financing.

The Brazilian Case[2]

Both the development of the capital market and the creation of the Brazilian Savings and Loan System took place in the context described above, and both played a very important role in the economic policy of the military regime that has governed Brazil since 1964. The plan for restructuring the capital market was directly formulated and submitted to the Brazilian Central Bank by AID (U.S. House of Representatives, 1972), while the SBPE was created according to the American model. The SBPE is a system of financial institutions that channel savings from small savers through passbook savings accounts to the real estate investment sector. The following institutions are members of the SBPE: federal and state savings associations (public institutions); savings and loan associations (mutuals) and real estate credit societies (stock companies). The voluntary savings deposited in passbook savings accounts in these institutions by SBPE are indexed quarterly, and the interest rate is 6% per annum.

The SBPE was set up by the National Housing Bank (BNH) as part of the Home Financing System (SFH), and by 1977 it had financed about 850,000 homes. Like the housing policy as a whole, its organization was financed with resources from the "Unemployment Insurance Fund" (FGTS), a mandatory savings fund created in 1966 by the government to solve two problems: first, to replace one of the provisions of the existing labor laws, which had hindered the turnover of the labor force and, secondly, to finance the housing program. The FGTS is a kind of unemployment benefit fund and consists of contributions from all the companies covered by the Consolidation of Labor Laws. These companies must deposit 8% of each employee's previous monthly salary into individualized bank accounts. The workers are the legal owners of the resources and can make use of them under certain conditions, but the administration of the FGTS was given to the BNH in order to finance its program. From 1967 to 1977 the BNH controlled about 11 billion (gross collected) from the FGTS; part of these resources were used by the BNH as start capital to set up the SBPE (see Ministério do Interior/Banco Nacional da Habitação, 1968).

According to the Brazilian Association of Real Estate Credit and Loan Institutions (ABECIP) the passbook savings, "implemented to collect the saving of workers, housewives, civil servants, in short, of all those people who can only save a small part of their salary" (see ABECIP, 1977: 10), became by far the most important instrument for the public channeling of savings. How was this possible?

The promotion of passbook savings was launched through a very large publicity campaign in the mass media, especially over television. This massive campaign, financed with the workers' resources from the FGTS, stressed first of all the image of the passbook savings as a mechanism to obtain "security" and a "guarantee for the future" (see Instituto Gallup, 1973-74). And the campaign was most successful: The number of passbook savings account holders increased from 157,300 in 1967 to 13,265,000 in 1976, representing a growth rate of more than 8,000 percent. A tradition of saving became rooted in the country, and the channeled resources came close to $9.5 billion in 1976. This amount represented 28.1% of the total savings deposited in Brazilian financial institutions—a major source of financial capital drawn from Brazilian households (see U.S. AID, 1977). Today there are about 33 million passbook savings account holders in Brazil.

Conclusion

Unfortunately, the promises of the ad campaign of security, housing, and well-being for passbook savings account depositors have not, in the case of the low-income classes, been kept, as the following four-point summary argument shows.

(1) About 95% of the Brazilian passbook savings account holders, responsible for about one-third of the channeled resources, come from the low-income classes.
(2) As shown by surveys that evaluated the promotion of passbook savings, the deposits do not always represent a real savings. Some people do not restrain their spending habits while trying to save. On the contrary, they buy on credit so that money "saved" can be deposited into a passbook savings account (see Instituto Gallup, 1973-74). Consequently, the inverse relationship that normally holds between consumption and savings is reversed. In the Brazilian case one could say that "savings" are merely another form of consumption, the idea of "savings" being marketed as any other commodity is.
(3) Since almost the entire amount of the housing credit given through the SBPE goes to high-income classes, the savings of the low-income classes do not return to them in the form of housing.
(4) Although the resources channeled by passbook savings are officially designated for the financing of housing programs, they can also function simultaneously as a form of financial capital that can be inserted into any kind of national or international financial circuit. They can and have been used, for instance, for speculation on the stock market, or on the open market.

These points demonstrate a very important link between wage income and financial capital and thus between Brazilian households and the world-economy. The transformation of parts of the wage into small savings serves not only to create and establish financial institutions; it means also that, in reality, this part of the wage is regained in this way by the financial capital. If this is true, then this kind of savings must be seen as a mechanism to reduce the wage-income and, consequently, to augment in this way (financially) the relative labor surplus.

NOTES

1. Consider two statements made at the hearing on the development of capital markets in Latin America held before the Subcommittee on Inter-American Affairs:

The creation of capital markets would make possible for the first time the establishment of large enterprises that would be locally controlled. Until now, because domestic capital markets have remained undeveloped, the only equity capital that the individual groups, or families, could commit to an enterprise were their own limited resources. These are not adequate to furnish the vast amounts of capital that modern, large-scale enterprises require.

This, of course, has political implications. Some developing countries have expressed concern with the role that foreign capital has played in their countries. If we would encourage a model that would make possible the development of locally controlled large enterprises, then the American and the foreign sectors in general would also benefit. While enjoying greater business opportunities in absolute terms, they would at the same time appear as less significant as the local sector expands rapidly (U.S. House of Representatives, 1972: 10-11).

We must look for the key for the entire development process and how it starts. The key, in my opinion, to achieving political stability, high rates of economic development, and ultimately effectively functioning social services is a well functioning capital market capable of mobilizing the domestic savings for rapid economic development (1972: 21).

2. The data without any explicit references are taken from my dissertation (to appear shortly), which deals with the housing policy in Brazil in the period from 1964-1977.

REFERENCES

Associação Brasileira de Entidades de Crédito Imobiliário e Poupança [ABECIP] (1977). "Savings and Loan: Their Relationship to Competing Activities and their Importance for Internal Development," unpubl. paper presented at the XV Interamerican Savings and Loan Conference, Washington, DC.

Instituto Gallup de Opinião Pública (1973-74). "Relatório Sintese: pesquisa sobre atitudes com relação a poupança," São Paulo.

Ministerio do Interior, Banco Nacional da Habitação (1968). Relatório de atividades, Vol. I. Rio de Janeiro.

Research Working Group on Households, Labor-Force Formation, and the World-Economy (1982). "Household Structures and the World-Economy," unpubl. ms., Fernand Braudel Center, SUNY-Binghamton.

U.S. AID/Institute of Financial Education (1977). "O Progresso do Sistema de Poupança e Empréstimo na América Latina," Relatório preliminar para a XV Conferencia Interamericana de Poupança e Empréstimo na América Latina," Relatório preliminar para a XV Conferencia Interamericana de Poupança e Empréstimo, Washington, DC.

U.S. House of Representatives (1972). "Capital Markets and Economic Development: The Kleinman Plan," Report to the Subcommittee on Inter-American Affairs of the Committee on Foreign Affairs, Ninety-second Congress, Second Session, July 25. Washington: U.S. Government Printing Office.

11

THE CONTRIBUTION
OF PUBLIC GOODS
TO HOUSEHOLD REPRODUCTION
Case Study from Brazil

Johannes Augel

Sociology of Development Research Center
University of Bielefeld

Living conditions depend upon a variety of sources other than wages, for instance, the following:

- other monetary income;
- use values generated in the household;
- the use of goods such as private property, knowledge, experience, positions, and social networks;
- indirect income, payments in kind, or other advantages based on employment or on one's own enterprise;
- the use of public goods; and
- the time necessary for, as well as the effort spent on, the above-mentioned direct and indirect incomes.

The relative importance of each factor varies according to the pervasiveness of market relations and the specific combinations of these factors at the household level. In less urbanized societies, private household production is supposed to be relatively more important, and the participation in public goods to be less important, than in industrialized countries, where one also finds a greater degree of social differentiation in the use of the different types of income. The modernization process reduces the significance of the subsistence-oriented sector and transforms it into a functionally integrated, dependent, and complementary sector without destroying it. Simultaneously, the importance of public infrastructure, services, and grants increases, and the individual's survival and welfare conditons tend to depend less on subsistence and/or monetary income. The public sector comes to assume the role of providing income equivalents that complement or even replace personal labor income.

Income-Pooling Functions of the Modern State

Important (but sometimes neglected) is the contribution of public goods to the livelihood of households. A primary role of the modern state is to pool and redistribute society's resources. Taxes and social security contributions absorb an increasing part of the social product, from about 15% of the gross national product (GNP) in the less developed countries, to about 30% in the United States and about one-half of GNP in Sweden. Furthermore, the growth rates of public spending surpass those of private consumption.

Social Differentiation in the Use of Public Goods

However, the redistribution of resources is structured to the disadvantage of those who need them most. Theoretical studies are in disagreement on this point, and there has been a lack of empirical work on it. On the taxation side, as well as in relation to the distribution effects of public budgets, such important problems as the shifting of tax burdens and of public expenditure benefits have not yet been solved, and discussion on the distribution effects of public infrastructure and public services is totally controversial. Even the differentiation effects of "pure public goods" (e.g., the maintenance of public order) are being questioned. Differentiation is more notorious in the case of mixed public or merit goods. The basic problems are the definitions of the socially differentiated effects of the complementary goods, which can be material as well as immaterial. Neither theoretically nor empirically has the private disposal of complementary goods been defined as the decisive "purchasing power of public goods". Social indicator studies and global budget analyses, as well as studies on the use of public administrative services and of social and material infrastructure investments, have produced a plethora of evidence about the socially differentiated effects of public goods.

Public Goods in Relation to
Relative and Absolute Poverty

The use of public goods depends on the individual capacity of providing complementary goods, of either material or immaterial nature. Under conditions of relative or absolute poverty the individual capacity to "buy" public goods, even if they are free of charge, seems to be reduced or even completely absent. Not only the lack of complementary material goods, but most especially the absence of a set of specific living conditions, renders the access of individuals to public goods more difficult or even impossible. Young people and even children who have to earn their own livings do not have the free time left over as a complementary good with which they can take advantage of the public offer of free education or even health services. Among other important complementary goods that they lack are a consciousness of the value of an educational system, information about the appropriate type of school for them, and perspectives of social mobility. Therefore, personal participation in the public expenditure for education, science, and research varies according to the social and economic status of the individual.

Below a certain degree of poverty, the individual's difficulties in making use of public goods are mostly immaterial and reflect deficiencies in general living conditions. Political efforts to extend the range of public goods must be more than merely quantitative. The specific deficiencies of the poor and the causes of non-material restrictions on the access to public goods are as yet largely unknown. Especially in less developed countries social politics will have to pay more attention to non-material complementary goods as prerequisites in order to reduce the differentiation effect of public goods.

Distributive Effects on Urban Infrastructure

Urban infrastructure is an important part of the general means of social reproduction as well as of public expenses. The urbanization and (urban) industrialization process produces concentrations of public goods as well as increasing proportions of national populations in urban areas. Distributive effects can be analyzed from the macro and micro points of view; the sectoral and socio-geographic incidence of public expenditure as well as the individual or household participation in them must be considered.

The use of urban infrastructure is extremely differentiated. A significantly large part of the urban population is excluded to a great extent from the modernization process and cannot afford the complementary goods necessary to ''buy'' its share of public funds invested in the urban infrastructure, such as transportation, communcation, education, public health facilities, provision of water and electricity, and sewage disposal. True, there are always some benefits to the urban poor from such facilities, but their relative share of these benefits is small because the poor typically lack the (material and immaterial) complementary goods necessary for their realization.

The urban infrastructure forms an essential part of the living conditions of the impoverished urban masses. More than just transportation facilities

alone form an important part of living conditions in "marginal" urban set-
tling areas. Even if public facilities are under-provided, there is always a
certain participation in public expenditures for transportation, roads and
streets, provision of water and electricity, sewage disposal, public health,
public education, public administration, courts, security forces, and so on.
Urban settlement, even where "marginal", cannot be considered without
the support of public goods for the living conditions of the poor urban
masses.

Negative Distributive Effects of Urban Infrastructure

Participation in public goods does not always feature a favorable balance
for poor people. Even "purely public goods" such as general security, public
administration, and justice are used in different ways by various individuals
and by different social strata, and they can be used directly against certain
individuals, social groups, or classes. More recalcitrant to analyses and
theoretically more controversial is the problem of the net contributions by
and profits of the lower social strata in the context of the total system of
social reproduction.

Land use, as one of the basic living conditions, is dependent on two different types of public goods: First, to be used, land requires public or private
investments (the latter being individual or collective). Secondly, land ownership is regulated by legal, administrative, and police action. Since
"marginal" land use occurs under conditions of legal instability, public,
private, individual, and collective investments as well as use values risk
being withdrawn from "marginal" users in order to be "restituted" to their
"legal owners", thus representing a decisive negative distributive effect
of public goods.

The marginal occupation process results in a number of investments that
are needed in order to make the land suitable for use. As a result of this
process, the legal owner of land will try to recover the right to the property. This can be done by force (e.g., the expulsion of illegal settlers, the
burning and destruction of their huts) or in a "legal" way. According to
Brazilian legislation, the occupier of undeveloped land and the houseowner
acquire the right of "usufruct": The landowner can expel the occupier legally only by paying indemnity. The latter is not necessarily felt as expulsion
by the occupier; people who have taken over a fallow estate, acquiring the
usufruct of a plot according to the existing legal situation, or perhaps due
to the protection and self-defensive capacity of a great marginal mass, will
consider it a good opportunity, if they are able to sell their rights and the
improvements realized on the plot. The price will correspond to the individual investment and to part of the collective and public investment made
in the marginal settlement.

Urban land struggle can be considered a struggle for the use of public and private investment that have been undertaken, and of the values they have created.

Some Empirical Results from Brazil

In an analysis of the socially differentiated use of public urban infrastructural investments in the Brazilian context, both concentration and distribution effects of public goods can be found. Since the 1950's, and especially since the end of the 1960's, Brazilian growth policy and the "Brazilian miracle" have led to overurbanization. On the one hand, public entities invest extensively in urban infrastructure, while on the other hand, increasing parts of the urban population and urban settlements remain under provided in terms of all kinds of public investments.

There seem to be only a few empirical studies analyzing advantages for or injuries to individuals, households, or social groups by various specific, public, urban infrastructural investments. In the case of Brazil, the problem has been discussed in several publications. A study of the role of land tenure in the urbanization process of Salvador (State of Bahia) brought out a series of important insights.

From about 1966 onwards, Salvador experienced an urban construction and modernization boom, which led to unprecedented physical expansion and land speculation. Traditional forms of land tenure, especially the usufruct of public land, were transformed into full property. Land speculation occurred in two principal forms: private land purchase in areas of public investments (even during the planning process), and large-sized parceling projects.

According to existing legislation, land parceling projects have to provide internal physical infrastructure such as streets and canals, reserving certain areas, such as school buildings and leisure areas, for communal purposes. The municipality assures the connection of the single project to the existing urban infrastructure by streets, water-piping, and so on, and assumes the maintenance of the local infrastructural installations.

In this way, the land developing process is carried out in cooperation between private and public action, idealized as being in agreement with general social interest. It represents, however, a large-scale transfer of public resources to private profit and a socially differentiated use of public funds:

(A) The denationalization of public land and the transformation of land use rights into full land property did not benefit the landless urban poor, but instead the middle and upper strata and the old land-tenure aristocracy; furthermore, public or uncontrolled urban land was reduced, so that many "invasions" (spontaneous settlements, squatter settlements) were dissolved, and the "marginal masses" were pushed to distant areas.

(B) The land-developing enterprises contributed to an extremely wide-ranging expansion of urban settlement, stimulating the set-up or urban infrastructure in these newly developed regions, while about 70% of the towns' populations live in marginal areas with a high degree of underprovision of urban equipment and services.

(C) The land valorization is carried out by the landholders sale of the parcels; in each parceling project they sell only a part of the lots. The others remain in their ownership for "fattening". The landowners not only use the benefits resulting from the occupation process, but also profit from the valorization of the land by public investments.

(D) In marginal areas, physical infrastructure, with the exception of a few public investments, is the result of the occupation process substantialized in the individual and collective investments of the "invaders"; the legal and factual situation of the squatters, however, is unstable, so that they can easily be expelled from their settlements. For the urban poor, public goods are not only almost totally absent, but assume the character of "public bads": Public entities contribute to the instability of the urban poor settlements by the development of urbanization projects, by legal and police action, expulsion, and the like.

Conclusions

Household reproduction depends on a set of resources. Beside monetary and non-monetary incomes, there are some other types of goods of great importance for living conditions, for the quality of life, for social mobility, and even for survival. Public interference is exercised through the appropriation and the redistribution of important parts of the social product. The benefits of public action are socially differentiated. Because the individual capacity for the consumption of public goods depends mainly on the availability of private complementary goods (be they material or immaterial ones), poor masses risk being excluded from their use. Participation in the use of public goods such as physical infrastructure or social, educational, and other public facilities is an important aspect in urban movements and social struggle.

Empirical research done in Salvador/Bahia (Brazil) shows on the one hand the process of appropriation of urban infrastructure by the upper strata and the traditional land-tenure bourgeoisie, which was able to channel big shares of public infrastructural investments to its own advantage. On the other hand, the urban poor are shown not only to have participated less in public expenditures, but also to have suffered from the negative distribution effects of public action.

REFERENCES

Augel, Johannes (1978). "The Poor in the Urban Infrastructure," *Bulletin of the Society for Latin American Studies*, No. 29, Nov., 31-46.

Augel, Johannes (1979a). "A ocupação do solo urbano," in Secretaria do Planejamento, Ciência e Tecnologia, Fundação de Pesquisas—CPE, ed., *Habitação e urbanismo em Salvador*. Salvador/Bahia: Grupo de Trabalho de Estudos e Pesquisas, 9-25.

Augel, Johannes (1979b). "Notas acerca de la función social de la infraestructura urbana," Eca. *Revista de Extensión Cultural*, año XXXIX, Sept. San Salvador: Univ. Centroamericana José Simeón Cañas, 765-78.

Augel, Johannes (1981). "Sobre algunas funciones sociales de los bienes publicos," *Homines: Revista de Ciências Sociales*, V, 2. San Juan: Univ. Interamericana de Puerto Rico, 103-18.

Boulding, Kenneth E. & Pfaff, Martin, eds. (1972). *Redistribution to the Rich and the Poor: The Grants Economics of Income Distribution*. Belmont, CA: Wadsworth.

Bowers, Patricia F. (1974). *Private Choice and Public Welfare*: Hinsdale, IL: Dryden.

Gilbert, Alan & Gugler, Josef (1982). *Cities, Poverty and Development: Urbanization in the Third World*. Oxford: Oxford Univ. Press.

Grand, Julian le (1982). *The Strategy of Equality: Redistribution and the Social Services*. London: Allen & Unwin.

Griliches, Zvi, Krelle, Wilhelm, Krupp, Hans-Jürgen & Kyn, Oldrich (1978). *Income Distribution and Economic Inequality*. Frankfurt: Campus.

Lojkine, Jean (1977). *Le marxisme, l'Etat et la question urbaine*. Paris: Presses Univ. de France.

Musgrave, Richard & Musgrave, Peggy (1976). *Public Finance in Theory and Practice* New York: McGraw-Hill.

Pottier, Claude (1975). *La logique du financement publique de l'urbanisation*. Paris: Mouton.

Preteceille, Edmond (1973). *La production des grands ensembles*. Paris: Mouton.

Ribeiro, Elisabete Maria Andrade & Debeffe, Charles (1979). "Poder público municipal e propriedade fundiária urbana," in Secretaria do Planejamento, Ciência e Tecnologia, Fundação de Pesquisas—CPE, ed., *Habitação e urbanismo em Salvador*. Salvador/Bahia: Grupo de Trabalho de Estudios e Pesquisas, 81-220.

Skarpelis-Sperk, Sigrid (1978). *Soziale Rationierung öffenlicher Leistungen*. Frankfurt: Campus.

Topalov, Christian (1973). *Capital et propriété foncière. Introduction à l'étude des politiques urbaines*. Paris: CSU.

12

STATE, COLLECTIVE, AND HOUSEHOLD
The Process of Accumulation in China, 1949-65

Lanny Thompson

Fernand Braudel Center
State University of New York—Binghamton

The thesis of this chapter is that rural households in China were reconstituted through the process of collectivization, and similarly with the decentralization of communes, and were a result, on one hand, of peasants' struggles to improve their consumption and, on the other hand, of endeavors by collectives and later communes to restrict peasant incomes. A central contradiction of the socialist development of agriculture was the creation of a mass of paid laborers, despite the attempt to keep the costs of such labor to a minimum, even in the face of peasant resistance to threats to their standard of living. In what follows, I will demonstrate that collectivization transformed households from units of combined production and consumption into spheres of activities for the reproduction of socialized labor, and that unpaid household work benefited socialized accumulation precisely by subsidizing the reproduction of labor, but also that peasants strove to expand these activities at the expense of socialized accumulation in order to improve their livelihood. The analysis will show the existence of struggles over the extent and kinds of household activities, manifested in the competition between households and socialized spheres over the use of resources, labor, and its product. Finally, I argue that the reconstitution of households resulted in a double shift for women. I will demonstrate that this reconstitution posited women, first as generational reproducers of socialized labor and, secondly, as second-class socialized labor itself. Family and kin structures were in part an expression of this double participation of women.

The Household and Land Reform

From the outset of land reform that erupted from below in the 1940's, the interests of the peasantry in ending "feudal exploitation" and distributing land to the tiller coincided with those of the Communist party and the fledgling state apparatus. The key objectives of the Party were to spur agricultural output by stimulating peasant household production through land redistribution; to loosen resources for agricultural investment by eliminating landlord appropriation and luxury consumption; and to smash the landlord class as the dominant political force in the countryside in order to consolidate state power under the direction of the Party. Even before the redistributive movement was complete, the Party began to encourage rich, middle, and poor peasants to increase their productivity and marketable output—to lay the groundwork for the road to modernization. The phrase *"fa chia chih fu"* served to sum up the promise of the future for the peasantry and to mobilize these masses under the direction of the Party. Translated literally, the phrase means "to set up a household and make one's fortune", which expresses the image of household production revitalized by the newly allotted land, with peasants encouraged to improve their livelihood at the hearth, in the fields, and in the marketplace. In the early 1950's, the rapid agricultural recovery from protracted war was encouraging, and peasant incomes were on the rise (Shue, 1980; Selden, 1979: 29-39).

Household production at that time in China meant the organization of family members in agricultural and handicraft production, and the provision of the daily and generational reproduction of that family. Put quite simply, the peasant household was a unit of both production and consumption, and it was nearly always a family unit. The culturally prescribed ideal was a patri-local joint family; however, the land base of middle and poor peasant households did not usually provide sufficient area to support the members of a broadly extended family. In reality, stem families were prevalent and viable, followed by conjugal families (Baker, 1979: Ch. 1; Yang, 1959: 91). The great political and economic instability of the 1930's and 1940's had created profound social disintegration in many rural areas. Countless families were weakened, were separated, or failed to reproduce altogether, as the normal functioning of the household, clan, and village were disrupted. An aspiration of the peasantry was for the establishment of a stable, traditional family. The main thrust of the peasant movement, and of Party practice, in the late 1940's and early 1950's was for private property, increased production, and family—the bases of a prosperous and secure household organization of production (Croll, 1981: 151-52; Johnson, 1983).

However, the period was not simply one of the retrenchment of traditionalism with a new virility rooted in the soil. The promotion of "woman-work'', beginning in the 1940's as a part of the war effort in the liberated areas and subsequently extended nationwide, actually expanded women's activities in agriculture and handicrafts. During the late 1940's and early 1950's the Party organized special women's groups to mobilize women to participate in the land reform, in hygiene and literacy campaigns, and obstensibly to promote women's equality. Laws were passed giving women equality in land inheritance and the freedom of marriage and divorce. Through women's organizations they began to participate in village politics in a way unheard of in pre-revolutionary China. Their markedly increased contribution to production and politics, and the legal reforms centered on the 1950 Marriage Law, signaled important steps in the women's movement, especially for rural women (Davin, 1979).

Still, the practice of female inheritance and freedom of marriage and divorce directly conflicted with the patri-lineal, patri-local kinship system. The promotion of woman-work had been encouraged primarily to increase production, and this did not imply a radical reform of the fundamental structure of the family. Rather, harmonious family relations were encouraged, with the worst abuses criticized (Johnson, 1983). But to stress the independent importance of ''patriarchy'', as do some scholars, is to state the case too one-sidedly. The family system was part and parcel of the whole organization of production and reproduction. Only with membership in a strong family was there hope of prosperous growth and old age security, which is why many women were in fact wary of even the liberalization of the family, given the existing relations of (re)production. There was nothing more hopeless than an abandoned, widowed, or childless woman (Baker, 1979: Ch. 1).

The Dilemma of the First Five Year Plan

The first program of coordinated national development, the First Five Year Plan (1953-1957), followed closely the Soviet model, with the investment priority going to capital-intensive, ''heavy'' industry, primarily producer goods manufacture in centralized urban-based complexes. Yet there were great expectations with regard to agricultural growth, and it was crucial to the success of the industrialization strategy. Agriculture was expected to increase output rapidly to furnish a tax base for the state, to provision the growing urban population, to provide inexpensive raw material for industry and for exports (with which to gain foreign exchange necessary to pay for the import of machinery, equipment, and even complete factories). By taxing and manipulating prices against agriculture, the countryside was to be the basis of the proposed development plan (Eckstein, 1977: 50-51).

The expressed strategy for agriculture was to proceed in a step-by-step manner; improving technology, increasing productivity, and transforming social relations in a series of stages, beginning with land reform and proceeding through mutual aid teams and cooperatives, and eventually, collectivization (Walker, 1966: 2-4). The measure of success would be that each progressive stage should outperform the preceding one in the marketed outputs of agricultural products and levels of household consumption. This was in keeping with the early principles of aligning the interests of the state and the peasantry (Selden, 1982).

In 1949 supply and marketing cooperatives were established as the direct link between peasant producers and the state. They were instituted to control local retail markets, and to collect produce to be taken up by the state trading companies for wholesale trade. The supply and marketing cooperative offered goods for household production and consumption, and market outlets for handicrafts and produce. Although prices were attractive overall when compared to the still-existing private trade, the biggest incentive for peasants to deal with the marketing co-ops was the production contract. If the peasant agreed to sell a fixed amount of produce from the next harvest, the marketing co-op would supply interest-free credit at the beginning of the season. As a result of the elimination of rents and debt payments, and because of price incentives and the improvement (but not reversal) of the terms of trade for agriculture, household incomes were rising, and peasants were improving their consumption (Shue, 1980: Ch. 5; Selden & Lippit, 1982a; Solinger, 1980).

In conjunction with the First Five Year Plan, the Unified Purchase and Supply degree was put into effect in order that agriculture be directly integrated into the network of national economic planning and accumulation. All primary commodities were monopolized by the state, and private trade was forbidden. The remaining infrastructure still in the hands of private merchants was seized. Unified Purchase and Supply was an order of compulsory sales, mandating that peasants sell their surpluses according to the regulations, quotas, and prices set by the state. Despite the success of the state in gaining control over rural markets, throughout 1954 the Party became increasingly concerned over the slow growth of marketable agricultural outputs. Already key targets for grain and cotton were not even close to being met. Grain production barely kept up with population growth, and cotton output showed a negative growth rate. The resulting supply bottlenecks of staple grains, industrial raw materials, and export products were threatening the very success of the industrial development drive of the Five Year Plan (Walker, 1966).

To reduce the planned speed of industrialization would have eased the demand placed upon the agricultural sector, but this ran counter to the commitments and objectives of the Five Year Plan. If a much larger share of investment has been allocated to agriculture, perhaps output could have increased, but again at the expense of high-priority industry. Another option was to continue the price-planning tools and intensify the reliance on the market, offering incentives for peasants to increase marketed outputs. This would result in higher peasant incomes, but there was no guarantee that peasants would not simply raise their own consumption, as they had done following the land reform, rather than purchasing more modern production inputs and increasing further output. Thus, to resort to price-planning would increase the resources available to the peasantry, with little assurance that they would not act counter to the interests of the state planning apparatus (Eckstein, 1977; Solinger, 1980).

Transformation of
Rural Relations of Production

In 1955 Mao sought to cut through this dilemma by pushing for immediate collectivization. It was an attempt to increase both production through the mass mobilization of labor and productivity through the reorganization of rural relations of production. In contrast to previous policy assumptions, mechanization did not serve as the technological foundation of collectivization. Rather, collectivization was advanced as a means of accelerating the rate of rural accumulation to provide for the eventual mechanization of agriculture. The property basis of household production, which had been strengthened by the land reform, was eliminated, and the household organization of production was consequently curtailed. Production was now structured among many households on collectively owned land. In the majority of cases the guiding principle was to form the collective around the natural village. On the average, one village, hence one collective, encompassed 250 families. Production teams (roughly 20 families) became the new unit of family labor-organization and accounting within the collective (Yang, 1959: 238-39; Walker, 1966).

This transformation of rural relations of production created the means for direct appropriation of labor, and established a new locus of accumulation. Peasant production teams were organized, producing for the collective, with households receiving remuneration based upon their earned workpoints. After the collective had provided for all its costs, and set aside funds for investment, the balance would be distributed to households on the basis of their workpoints. The collective determined investment levels and priorities, and was required to finance its development from its own savings. This arrangement allowed the socialized planning of both investment and consumption, with the purpose of accelerating the former by limiting the latter. By restricting household property, activities, and income, households did not become significant loci of accumulation. Further, in cooperation with the planning apparatus, the collective enforced production targets and gathered produce to be purchased by the state at fixed prices. The price scissors maintained by the state ensured an unequal exchange between agriculture and industry. Thus labor contributed by households provided the surplus appropriated by the collective, and indirectly appropriated through the state's maintenance of unequal exchange (Kojima, 1982).

The collective organization of land and labor provided an institutional framework for the increased mobilization of rural labor. From 1954 to 1957 the total annual labor days worked by peasants increased by nearly 50 percent. Some of this work went directly towards capital construction projects. It was anticipated that the increase in labor involved in the building of terraces, dikes, and waterways would lead to an eventual rise in productivity. Farm labor also increased dramatically as peasants were enjoined to intensify their labor in order to increase output rapidly. Thus the state mobilized its most potential resource, labor, in an attempt to raise output immediately and provide for long-term growth (Table 12.1; Schran, 1969: Ch. 4).

Where did the collectives discover this great reserve of labor to be tapped? The bulk was provided by women, who were drawn out of the house into collective production, the sphere of accumulation. Throughout the early 1950's a combination of measures applied in conjunction with the organization of mutual aid teams and cooperatives had encouraged women to enter socialized, remunerated production. Special women's teams and political groups were formed, and the promise of greater respect, authority, and material well-being resulting from the income acted as an incentive for women to participate. But the watershed of women's participations was collectivization. Women apparently accounted for 80% of the increase in labor days from 1955 to 1957. It is clear that in each successive stage of organization, from mutual aid to collective, labor days increased, and that women accounted for most of this increase (Table 12.2; Croll, 1979: Ch. 2).

While it is true that the First Five Year Plan resulted in high growth rates in industry, collectivization did not solve the problem of sluggish agricultural growth. The rapid accumulation in industry, at the expense of a great disparity between agriculture and industry, had led to severe bottlenecks and imbalances that were still undermining the anticipated role of agriculture in the overall development plan. Again the Chinese leadership was more than reluctant to divert investment from heavy industry into the mechanization of agriculture (Eckstein, 1966: 29-31). Besides, there is evidence that the existent capacity for tractor and fertilizer production was far too low to make such a plan feasible (Lippit, 1975). The innovation

TABLE 12.1 Average And Total Annual Labor Days, 1950-59

Year	Average Annual Labor Days	Total Annual Labor Days (in billions)	Indices: Total Labor Days in 1952 = 100.0							1952 Man-Year Equivalent of Total Annual Labor Days (in millions)
			Total Labor Days	Subsidiary Work	Farm Work	Corvée, Basic Construction	Collective Affairs	Communal Services	Communal Industries	
1950	119.0	26.489	97.3	19.2	75.2	3.1				222.6
1951	119.0	26.833	98.8	19.4	76.1	3.2				225.5
1952	119.0	27.168	100.0	19.7	77.1	3.2				228.3
1953	119.0	27.537	101.4	20.0	78.1	3.2				231.4
1954	119.3	28.155	103.6	20.4	79.9	3.3				236.6
1955	121.0	29.439	108.4	21.0	83.0	3.9	0.4			247.4
1956	149.0	38.084	140.2	23.7	104.3	8.7	3.5			320.0
1957	159.5	41.518	152.8	25.8	113.4	9.7	3.8			348.9
1958	174.6	47.474	174.7	28.8	120.3	10.9	4.2	6.7	3.9	398.9
1959	189.0	58.420	215.0	29.5	151.7	12.3	4.4	9.5	7.5	490.9

SOURCE: Peter Schran, "Average and Total Annual Labor Days, 1950-1959," (p. 75) in *The Development of Chinese Agriculture, 1950-59.* Copyright ©1969 by University of Illinois Press. Reprinted by permission.

TABLE 12.2   Changes in Labor Utilization Rates, 1955-57

| | | | *Percentage Increase with Collectivization Compared to the Days of —* | | |
Labor type	Number of persons	Work Days	Individual farming	Mutual aid teams	Lower-stage agricultural cooperatives
Male full-time labor	267	259	50	24.5	9.8
Male part-time labor	42	197	112	72.0	41.7
Female full-time labor	132	162	184	85.2	42.1
Female part-time labor	95	75	650	29.7	41.5

SOURCE: Elizabeth Croll, *Women in Rural Development: The People's Republic of China*, p. 18, Table 3. Copyright ©1979 by the International Labour Organisation, Geneva. Reprinted by permission.

of the Great Leap Forward, launched in late 1958, was to reorganize and mobilize *rural* labor for the fabrication and expansion of small-scale industry, especially in farm tool improvement, mechanization, and electrification of agriculture (Stavis, 1978). This involved combining agriculture and industry into an interlocational structure—the rural commune, which was to finance this rural modernization out of its own savings. That is, commune labor itself was to be the direct source of accumulation. Agriculture was greatly centralized as many collectives were merged under a single administration. The commune expanded its activities into small-scale industry and handicrafts, as well as into defense, education, health, and child care. The political apparatus was merged with the commune management, creating a combined and expanded political and economic administration (Walker, 1968).

The Great Leap Forward involved even greater recruitment of labor than the collectivization drive. Agrarian capital construction and the intensification of labor were carried out in much greater dimensions than previously, and, on top of this, labor for industrial production was mustered (Schran, 1969). Again, women provided the bulk of the labor contribution. It is estimated that 90% of rural women were employed in socialized production, engaged in 250 labor days each a year, which in 1959 constituted 40%-45% of total labor days (Selden, 1979: 82).

However, the immediate results of the Great Leap Forward with respect to production were disastrous; already by the end of 1959 the crisis in the countryside had become catastrophic. Grain production fell sharply n 1959 and 1960, and there were shortages of food; peasant consumption dropped miserably, approaching famine conditions in many areas (Eckstein,

1975: 24). By 1961, 32% of China's imports were foodstuffs, up from 2.5% in 1960, while at the same time imports of machinery, equipment and plants, all crucial to China's development, were cut back from 62% to 21% of total imports (Eckstein, 1966: 107). Many of the small-scale industrial endeavors proved to be technologically inefficient, particularly the infamous backyard iron furnaces, most of which produced an unusable product, as did most of the outcomes of the tool reform campaign (Stavis, 1978). In 1958 cadres had merged collectives and townships disregarding traditional economic areas and centers, aiming instead for the largest size possible. Skinner (1965) argues that giantism made the commune too unwieldy because it was incompatible with existing transportation and administrative infrastructure, land use patterns, and traditional bonds of village solidarity.

In late 1959 and throughout 1960, a progressive decentralization was carried out, and by 1961-62 the commune would take the form that would endure the remaining years of the 1960's. Thereafter the commune resembled a combination of agricultural collectives and industrial and handicraft enterprises, joined together by the central planning administration of the commune. What developed was a three-tiered structure: the communes, which were formed from roughly 10-15 brigades (corresponding to villages), each of which consists of 10-15 teams (corresponding to neighborhoods). The commune was the lowest level of direct state authority and was the link between rural households and the centralized planning apparatus. This level managed the plan for production within the commune, setting quotas, administering compulsory sales, and projecting growth targets. Communal industry was reorganized around what was technically feasible and cost-effective, including many small, but relatively modern factories. Modern means of production and land were owned by the commune, or by the brigades that managed large-scale agricultural and capital construction projects, and operated machine stations, workshops, and social services. The teams were the units of daily production and accounting, usually specializing in agriculture (Lippit, 1977).

With respect to labor, key assumptions behind the collective and communal strategies were these:

- A substantial portion of rural labor was underemployed, thus consuming, but contributing little to output.
- This labor could be effectively employed without burdensome capital investment and transportation development.
- Most important, such employment would not lead to increases in household consumption (Eckstein), 1966: 32)

A central contradiction emerging with the rural development strategy was the creation of masses of paid laborers, while attempting to keep low the collective cost of labor, in order to sustain high rates of investment. This was the context of the reconstitution of peasant households.

The Reconstitution of Households

As we have seen collectivization was premised on the maintenance of low remuneration to labor. Indeed, while average peasant income increased 18% from 1952-56, it did not increase significantly in the course of the following two decades; at the same time, the number of labor days worked by peasants more than doubled from 1952-59 (Selden & Lippit, 1982a). Collectivization was imposed by the state upon the peasantry precisely as a means of limiting consumption and accelerating planned accumulation and labor employment. Although the process was not accompanied by overt violence in most cases, it was marked by the economic and political coercion of the peasantry, many of whom saw nothing to gain from the socialization of agriculture, especially those relatively well-off rich and middle peasants (Selden, 1982). From the beginning of collectivization, peasants struggled to maintain the level and security of household consumption through asserting the right to raise crops and livestock for subsistence and exchange. Official policy underlined the importance of these activities, a lesson learned from peasant resistance in earlier attempts at cooperativization in northern China. Cadres were supposed to set aside 5% of the collective's arable land for private use by households, and allow the exchange of produce for consumption. Yet in some locales overzealous cadres attempted to overstep these limits, socializing all, or nearly all, land and livestock and disallowing markets during the collectivization drive of 1955-56. Peasants resisted this encroachment on their livelihood, in the main by slaughtering their livestock, but also by neglect of, and passive resistance to, socialized agriculture (Walker, 1965: Ch. 4; Walker, 1966).

A result of the conflict was an unstable and shifting compromise between cadres and the peasantry. The limits of collective and household were a continuing source of contention. This was expressed in part as the competition between collective and household for labor and resources. Specific issues included the amount of labor to be contributed to the collective, usufruct of land and water, and the use of manure produced by household pigs but needed as fertilizer for the collective. The excessive use of labor and resources in household activities could have increased incomes but at the expense of collective production and investment; yet socialized agriculture itself rarely could generate the incomes, the products, or the services for an adequate living. Despite the increasing contribution of household labor to collective production, the remuneration to households was generally below the social standards and expectations of the peasantry.

In order to supplement the collective payment, a host of traditional activities were retained in form, although transformed in essence. Households secured rights to small garden plots of marginal land on which they cultivated various fruits and vegetables, and raised pigs and poultry. They were allowed to collect fodder and fuel from hillsides and embankments, and to tend fruit trees and bamboo groves. Handicrafts were allowed, even though most raw materials (e.g., cotton) were monopolized by the state. These agricultural and handicraft products were either consumed directly, or exchanged in periodic village markets, which were generally characterized by an exchange of use-values between direct producers. These markets were sources of food and handicrafts important for daily living but not available through socialized channels. While the state tightly controlled national and regional markets of primary commercial products, a host of "third category" items were freely traded in village markets (Skinner, 1965).

Walker (1965: 23-41) concludes that household activities on garden plots (1) provided the foods needed for a balanced diet; (2) raised the standard of living, in many cases from the margin of subsistence to tolerable levels; (3) were a source of cash; and (4) provided a margin of security in contrast to the uncertainties of the collective. He found that in 1957 income from garden plots, including the value of produce consumed, amounted to 19%-34% of total household income.

Household activities were reconstituted as the necessary tasks of reproducing socialized labor in the context of insufficient incomes and consumer goods. Households were transformed into spheres of organizing reproductive work in relation to the sphere of accumulation, the collective. This reconstitution was characterized by the positing of women, children, and the aged as the predominant, although by no means exclusive, contributors to household work. But it was women that bore a particularly heavy burden. Not only were they relegated to the privatized tasks of reproduction, but they were also mobilized for collective labor; working women carried the weight of a "double shift". The particular household chores that conflicted with employment could be assumed by other women of the family. For example, older women, who traditionally had gradually turned their work over to daughters and daughters-in-law, took over a heavier household work load in order to allow the younger women to particpate in socialized production. Thus the work of women who stayed at home was also intensified (Davin, 1979: 125-26; Parish & Whyte, 1978: 242-44).

The importance of unpaid household work was brought out in graphic fashion during the tumultuous years of the Great Leap Forward. The increased employment of women invovled in the drive to create rural communes in 1958-59 was possible only if they were released from their usual household duties. Consequently, communes attempted to socialize a large share of household activities, although the extent of this socialization varied so greatly throughout China, and it was so brief, that an accurate account has not been made. However, one can generally say that, for a brief period lasting no later than 1960, communes radically circumscribed the household as a locus of reproduction, and tried to draw practically the entire family into socialized production and consumption. In many communes, crèches and nurseries were formed to provide child care, and public dining halls provided communal meals. Some communes may have gone so far as to abolish household incomes, distributing goods and services "according to need" through communal channels. Brigades expanded into the production of light consumer goods, such as clothing and shoes, which had been previously produced in households. Most important, access to garden plots was abolished, and household livestock and tools were confiscated as the communes attempted to organize this production. Periodic markets were simultaneously abolished (Croll, 1979; Selden, 1979).

Most of the new services provided by communes proved to be too expensive and unsatisfactory to be continued. This was particularly true of dining halls, which were beset by the costs of wages and fuel and subject to criticisms about the quality and variety of meals. The operation of dining halls required the hiring of laborers and the use of expensive coal to fire the large kitchens used unpaid work and fuel gathered from hillsides and embankments. Child care, especially during the youngest years, could be provided at less cost to communes if left primarily to unpaid mothers and grandmothers. Many daily tasks such as these fared no better under commune management; the maximum use of labor, with the least expense, called for a revival of unpaid household work (Crook & Crook, 1966).

With the decline in household activities in handicrafts and agriculture, the countryside was hit with shortages of meat, vegetables, light consumer goods, and the like. The scarcity of pig manure for fertilizer seriously undermined communal agricultural output. Most commune experiments to absorb this production resulted in higher costs and declining output. The emphasis on capital construction in agriculture, and the high priority given to rural industrial development, led to neglect of production and marketing serving local consumption needs. For example, the socialization of livestock, especially pigs, was quite costly and inefficient, requiring the construction of special barns and the hiring of labor. Overall pig output fell sharply during the Greap Leap Forward. Further, while periodic markets were abolished, no satisfactory alternatives were systematically developed. In the face of peasant unrest and falling production on all fronts, cadres returned garden plots, livestock, and tools to households during 1960, and local markets were officially sanctioned after 1961 (Walker, 1965; Skinner, 1965).

During the crisis of the Great Leap Forward, household production was in many cases temporarily re-established on a contractual basis with the commune. Under this arrangement, production quotas were contracted out to households. These were short-lived however, as the organization of production was soon restored by the brigades and teams. Although the establishment of socialized agriculture was conclusive by 1961, documents from Lien-Chiang County revealed pressures in some teams to break up into household contractual production as late as 1963 (Chen, 1969: 99-106).[1] The Socialist Education Campaign (1962-63) was in large part directed against this "spirit of individual enterprise". The documents contain repeated refuations of such alleged peasant statements as the following: "With individual enterprise we eat to the full"; "Individual enterprise is not a class struggle, but simply a way to eat well"; "The government is afraid the masses will eat too well, and so they promote collectives" (Chen, 1969: 105-06, 112-17, 142-43).

The Lien-Chiang documents suggest that the positing of households exclusively as spheres of reproduction was actively pursued, and one means of this was to encourage women, but not men, to engage in household activities. As a general rule, women had smaller labor obligations than men, at a time when labor quotas were being increased and strictly enforced. One document of general policy stated, "The regulations stipulate that the production teams should organize all persons able to work for participation in labor," but continued, "When determining the basic labor quota for female commune members, consideration should be given to physiological conditions and the practical demands of household duties" (Chen, 1969: 126). In one brigade, women, but not men, were allowed special additional exemption for child care, and especially for expanding pig production on the garden plot. A ten-day per month exemption was granted for those women having a sow with a litter, the same exemption given for the care of three young children. Furthermore, fertilizer (pig manure) quotas were assessed individually, with women laborers and "nonworkers" required to deliver 40% and 80% more, respectively, than male laborers (Chen, 1969: 66). Another brigade conducted an education campaign, in which the "masses" were encouraged

> to effect production economy and frugal commune management, unite in strengthening the collective economy, and complete winter production effectively in a struggle for attaining a rich harvest next year, meet the new high tide of the nation's economy, and achieve a new victory of socialist construction (Chen, 1969: 147).

In contrast, the "women masses" were called upon,

> to participate actively in collective labor, make precise calculation, consolidate their household duties and manage them harmoniously, and, with the prereq-

uisite of not affecting the collective interest, strive to expand household subsidiary enterprises and increase their income (Chen, 1969: 147).[2]

After collectivization, and again after the decentralization of the communes, household work, including participation in periodic markets, was
established as a sphere of reproduction in relation to the sphere of accumulation (socialized agriculture and, especially, industry). This was beneficial
to the collective, and later the commune, as well as to the state planning
apparatus. These activities served to cheapen the costs of reproducing labor
power and permitted a focus upon the development of producer industry.
To increase remuneration and provide services would have cut into the funds
available for investment. To modernize periodic markets would have required investment in transportation and warehousing, and would have added a burden to administration and logistical problems to central planning.
Moderately restricted, the markets did not become avenues for household
accumulation; rather, they were tied up with efforts directed towards increasing consumption.

But precisely because the household competed with the collective and
the commune for labor and resources, the limits of household activities
became a point of antagonism. Peasants continued to struggle for the social
space for household work through which to improve their livelihood. The
documents from Lien-Chiang County show how the conflict between
household and commune was manifested on an everyday level. One finds
there repeated references to problems with the peasantry: poor job discipline
and the failure to fulfill labor quotas; the watering down of fertilizer sold
to the commune and excessive bickering over its price; theft, including stealing of communal tools and materials and the felling of socialized trees; opening up of uncultivated land for household use and excessive size of garden
plots; abandoning agriculture for peddling or odd jobs; and so on (Chen,
1969: 48-49, 99-102, 145-46, 210-11). Peasants sought to expand household
activities as a way of improving their consumption, while the cadres sought
to restrict it as a way of augmenting accumulation.

Women and the Family

Make no mistake, women have made significant gains in Chinese society, and some are highly visible in important positions in political and
economic jobs. As women entered socialized, remunerated production in
collectives and communes they gained higher status and well-being in the
family and in the society. Davin concludes,

> As a result of marriage reform greater economic independence, better educa-
> tion, increased contacts with society, and a heavy commitment to sexual equali-
> ty by the previaling ideology, women's position within the family has
> undergone a marked improvment. However, many problems remain, and since
> these are related to complex general socio-economic problem they are unlikely
> to be quickly resolved (1979: 114).

It is painfully clear that women had not, as a whole, obtained equality. In
the commune, women's labor was concentrated in agriculture, especially
in the lowest paid, part-time and seasonal tasks; in brigade workshops for
making consumer goods; and in service sectors, in which the pay is lower
than in commune industries. Women's workpoint rates were commonly
50%-80% those of men (Croll, 1979: 29). This was symptomatic of the
continuing sexual division of labor and the relative devaluation of "woman-
work". But lower work point evaluations were regularly given to women
who performed the same tasks as men. Many struggles emerged over the
issue of equal pay for equal work, sometimes with women challenging men
in work competitions to prove the quantity and quality of their work was
equal. Women's pay status was also adversely affected by their fluctuating
participation. One survey of 29 collectives in Zhejiang showed that while
only 14% of employed men were part-time laborers, 42% of employed
women were part-time (Table 12.2). Women could be seen entering and
leaving emkployment, depending upon the life cycle, agricultural seasons,
and policy vacillations, functioning in part to smooth out disruptive cycles
of the economy. They were involved in the economy as seasonal, part-time,
temporary life-time, as well as full-time laborers, according to their ability
to fulfill household obligations first. It seems that women did not enter
socialized employment on an equal footing with men. Women split their
responsibilities between socialized labor and household work, while men
dominated the socialized sphere, holding the regular, highest paid jobs, and
being most active in politics and administration (Croll, 1979: Ch. 3). Not
only did women contribute the bulk of the unpaid household work, they
provided cheap, flexible labor to socialized spheres.

   In traditional China households came under the unquestionable authority of the male head, who dominated the management of land and work.
The relationship between the father and son(s) was the nucleus of the
household. Sons were highly valued for their important contribution in
agriculture. They were quite necessary for the prosperity of the family and
the old age security of the parents, not to mention the fate of the lineage;
a family with many sons was considered to be quite fortunate. Patri-local
marriage was the means by which young women were recruited in order
to reproduce the household as a unit of production and consumption.

Women's primary obligations were in the house, and in southern China they did signficant agricultural work as well. Women were expected to feed and clothe the family, to bear and raise children (preferably sons), and to participate as needed in adjunct and seasonal agricultural work.

After collectivization, patri-local marriage remained customary, and a woman often joined her husband's production team, as well as his residence. During collectivization, and after the decentralization of the commune, the organization of production units (especially teams) around traditional bonds, particularly kinship, was favored as a means of promoting cooperation and stability. Together as a team, a group of male kinsmen held usage rights over socialized land, water, and equipment. Many of the small teams were referred to by family name, and in the village members of one family may have held the most prominent position. This is not surprising considering that a village usually consisted primarily of one or two lineages, and that the collectives (and later communal brigades) were structured around the traditional village (Diamond, 1975; Croll, 1981: 176-78). Parish (1975) reports that both villagers and commune officials objected to the movement of men that would result from frequent matri-locality. Such as choice would have tended to deplete poorer teams of higher-earning, more-valued male laborers, as they were deserted for richer teams where laborers would have been better off. Patri-locality was one way to prevent this and other problems of labor migration.

They were further pressures for the maintenance of patri-locality. The Marriage Law (1950) stated that children had the duty to support and assist their parents in old age. Although the communal brigades would have supported the aged as a last resort, the standard of living was quite low and insecure, and carried a less than desirable status. Stem families werer a common arrangement between the paretns and a son, in which the elders were dependent upon the remuneration to the young, and the young were dependent upon the elders for their unpaid work in the household. The ability of young women to engage in socialized employement was often possible because their household duties were assumed in part by mothers-in-law. Aged fathers could cultivate a few vegetables on the garden plot, even if they were unable to put in a full day of heavy labor for the work team. With incomes derived for the most part from socialized employment, the authority of parents actually declined as they contributed fewer and fewer earnings to the household. With collectivization, the authority of fathers over sons began to weaken, as the main source of their authority—the land— was socialized. The father-dyad, which dominatcd the traditional family, was replaced by the husband-wife dyad as the primary relationship, even among the remaining stem families (Parish & Whyte, 1978: 209-21; Parish, 1975; Yang, 1959: 53). Studies conducted in the 1970's report that 37%

of families were of a stem structure, compared with 60%-63% in 1936 (Parish & Whyte, 1978: 131-38; Croll, 1981: 143-50). For this reason it has been argued that the conjugal family was the trend in rural China. However, virtually all aged parents were a part of a son's household, and a spatial closeness was found even between parents and sons with separate households, facilitating mutual support. Parents were assured that they would not be forgotten in their old age, and were able to provide domestic chores for their married sons. Parish and Whyte (1978: 137) characterized the majority of households as "stem-and-associated-nuclear-family combinations". This interdependence between generations upon earnings and unpaid work promoted further the maintenance of patri-locality.

The continued functioning of patri-locality meant that young women were neither encouraged to develop politically, nor recommended for special education and technical or administrative training, because it was expected that they would leave the village upon marriage and these skills would be lost to the family, team, and brigade. Since parents depended upon their sons in old age, and teams relied upon men for high productivity, they made certain that as boys they acquired the skills necessary for high earnings and production. Income-earning laborers were the basis of a prosperous household, and women were recruited primarily as the reproducers of that labor, although they were also valued for their own contribution to household earnings. With the overlapping of kinship and team, patri-locality also served as means for recruiting labor for the team, not just the household. Thus, women were recruited into households to maintain and renew its laborers; to produce a new generation, as well as caring for the old; and also to contribute to income through subsistence work and socialized employment (Croll, 1981: 152-59).

Women contributed in a double way: The prosperity of households owed much to their valuable household work and employment earnings, and the processes of accumulation were based upon their cheap labor and unpaid work. The gains made by women coincided with the emergence of the double shift. On one hand, the intensification of household work was the means by which families improved their standard of living, and life-long prospertiy for peasants, men or women, could be found only as member of a household. On the other hand, household work was shouldered in particular by women, and its intensification at the expense of socialized employment on the part of women could only undercut their advances. The double burden was in part the liberation of women becasue they entered socialized employment, and as a result won greater independence, participation, influence, and status. Yet at the same time it was the continuation of their subordination because they worked twice as much, were paid less, and had little to say about it politically.

Conclusion

Households mediate the contradiction of creating a mass of paid laborers while needing to keep low the costs of remuneration; they mediated the contradiction between keeping low remuneration and the demand of the peasantry to improve their standard of living. Households were both the means by which the state attempted to restrict the level and the costs of consumption, and the means by which the peasantry struggled daily for the social space to improve it. Households were the expression of the articulation between paid socialized labor and unpaid work; thus both households and processes of accumulation were predicated on women's double shift.

Households mediated the tension between accumulation and consumption, in which each threatened to cut into the other. The result of over-accumulation is the improverishment of the masses, but the result of over-consumption is the harsh sentence of continued backwardness. Households were not remnants of the past awaiting modernization; they were posited as one of the foundations of modernization, which is to say that women held up somewhat more than half the sky.

NOTES

1. In 1964 Chinese Nationalist commandos raided Lien-Chiang County and stole certain documents relating to communes in the country. Twenty-five of these documents have been translated and published under the editorship of C. S. Chen (1969).

2. Although the term is not made clear in this particular brigade report, a document sent down from the Fukien Provincial Committee of the Communist party refers to "domestic subsidiary production" as cultivation of garden plots, raising domestic livestock, handicrafts such as knitting, sewing and embroidery, keeping of trees and bamboo groves, and the like (Chen, 1969: 118-19).

REFERENCES

Baker, Hugh (1979). *Chinese Family and Kinship.* New York: Columbia Univ. Press.

Burki, Shahid (1969). *A Study of Chinese Communes, 1965.* Cambridge: Harvard Univ. Press.

Chen, C. S., ed. (1969). *Rural People's Communes in Lien-Chiang.* Stanford: Hoover.

Croll, Elisabeth (1979). *Women in Rural Development: The People's Republic of China.* Geneva: ILO.

Croll, Elizabeth (1981). *The Politics of Marriage in Contemporary China.* Cambridge: Cambridge Univ. Press.

Crook, Isabel & Crook, David (1966). *The First Years of Yangyi Commune.* London: Routledge & Kegan Paul.

Davin, Delia (1979). *Woman-Work in China*. Oxford: Oxford Univ. Press.

Diamond, Norma (1975). "Collectivization, Kingship and the Status of Women in Rural China," in R. Reiter, ed., *Toward an Anthropology of Women*. New York: Monthly Review Press.

Eckstein, Alexander (1966). *Communist China's Economic Growth and Foreign Trade*. New York: McGraw-Hill.

Eckstein, Alexander (1975). *China's Economic Development*. Ann Arbor: Univ. of Michigan Press.

Edkstein, Alexander (1977). *China's Economic Revolution*. Cambridge: Cambridge Univ. Press.

Eckstein, Alexander, Galenson, Walter & Ta-Chung Liu, eds., (1968). *Economic Trends in Communist China*. Chicago: Aldine.

Johnson, Kay (1983). *Women, the Family, and Peasant Revolution in China*. Chicago: Univ. of Chicago Press.

Kojima, Reiitsu (1982). "Accumulation, Technology, and China's Economic Development," in M. Selden & V. Lippit, eds., *The Transition to Socialism in China*. Armonk, NY: Sharpe, 238-65.

Lippit, Victor (1975). "The Great Leap Forward Reconsidered," *Modern China*. I, 1, Jan., 92-115.

Lippit, Victor (1977). "The Commune in Chinese Development," *Modern China*, III, 2, Apr., 229-55.

Parish, William (1975). "Socialism and the Chinese Peasant Family," *Journal of Asian Studies*, XXXIV, 3, May, 613-30.

Parish, William & Whyte, Martin (1978). *Village and Family in Contemporary China*. Chicago: Univ. of Chicago Press.

Schran, Peter (1969). *The Development of Chinese Agriculture, 1950-1959*. Urbana: Univ. of Illinois.

Selden, Mark (1979). *The People's Republic of China*. New York: Monthly Review Press.

Selden, Mark (1982). "Cooperation and Conflict: Cooperative and Collective Formation in China's Countryside," in M. Selden & V. Lippit, eds., *The Transition to Socialism in China*. Armonk, NY: Sharpe, 32-97.

Selden, Mark & Lippit, Victor (1982a). "The Transition to Socialism in China" in M. Selden & V. Lippit, eds., *The Transition to Socialism in China*. Armonk, NY: Sharpe, 3-31.

Selden, Mark & Lippit, Victor, eds. (1982b). *The Transition to Socialism in China*. Armonk, NY: Sharpe.

Shue, Vivienne (1980). *Peasant China in Transition*. Berkeley: Univ. of California Press.

Skinner, William G. (1965). "Marketing and Social Structure in Rural China, Part III," *Journal of Asian Studies*, XXIV, 3, May, 363-400.

Solinger, Dorothy (1979). "State versus Merchant: Commerce in the Countryside in the Early People's Republic of China," *Comparative Studies in Society and History*, XXI, 2, Apr., 168-94.

Solinger, Dorothy (1980). "Socialist Goals and Capitalist Tendencies in Chinese Commerce, 1949-1952," *Modern China*, VI, 2, Apr., 197-224.

Stavis Benedict (1978). *The Politics of Agricultural Mechanization in China*. Ithaca, NY: Cornell Univ. Press.

Walker, Kenneth (1965). *Planning in Chinese Agriculture*. Chicago: Aldine.

Walker, Kenneth (1966). "Collectivization in Retrospect," *China Quarterly*, XXVI, Apr.-June, 1-43.

Walker, Kenneth (1968). "Organization for Agricultural Production," in A. Eckstein, ed., *Economic Trends in Communist China*. Chicago: Aldine, 397-458.

Yang, C. K. (1959). *Chinese Communist Society*: Cambridge: M.I.T. Press.

13

GENDER DIVISION WITHIN THE U.S. WORKING CLASS
Households in the Philadelphia Area, 1870-1945

Torry Dickinson

Fernand Braudel Center
State University of New York—Binghamton

As the United States became part of the core (or of the economic and political center) of the capitalist world-economy by 1900, changes in industrial and political organization restructured the ways that working-class households were sustained or reproduced. Working-class households within the capitalist world-economy have their labor (or their profit-yielding work) organized within capitalist production processes and receive wage incomes that cover a portion of the costs of their daily and generational reproduction. Working-class households in the core receive higher wage incomes that cover a greater portion of the costs of their maintenance than do households in the periphery (or in the Third World). In order to cover the costs of the daily and generational reproduction of households, these economic units must also rely on a portion of non-wage income, which varies proportionately depending on the location of households within the zones of the world-economy. The global reorganization of production associated with the decline of Britain as the hegemonic power within the capitalist system and the rise of the United States as a major power by the end of the nineteenth century transformed the ways that U.S. working-class households were reproduced. This transformation of household relations changed the ways that males and females were economically and socially related.

AUTHOR'S NOTE: This research was made possible partly by a Susan B. Anthony Dissertation Grant from the American Association of University Women. Robert Schaeffer, a fellow graduate student, helped me with writing and editing.

As the United States assumed its new position as part of the core of the global economy by the turn of the century, changes in the structure of capitalist production processes made working-class households more dependent on wage income and market consumption. The growing dependence of households on wage income earned within the context of capitalist production fundamentally changed wage and non-wage work relations between household members. As households depended more on capitalist production to meet their economic needs, capitalist production became more efficient and more automated which redefined and restructured the demand for labor. In relation to the restructuring of the labor force, non-wage work relations changed as well. The growing reliance on wage income and the declining reliance on certain forms of non-wage income, the form that proletarianization assumed in the United States between 1870 and 1930, fundamentally changed the character of wage and non-wage work relations between household members.

As the United States became part of the core, proletarianization restructured both work and social relations between household members, including relations between gender groups (or socially created male and female groups). Proletarianization in the United States brought the increasing integration of labor within capitalist relations. This economic process divided household members into hierarchically arranged groups that reflected patterns of gender and age stratification. The development of these patterns of stratification was rooted in the global, social division of labor. As households relied on more income from wage labor and on more consumer commodities purchased through the expanding capitalist market, more polarized work and social relations developed between socially constituted gender (as well as age) groups.

As industrial production became more mechanized and as higher wages were paid to laborers working within capitalist enterprises, the division of work and labor between household members changed. Adult males tended to become defined as the dominant wage laborers and adult females tended to become defined as subordinate, lower-paid wage laborers. As machines began replacing a portion of human laborers within the industrial production process, adult females, older people, and younger people tended to become defined as "reserve army" groups. By the third decade of the twentieth century, adult females had clearly become etablished as secondary laborers within the area of domestic work. Proletarianization, which brought the growing integration of working-class households within the capitalist world-economy, made household members into different kinds of labor and work specialists. No longer were all household members part-time, temporary wage laborers as well as part-time non-wage workers during the entire "working day" (which once tended to be just as much as a non-wage working day as it was a wage working day). The increasing reliance of households on higher wages and on market consumption served to establish more divided polarized households along the lines of gender and age. This was even the case for lower-income, more economically deprived ethnic groups that relied on low wages and a relatively large proportion of non-wage income.

Historical research on the related areas of proletarianization, the commodification of household activities, and the formation of gender groups needs to be studied in such a way that global processes, regional developments, and household transformations are all taken into consideration. This chapter represents part of an effort to redirect studies in this area. In order to begin showing that the development of gender divisions can be explained through historical research, three areas will be examined here, including the institutionalization of gender inequality through an early "state" agency; the contribution of income by children and the polarization of gender groups; and cooperative relations between low-income people and resulting social alternatives (which may bring a reduced level of gender polarization). The form that the capitalist division of labor assumed in the United States both widened the gap between household members over the long run and sometimes, as a result of a low degree of integration within capitalist relations, promoted certain short-lived patterns of *relative* gender "equity".

Polarization of Gender and Age Groups in the Philadelphia Area, 1870-1945

The following historical section on households in the Philadelphia area demonstrates, with data drawn from archival records of social service agencies, that the redefinition of social relations between gender groups formed an integral part of proletarianization. As laboring households depended less on income from non-wage work and more on income from wage labor, sexist relations became institutionalized throughout more spheres of social life. Given the preliminary stage of research in this area, the method employed here, which links together theories of social change with historical records of neighborhood life and household structures, provides one way to develop a more comprehensive understanding of the development of gender divisions. Historical evidence for this study is drawn from a larger research project (Dickinson, 1983) on changes in households and ethnic groups in the United States. An interpretation of data on developing social relations is advanced here to support the thesis that capitalist social processes created more rigid, specialized work roles between household members as the United States became a major world power after 1870.

Archival records of Philadelphia's workhouse, the House of Industry (which operated in various forms from 1830 until the mid-twentieth century), provide evidence that divisions between males and females, between young and old, in households widened as industrialization proceeded. The House of Industry, like other early relief agencies, intervened increasingly into the ways that households in the neighborhood were reproduced. And, like other social agencies, this workhouse encouraged the development of households that were more integrated into capitalist relations. Social agencies, in response to the pressures of industrial production, promoted the dismantling of assistance networks organized by households and worked to establish stronger links between households, the labor force, and the capitalist market. In the long run, the increasing incorporation of households into the capitalist division of labor contributed to the gradual formation of new social relations of inequality.

Policies of the House of Industry and social conditions in the more industrialized areas of the East Coast changed significantly after 1880, bringing changes in the ways that household members were socially related to each other. Even though practices of social agencies did divide males and females during the mid-nineteenth century, the form that these divisions assumed changed as social relations were reconstituted after the United States became a part of the core of the world-economy. After 1880, major changes in the relief policies and practices of the House of Industry occurred as one part of the reorganization of the capitalist division of labor. Changes in the ways that relief programs were organized and relief income was distributed restructured the ways that materially deprived households were reproduced.

During this period, when the industrial production process in the United States became established as the primary way for producing goods, the House of Industry developed new ways to distribute relief income (whether it was in kind or in money), resocialize working people, and encourage further integration into large-scale industrial relations. Changes in these practices were not carried out by conscious agents of capital who worked to establish a strong state, but evolved both as a response to and, eventually, as a promoter of the slowly dominating, industrial production process. As the United States became part of the core, capitalist production, the state, and the structure of the working class all changed in relationship to each other. Changes in one institution of the capitalist world-economy both reflected and promoted changes in other institutions of the world-economy. These changing, interconnected relationships were an integral and necessary part of capitalist development. For working-class people a focal point for the transformation of these relationships between capital, labor, and the state was the restructuring of households and the shift in relations between household members. In the long run, the realignment of class relations in the United States after 1870 served to polarize the work and social roles of males and females.

After 1880 the House of Industry, along with other social agencies concerned with the maintenance of the working class, distributed income to economically destitute households only if some of the economic activities of the unit could be supervised by the House staff. This growing intervention by social agencies into household relations marked another stage in the increased supervision and regulation by "state-like" agencies of household economics. "State"-sponsored intervention acted to encourage a growing dependence on wage labor (which was organized increasingly by large enterprises) and on market consumption. Nonconformity with guidelines established by social agencies often led to the denial of any relief. As standards for relief eligibility increased, economically deprived households were left in even a more desperate struggle for their livelihood during the depression of 1873-1896. The increasing regulation of household economics by parastatal (and later state) agencies, along with the gradual disappearance of once-prevalent sources of income, served to reduce control households once had over their own reproduction. The reduction of household control over reproduction also meant a decline in certain kinds of control over the development of gender relations. In the long run, this became translated to mean a polarization between gender groups and the institutionalization of gender inequality throughout more spheres of the social division of labor.

Many of Philadelphia's low-income women found themselves appealing to the House of Industry for assistance, particularly during the depression years. The House staff attempted to integrate these women, who relied heavily on non-wage income within the industrial wave of the future. Relief recipients were encouraged to evaluate their own concepts of household economics and to redefine more household activities within the context of the labor force and consumerism. Before relief applicants could obtain low-paid wage work in the sewing room, these women's homes were inspected in order for the House staff to assess both economic need and the strength of industrious attitudes. Women were given work if they demonstrated that they were just as disciplined as were factory workers in industrial plants. Before the turn of the century, female sewers began receiving wages on a weekly rather than a daily basis. This form of payment helped workers save wage income in order to consume more expensive market goods (House of Industry Annual Reports, 1891: 10; 1874: 10; 1880: 8-10; 1897: 10; 1896: 12). It promoted the view that income should be saved for future consumption.

The sewing room women often worked on garments that they eventually purchased. Supervisors stressed the importance of making installment payments on the garments sewers bought. They often said, "By paying a little each week while a garment is being made, it is fully paid for before it leaves the room" (House of Industry, Annual Reports, 1904: 13; 1874: 10). The House staff promoted acceptance of increasing levels of consumption, which was associated with earning higher wages on a more regular basis.

The House of Industry helped to promote a new definition of "womanhood" by advocating that women assume primary responsibility for reproductive activities at home, which—particularly during the hours of the increasingly more masculine wage-working day—were performing domestic work and certain other kinds of subsistence activities. This new focus on what female work should be differed from the long-established view of low-income households that all household members—regardless of gender or age—should be responsible for subsistence work, including domestic work. In order to demonstrate that female parents should be primarily responsibile for their children's welfare, mothers' meetings were organized by social workers. As a reward for attending mothers' meetings, women had access to dry goods and coal at one-half the market price. As they sat together, supposedly discussing the educational futures of their children, these mothers—who were expected to be dutiful and domestically inclined—were to volunteer to sew garments for the House of Industry. If there was not enough income to purchase adequate clothing so that the children could attend public school, social workers chastised the mothers and called them neglectful. In order for these parents to develop their "saving skills", the House sold saving stamps for food and collected installment payments on coal purchases (Annual Reports, 1875: 8; 1877: 8; 1901: 3; 1899: 11).

Within the confines of this workhouse, polarization between gender groups became spatially established when males and females began being assigned to different floors for lodging. The increased regulation of lodgers partly meant that household members became physically separated according to gender and age categories. Reinforcing the division of male and female work roles, the new policy divided men and women and assigned children to the female quarters. New regulations limited and controlled social contact between males and females and reduced fraternization between all relief recipients. House practices ensured that "men and women were locked securely apart" and that "no communication was allowed". In fact, records of the agency indicate that "departments were practically distinct for each sex" (Annual Reports, 1901: 9-10; 1889: 8; 1895: 7). Dividing the relief population in this way both encouraged new conceptions of household relations to emerge and reduced the potential for any kind of a rebellion. Separating household members served as a means both to maintain social control and to reduce the control that laboring people had over their "free" (or non-working) hours. During the politically turbulent depression years, social agencies played a central role in ushering in the new industrial order by restructuring relations between gender groups.

Low-income households that depended heavily on non-wage income sometimes resisted parastatal intervention into reproduction relations. Some households opposed increased intervention by agencies into household activities by refusing to accept any relief income. For example, many neighborhood people opposed the House of Industry's 1902 regulation stating that non-vaccinated applicants could not work. Records indicate that, for over two years, some women were denied employment because they refused to be vaccinated (Annual Reports, 1904: 13; 1910: 10). Social agencies often worked to undermine the self-help networks organized by working-class households, but these attempts frequently were described by reformers as unsuccessful ones.

The Recomposition of Household Income and the Gender Polarization Process

The specific forms that processes of capitalist development assumed in different areas affected the rate at which the social polarization of gender groups proceeded. The development of different production processes and the formation of different patterns of household reproduction served to retard and/or accelerate the work role specialization of gender groups. Most of the time, these pressures were multiple, contradictory ones. Household members, particularly for low-income groups that were forced to reorganize their work routines on a continuous basis, generally felt themselves being simultaneously pushed together and pulled apart. By 1920 the pulling-apart processes became the dominant ones.

The archival records of the House of Industry provide data on the differentiation of work roles between male and female children from the same household. By the last third of the century, the ethnic composition of the neighborhood surrounding the workhouse changed. This change reflected the relocation of ethnic groups within the global and regional labor forces, the growth of industrial production, and redefinition of urban and rural spaces. Ethnic groups from western Europe, and later Afro-Americans, moved to other areas in Philadelphia, and Italian-Americans (one of the newly-arrived ethnic groups from southern Europe) settled in the neighborhood. The data on the gender differentiation of child labor refers to working people from this group of materially deprived Italian-Americans.

Records from the Industrial School, which was managed by the House of Industry, can be used to study the social gender gap. Although the gap between males and females widened for this group of low-income immigrants, certain processes of capitalist production simultaneously retarded the polarization process between 1870 and 1930. Both capitalist structures and household structures, which were partly organized by working people, continued to define many Italian-Americans as a group that relied heavily on non-wage income. Within the organization of capitalist production and within the area of non-wage work, the types of work performed by household members sometimes retarded the polarization process. An examination of the different linkages between household activities and capitalist production contributes to an understanding of how household members were pulled apart.

As households became more dependent on wage labor and market consumption, the work of male and female children tended to be unequally divided into opposing spheres. Between 1871 and 1895, letters written by the teacher of the Industrial School show the types of economic contributions made by male and female children became divided along gender lines. When children left school to go to work, or when new positions opened up in the labor force, females tended to work in the home and males tended to work in the streets. By the turn of the century, domestic work became primarily a female occupation. Girls often left school to become full-time domestic workers in the homes of higher-paid wage workers or farmers. Sometimes girls remained in school and worked on a part-time basis as domestic workers. Boys, in contrast, often left school to become errand boys or messengers, hired hands on farms, or street vendors selling fruits and vegetables from carts. Male children worked as boot blackeners on an unsteady basis and sometimes found work in small shops. At times boys went to school on a part-time basis and earned an income during the rest of the day by stripping and selling willows for basket-making. While the work of girls often took place in their own home or in the well-supervised house of a higher-income household, the work of boys usually took place outside of the home and often in the street (House of Industry, 1871-1895). As capitalist enterprises expanded the scope of their operations and began taking over these operations, which once directly provided income for working-class households, new consumer-goods industries divided the labor force into male and female groups. The gender gap in work relations became even further institutionalized as the largely cultural base for gender divisions became replaced by an economic base, which was rooted in the logic of capital accumulation.

The linkages of male and female labor within different capitalist production processes affected how extensively gender groups became polarized. Data from the Industrial School's records suggest that capitalist production that depended on the labor of all household members, and that organized the whole household as a unit within the production process, tended to minimize the extent of gender polarization within households. For younger workers, however, the demands of live-in work separated children from their households of origin. This physical and occupational separation probably tended to polarize household members along ever-more-dominant gender lines. On the one hand, the organization of units of household labor within capitalist enterprises may have served to create household cohesion and to reduce gender differentiation. This probably occurred more frequently in rural, agricultural areas or in low-income, immigrant neighborhoods that had one main industry. On the other hand, the geographical and occupational dispersion of children, which took place as part of capitalist expansion, accelerated the division of members along gender lines and institutionalized sexism within the labor market.

Letters of the Industrial School suggest that geographical and occupational mobility was experienced differently and unequally by males and females. Siblings from the same household often were pulled apart in divergent directions, with boys and girls finding different kinds of work and moving to different places. Both the larger boys, who found work as live-in hired hands on farms, and the larger girls, who found work as live-in domestics, were forced to loosen ties with the household of origin (House of Industry, 1871-1895). The maintenance of the household of origin as a fairly flexible, cooperative working unit and/or the household's relative independence from the capitalist market, and not ruralness itself, permitted the formation of household members as "socially-like" beings. As the movement of urban boys to rural areas indicates, certain rural conditions did polarize household members. Although capitalist relations that established "urbanness" generally tended to institutionalize sexism more rapidly than capitalist relations in rural areas did, a complex of social processes in urban and rural areas created contradictory tensions for household members. Certain work and social relations pulled household members apart along gender lines, and other relations made household members rely directly on each other for their similar economic contributions. Even though both cohesive and divisive processes developed, overall people became more divided as sexism became institutionalized through the capitalist division of labor.

Social and Economic Alternatives Within and Outside of the Capitalist System

Inequalities within the labor force and throughout work relations in general created some ethnic groups as low-income groups. Households making up these ethnic groups received low, unsteady wages and depended heavily on non-wage sources of income. In order for these households to maintain themselves, cooperative working traditions emerged, which made household members recognize the contribution of all household members. Resources for this group were shared reciprocally within and between households. Networks of households within low-income groups were linked together through self-defined relations of sharing income, goods, and work. As one settlement worker in Philadelphia noted, "There is a great deal of true charity among this class of people" (Starr Centre Reports, 1913: 6).

Settlement records provide many examples of Afro-American households sharing income and organizing work collectively during the first decades of the twentieth century. In one case, a paralyzed mother and her daughter received economic support from friends in the neighborhood who also faced extreme poverty. When the daughter became almost exclusively involved in taking care of her mother and could not earn enough income from iron-ing, friends provided economic assistance (Starr Centre Reports, 1913: 6).

As well as distributing income between households and organizing work cooperatively in order to supplement low wage incomes, Afro-Americans often shared their homes with each other. The Works Progress Administra-tion (W.P.A.) Survey of 1939 shows that low-income households often had to share their homes with each other during the depression in order to sus-tain themselves. Within low-income Black neighborhoods, the poor shared with the poor. Twice as many Black households doubled up as compared to White households, according to the W.P.A. survey. Both as a means of increasing or stretching income and as a way of sharing housing with people facing similar conditions, Afro-Americans often brought in unknown lodgers (Philadelphia Housing Authority, 1939: 52-56).

A study by Sadie Tanner Mossell of the ways that Black households sus-tained themselves in Philadelphia during the First World War shows that household members shared work roles and material goods. Within this group of recently relocated people, households shared income and housing with members of other households. In response to the economic and social hard-ship brought on partly by racism, relatively flexible, unspecialized work roles emerged. Two-thirds of these households in Philadelphia relied on income from the father, the mother, the children, and/or lodgers. While mothers worked, children often did domestic work, which included taking care of younger children, buying food, and preparing meals. Household members shared clothing and did not conceive of belongings as one indi-vidual's private property. The girls shared the clothes that had been pur-chased, as did the boys. Non-working children got cast-off clothes, and mothers remade some clothes to fit younger children. Other clothes were simply handed down and worn without being remade. Minimal consump-tion through the market sometimes served to create conditions under which

household members considered material goods as collective belongings and
not as the property of one person (Mossell 1921: 6-35).

Working together minimized the extent to which members of gender
groups perceived members of socially opposing groups as "others". In
Philadelphia, during the opening decades of the twentieth century, Italian-
Americans often found themselves in similar work situations. Members of
the same household sometimes worked together at the same shop and even
at the same bench. Sharing work experiences, even if they occurred within
the context of capitalist production, did encourage household members to
organize alternative work relations. One alternative was to recognize the
common humanity of all household members. Before relations became extensively commodified, when cultural traditions of ethnic groups were just as
strong as the economic imperatives of the capitalist division of labor,
household members had a better chance of seeing each other as similar
beings.

Within the context of capitalist production processes, working people
organized alternative reproduction relations. Italian-American, male,
migrant laborers resisted the pressures linked to the commodification of
personal life by organizing alternative reproduction relations. Male, migrant
construction workers formed part of both long-term households (or their
households of origin) and short-term households (or domestic networks made
up of a group of co-workers). These migrant workers transferred income
to their households of origin and also collectively organized their domestic
work at the camps. These workers shared income formed outside of the
market with each other; their domestic work yielded income and allowed
them to remain more independent from the market. Their work and their
sharing enabled them to avoid individually consuming services and goods
sold at the camp. Purchasing services and goods from the camp owners
reduced the workers' savings. These male construction workers bought only
necessary goods; for example, they collectively purchased food for cooking. Wages generally were not spent in the dining room and were spent
only in the company store when essential provisions were purchased. Italian-
American men pooled their resources and bought all their staple items in
large quantities from the company store. In order to avoid paying for food
in the dining hall, all cooking was done by the migrant laborers (Works
Progress Administration, 1940-41). This collective way of organizing
domestic work was one way of sharing work and income within a low-
income ethnic group. However, this phenomenon occurred because the social
division of labor had already selected males as the wage workers for these
camps. These men became effective, cooperative domestic workers because
they had become spatially separated from their households of origin and,
more specifically, from women. They rejected commodities and lower incomes and accepted the collective responsibility of "housework".

Conclusion

As the United States became a part of the core of the capitalist world-economy by 1900, the global reorganization of industrial production and the expansion of the world market changed the ways that the U.S. working class was reproduced. Working-class households depended on higher wage incomes (with adult males increasingly tending to earn the highest, steadiest wages). Certain kinds of non-wage work and non-wage income declined. Domestic work, which was increasingly the primary responsibility of adult females, reflected the growing integration of households within capitalist relations. The commodification of household activities and the institutionalization of sexism within capitalist production and by the state (a non-conscious process that was integral to the capitalist division of labor) served to create a widening economic and social gap between males and females.

The development of the capitalist world-economy necessarily both polarizes household members and, because of inequality resulting from the commodification of labor and work relations, creates conditions that may encourage people to work together. By thinking about how this contradictory process takes place, working-class people may be able to construct social alternatives within and outside of the capitalist system.

Although it is not analyzed here, after 1930 growing state intervention in the reproduction of labor made households more dependent on the state in ways that probably reinforced gender divisions. It was not until the democratic protest movements of the 1960's and 1970's, which began posing social alternatives—alternatives partially reflected in subsequent state policies—that people began thinking seriously about restructuring social relations. A re-examination of working-class history can and should contribute to the discovery and establishment of a new system of social relations that creates social equality instead of social injustice.

REFERENCES

Barrett, Michèle & McIntosh, Mary (1980). "The 'Family Wage': Some Problems for Socialists and Feminists," *Capital and Class*, No. 11, Sum. 56-72.

Davidoff, Leonore (1979). "The Separation of Home and Work? Landladies and Lodgers in Nineteenth and Twentieth Century England," in S. Burman, ed., *Fit Work for Women*. Canberra: Australian National Univ. Press, 64-97.

de Brunhoff, Suzanne (1978). *The State, Capital and Economic Policy*. London: Pluto.

Dickinson, Torry (1983). "Redivided Lives: The Formation of the Working Class in Philadelphia, 1870-1945," unpubl. Ph.D. diss, SUNY-Binghamton.

Dowd, Doug F. *The Twisted Dream: Capitalist Development in the U.S. since 1776.* Cambridge, MA: Winthrop.

DuBois, W. E. B. (1972). *Black Reconstruction in America, 1860-1880*. New York: Atheneum.

Glassberg, Eunice (1979). "Work, Wages, and the Cost of Living: Ethnic Differences and the Poverty Line, Philadelphia, 1880," *Pennsylvania History*, XLVI, 1, Jan., 17-58.

House of Industry (1840-1930). *Annual Reports*. Philadelphia: Temple Univ., Urban Archives.

House of Industry (1871-1895). *Letters of the Industrial School*. Philadelphia: Temple Univ., Urban Archives.

Lefebvre, Henri (1971). *Everyday Life in the Modern World*. New York: Harper & Row.

Mossell, Sadie Tanner (1921). "The Standard of Living Among One Hundred Negro Migrant Families in Philadelphia," *Annals of the American Academy of Social and Political Science*, Vol. XCVII, Nov., 3-50.

Philadelphia Housing Authority and the Works Progress Administration (1939). *Real Property Survey and Low Income Housing Survey*. Philadelphia: City Archives.

Robinson, Elizabeth (1870-1895). "Monthly Letters to the Supervisor," Philadelphia: Temple Univ., Urban Archives.

Scott, Joan & Tilly, Louise A. (1975). "Women's Work and the Family in Nineteenth-Century Europe," *Comparative Studies in Society and History*, Vol. XVII, 36-64.

Starr Centre Reports (1913). "Some of the Individual Cases Helped," *Pennsylvania Historical Society, Philadelphia Annual Reports*, Occasional Paper No. 4, May 23.

Wallerstein, Immanuel (1980). "The State in the Institutional Vortex of the Capitalist World-Economy." *International Social Science Journal*, XXXII, 4, 743-51.

Works Progress Administration (1939-41). *Ethnic Survey: Italians and Blacks in Philadelphia, 1939-41*. Philadelphia: Balch Institute for Ethnic Studies.

Zaretsky, Eli (1976). *Capitalism, the Family, and Personal Life*. New York: Harper Colophon.

III

Internal Structure
of Households

14

WORKING OR HELPING?
London Working-Class Children in the Domestic Economy

Anna Davin

Fernand Braudel Center
State University of New York—Binghamton

The Domestic Economy and the Neighborhood

Much employment in late nineteenth-century London was seasonal or irregular. The "season" of fashionable residence in London was one cause of irregular demand, in the important luxury trades especially. In other cases either the raw material or the market was seasonally limited, as with various forms of food processing or matches, soft drinks, or umbrellas. Weather was crucial in some cases: Building, for instance, stopped during much of the winter, and dock work too was slack then—though that was always fairly unpredictable, depending on the arrival of ships and the nature of their cargoes. Gareth Stedman Jones, in *Outcast London* (1971), shows how within this overall pattern of irregular or seasonal unskilled work, men's and women's employment had patterns that were partly complementary.[1]

In other cases work might be regular but poorly paid, requiring supplement if more than one or two people were to be supported by it. Charles Booth, in his classification of the London population towards the end of the nineteenth century, estimated that 41% of the working class were "in poverty", that is, had at best "means ... sufficient, but ... barely sufficient, for decent independent life," and not always that. The 41% broke down thus: 1%, "the lowest class—occasional laborers, loafers and semi-criminals"; 10%, "the very poor—casual labor, hand to mouth existence, chronic want"; and 30%, "the poor—including alike those whose earnings are small because of irregularity of employment, and those whose work, though regular, is ill-paid".[2]

The rest of the working class were in categories Booth called "comfortable" (artisans, shopkeepers, the "best class" of street traders, foremen and highly skilled workers, some small employers), and as "regularly employed and fairly paid" might seem to have enjoyed relative security and comfort. But the tidy categories and proportions leave out of account the ups and downs that families would go through over time. There was not much margin at the best of times, especially with more than one or two small children, and usually little chance of cushioning major blows like the death or injury of a parent or other wage earner, or even the briefer difficulties occasioned by temporary unemployment or illness. Long-term illness was another danger: tuberculosis, heart disease (often following on rheumatic fever, a common childhood illness), and work injuries were all frequent causes of prolonged dependence, medical bills, and economic difficulty. The fluctuations of the trade cycle (even though within an overall context of rising prosperity), the particularly precarious and seasonal character of much London employment, work hazards, and poor health provision all threatened security. "Disaster was always a real possibility for even the most secure of artisans" (Crossick, 1978: 174).

Whatever a man could earn, it was rarely enough for the regular and long-term maintenance (rent, heat, food, clothes, and shoes) of more than one adult and several children. For women breadwinners the problem was still more acute, since their wages were even lower. (The Poor Law authorities expected a widow to be able to support herself and one child, but not more; and a widow with several children would be expected to hand most of them over into institutional care if she was to get any help from the parish.) As the number of surviving children in a working-class family in this period averaged five, and many had rather more, it is easily seen that most families would experience difficulty as long as their children, or most of their children, were too small to earn or make other economic contribution. This "poverty cycle" in working-class life was observed and analyzed by B. S. Rowntree (1901) in his study of poverty in York at the turn of the century.

The ideal that the basic social unit should be a family-based household, headed and maintained by a male breadwinner, cared for by a dependent housewife, and rearing dependent children, was at this time almost unchallenged in the middle class. It was also accepted in the upper sections of the working class, if for different reasons and with some modification: Work would be expected from the children, for instance, and indirect earnings by the mother through letting lodgings or running a small shop were permissible.

But for most working-class households this idea—whether or not they subscribed to it—would be out of reach. Reality was quite different. First, as we have seen, men's wages were often inadequate or irregular; they could not necessarily support a family. Secondly, households did not always conform to the ideal either in composition or in economic structure. Illness, injury, or alcoholism might make the man dependent on others' earnings; or death or desertion might break the nuclear core. Women who lost their husbands sometimes set up with one or both parents, perhaps combining their limited earning power as washerwomen, or keeping house for a father and sharing or perhaps complementing his earnings. Sometimes eldest siblings maintained younger ones when one parent or both died, "broken" families would be joined through second marriages, or sisters and brothers might have joint households, with a variety of arrangements as to finances. In many cases a nuclear family would be joined by some extra member—grandparent, aunt, or uncle, more distant relative, even someone without blood ties—for longer or shorter periods. They would contribute to rent or food; they might technically count as servants or lodgers, but often they wre still part of the "family".[3] Sometimes, too, an elderly person living alone nearby would regularly eat with neighbors (or have food brought round by them), especially if they were kin.

The most common addition to a household would be a child. This could be a temporary arrangement during some crisis; it could be just a question of bed space, with the child eating at home but sleeping with neighbor or relative; or it could be intended as a long-term adoption, especially in cases of bereavement. In most households an extra child could be fitted in without much trouble because of the general flexibility of living arrangements. Beds were normally shared and expectations of privacy were low. Extreme crowding (or tension such as bad feeling between a child and step-parent) might make it desirable to farm out a child as company and as one who could perform chores and errands; or a harassed mother of small children might want a little nurse to take them from under her feet. Children's usefulness, actual or imminent, was undoubtedly an important consideration in the informal adoptions that took place, along with other factors such as pity and maybe affection for the children, or friendship for the mother, or hostility to the workhouse. A settlement worker in the 1890's commented that "if a woman dies it is seldom . . . that the children are allowed to go to 'the house with the big gates' " (Kimmins, 1899: 4); in a close-knit neighborhood it would probably be shameful for no alternative to be found to institutional care.

There was a general sense that responsibility for children extended beyond their immediate family. Adult supervision of children in the street tended to have a collective quality: Whoever was at hand—passing by, looking out the window, talking at the door, sitting out with their knitting or preparing vegetables on doorstep or pavement chair—would administer comfort or scolding or threats as required, no matter whose the children. In the neighborhood, and to some extent beyond, adults had a general right to exercise authority over children who were not theirs, or to ask them for services like running an errand. It was vested in them by virtue of age, and might be reinforced by ties of friendship and obligation with the child's parent. Occasionally, though, such exercise of authority might lead to rows between adults; while the extent to which asking a child to run an errand involved requesting a favor as well as, or rather than, demanding a right, it could be acknowledged by some reward, like a sweet or a coin or a slice of bread.

How far such authority and responsibility were thus generalized to adults outside the family-based household would vary considerably. Some neighborhoods would be too fluid and unsettled to allow the development of the networks of mutual help and obligation within which such conventions must be understood. Some communities had clearer rules than others and laid more stress on how children should or should not behave. Some families did not identify with local custom and, as newcomers, or because of different ethnic or religious background, or for reasons of family pride or aspiration, would hold themselves—or be held—apart. Nevertheless, it is safe to say that most children of the London working class in the second half of the nineteenth century would not have experienced supervision and discipline only from their parents (or other related elders) and teachers. Their range of acquaintance—people they knew by sight and by name (at least nickname), and who knew them—would include those in the same house certainly, but also most individuals and families in the same street, or even block, and some further afield again. Any of these might sometimes call on their services, or equally might offer support or reprimand. Those with whom such contact would be most frequent would probably be their parents' friends and workmates: participants in ramifying networks of neighbors and friends who gave each other reciprocal help, exchanging or lending skills, space, food, time, property, and children. These networks were to some extent separately male and female, and where child care was involved or loans of child labor, or temporary or permanent housing or feeding of children, it was most likely to be the female network that was brought into play.[4]

The neighborhood was an important context for the children, their relation to the living place being sometimes—especially as they grew older—quite centrifugal. There wasn't always room for much more than sleeping at home, which in poor families might well consist of only one room. (A school inspector in 1884 calculated that in inner-London poor districts, 30% to 58% of school children were in one-room tenements, and where there were more rooms it was often because the household was more numerous, and did not mean more living space.)

When the home was also used for some form of outwork, pressure would be still more acute. Material had to be stacked up somewhere, as did the finished work; the process would require at least a table and often other space if the pasted paper bags or boxes or the newly glued and painted toys and artificial flowers needed time to dry. Small children had to be removed. Arthur Harding's mother, in the years following his birth in 1886, was making matchboxes for their living, in their single room in Shoreditch. As a small child he would "be put in a box outside the door, or sent into the street with my sister," because "there was no room to move about. The matchboxes had to be spread out to dry and you couldn't afford to tread on them." A little older, he would come home hungry from school and "she would give me perhaps a couple slices of bread, put it on a saucer, and say 'Go on outside,' and I'd eat it on the street." Even for children less poor than Harding, food was not necessarily eaten at home. Sometimes mother and children would eat something together, but full family meals, unless perhaps Sunday dinner, were not usual except among the more prosperous and respectable. Children could fend for themselves if they had a penny or two, buying from the wide range of stalls and shops that sold cooked food. If they had no money and could find no one to provide any (as alms, or a gift, or a loan, or repayment of a debt, or in return for some service), they would go home for something like bread with dripping or jam, to be eaten in the street as like as not. Or often for the work they did they would be paid in kind with a cup of tea and bread, or even something more substantial.

The street was full of attractions for the young. Pavement and gutter offered many advantages—the company of other children, the chance of earning the odd copper or seizing some other advantage (such as coal "fallen" from a delivery cart, or a passing stranger from whom money might be extracted), access to important information through the child networks (concerning possible work or foraging opportunities for instance), and the continual interest and spectacle of street life. Most of all, child care—overwhelmingly the responsibility of the children—was much easier out of the cramped homes and in the company of others, and it was compatible with many of children's street activities.

Children and Work

Throughout the working class, children at almost any age—certainly from four or so—would be expected to do daily shopping, to look after any smaller children at least part of the time and sometimes almost entirely, to go on special expeditions (before breakfast on washing day to get scrap wood from workshops for fuel, or to a baker who sold yesterday's bread cheap, or to the gasworks for spilt coke) for any bargain or handout or leavings that could supply a household need, to help with housework on a daily basis, to run messages, and to help in the weekly turn-out in households where that occurred. Their time was at the disposal of their elders, especially their mother, and was used to save adult time and effort on every possible occasion. It also provided currency in the informal system of reciprocal favors already referred to, in which a kindness of one sort would sooner or later be repaid with some other help—child-minding for instance, or a loan, or a turn at nursing an invalid. Mrs. Walton, as a child in Mile End in the 1900's, used to go up most evenings to help "the lady upstairs," who made matchboxes: "[She] never used to give me anything but—I used to keep her company . . . she were on her own" (1902). Something might have been given to the mother, but more likely some other return was made. In the same way children would run errands for neighbors, being rewarded with a slice of bread or a sweet, or a coin they would hand over to their mother, or with no immediate recompense.

In some cases the family was jointly engaged in some enterprise in which children could be useful. This might range from the small corner shop in which they would help with weighing out and packing, renewing supplies, watching against thieves, cleaning up, and serving (or the market stall where their help would be similar), to woodchopping, where children helped to bundle the split logs and sell them round the streets, to laundry work, where they fetched and delivered the clothes and turned the mangle (used to extract water), or fetched clean and emptied dirty water, or helped hand out the clothes, to home work, where they would help directly in the work— always paid by the piece so the more hands the better—or go to get the materials or return the finished work. In these joint enterprises the working group was often composed only of women and children.

· In poorer families it would also be taken for granted that children would at all times be alert for anything that might be useful at home. This might be a question of lining up outside a hospital or restaurant that gave away surplus soup or dripping or broken meats. In markets and at shops they could ask for specked fruit, or collect aging vegetables and fruit discarded by stallholders, or grab anything dropped in unloading. Their eye for anything useful might occasionally be caught by items which, though accessible, had not yet been thrown out; that was fair game. The boundary here between foraging and theft becomes indistinct, and children did sometimes use their advantages of speed and size to abstract purses or steal displayed goods. Children's foraging also extended to fuel, and as with food, there was a spectrum between being sent out an errand, and simply keeping a weather eye open for whatever could be scavenged.

Child care was one of their most important responsibilities. Many children were, like Arthur Harding, brought up more by an elder sister or brother than by their mother. Even a four-year-old could help keep smaller children entertained and guarded, on the doorstep outside the house. The five- or six-year-old would be the recognized caretaker of younger siblings for more and more hours of the day, and with increasing license to roam. Almost every discription of life in London's poorer quarters in this period includes some mention of "little mothers" or "little nurses" cradling, watching, or playing with their little charges. Toddlers could be sat on step or curb, or pulled into a ring-dancing game; babies were carried everywhere, their weight only partly taken by the shawl which would be wrapped round nurse and charge and then pinned in place; or perhaps a home-made pram (usually a soap-box on wheels) would hold one or more babies while their young elders were busy.

In all of these kinds of work—errands, foraging, contributing to joint enterprises, domestic chores, child care—little account was made of children's work. It was help taken for granted, its value invisible—especially, perhaps, to the child. A clear example of this occurs in the autobiography of Grace Foakes, recalling her childhood in Wapping, where her father was a dock laborer, in the 1900's. He knew the cooks on two ships that regularly came down from Scotland, and when they docked he would buy from them a big bowl of dripping left over from roast meat. Grace would be sent "all round the tenements and surrounding streets" taking orders and collecting basins from those who wanted a share.

> Father first weighed the basin then put into it a half-pound of dripping. I had to return these basins one at a time so that I did not get them muddled up. . . . This took me a long time and meant a lot of running up and down tenement stairs. The profit he made paid for our dripping. We had the best of it, for there was always lovely dripping at the bottom of the bowl. I thought it well worth the trouble of coming and going, for nothing tasted as good as that gravy spread on our morning toast. Besides, it was free—and that make it all the nicer! (Foakes, 1972: 9).

In accounting for their share of the dripping "free", she of course discounts the value of her own time and labor, which in fact made the difference between the price her father paid for the big bowl of dripping, and the sum of all the neighbor's twopences for the little bowls she delivered.

Children also did work whose value was acknowledged by payment, however inadequately. Before the education laws of 1870 and after, which made school attendance (morning and afternoon five days a week) compulsory for children between the ages of five and at least ten (in London by the end of the century this had been pushed up to 13), there were full-time child workers in a variety of trades. Eight- or nine-year-olds were employed in workshops in the many branches of the clothing trade, in

Spitalfields by the silk weavers, in small factories as in the match industry, or in domestic service, as skivvies or child-minders.[5] After 1870 employers could not risk daytime employment of school age children during the week, at least on premises subject to inspection, as were factories and non-family workshops. So children's work was displaced into Saturday jobs and the hours after school, and tended more and more to be concentrated in service and trading. (This tendency was reinforced by subsequent legislation, which also attempted to control the number of hours worked and to ban or reduce street employments, especially for girls.) Indeed, their paid activities were by the end of the century much the same as the work they did within the framework of kin or neighborly obligation: helping on stalls and in shops or workshops, running errands, taking care of children, and doing domestic work.

The informal character of children's work by the end of the century, and the overlap between paid and unpaid work, make it difficult to analyze. Contemporary investigations tended to focus on paid and regular work, and on long hours. For example, an inquiry conducted by the London School Board in 1899 asked teachers how many of their pupils worked more than 19 hours a week outside school hours; their concern was with excessive work, but they did not try to gauge what was the norm, or how norm and excess were related. Again, witnesses to a major parliamentary inquiry in 1902 were asked about overwork and ill health, and it did not attempt to assess what was ordinary rather than pathological in children's work. Miss Holme, a manager of two South London schools who collected evidence for this enquiry, had asked teachers to obtain from children information on how many were earning, then verified their figures by interviewing some of the children. Out of 35 girls she checked, she dismissed 20 as not proper wage earners: They were just "running errands for neighbours at odd times." In such cases, she felt, "it was not work at all: The children like to make themselves out rather important" (Holme, 1902). She was of course in a position to impose her definition of work and to exclude theirs. It was, however, more likely that even children and certainly parents would understate the number of hours worked, being wary about all inquiries from authority, so we have here two indications of probable under-reporting, arising both from the investigators and from those under investigation.

The standpoint of the investigators deserves further discussion, though here it must be brief. This was a time when England's economic and military supremacy was being challenged, in trade by Germany and the United States, in empire by the Boers. A new sense of insecurity was provoking examination of the national assets, with a wider definition and a longer perspective than had been usual before. Children were clearly of key importance, as future labor force and army, and as parents of the succeeding generation.

Their health and training acquired a new significance in the 1900's, which dwarfed (though often if accompanied) humanitarian concern. Earlier generations of reformers had focused on education, but once the children were in the classroom other problems were perceived, and education was seen to be about more than lessons. The investigation and discussion of working-class childhood was carried out in this context by people whose experience and definition of childhood were middle-class. For them, as for European or North American historians today, children were dependents to be protected; children's waged work was exploitation of the helpless; and adults (whether parents or employers) who profited by their work had to be prevented and denounced. By the 1900's this is the generally expressed position whenever children's paid employment is discussed. Its implications for present purposes are twofold, alerting us first to the consequent distortions of their findings, and second to the gulf between such middle-class views of childhood on the one hand, and working-class views and practice on the other.

The middle-class assumption that work and childhood were incompatible was not a straightforward one about overtaxing the strength of growing children. This is shown by the investigator's concentration on paid work; physical strain could result as easily or more so from long hours of unpaid drudgery. Domestic work, even when paid, was also not taken very seriously. For at least some of the middle-class men who framed and conducted most of the inquiries, neither unpaid work nor domestic work really counted. Sir Charles Elliott, for instance, who had chaired the London School Board's 1899 enquiry, told the 1902 committee (which called him as first witness) that in his view, "Domestic service is of so intermittent a character that it is not usually severe, and to enquire into the hours when it begins would require such inquisition" (Elliot, 1902).

We have already seen how one investigator discounted errands as not actual work. Others went so far as to gather no information about girls, on the assumption that their work would be in the home; or acknowledged that an enormous amount of domestic work was done and many girls were drudges, but did not see how it could be "scheduled", let alone controlled (Chandler, 1902; Thompson, 1902; Holme, 1902; Neville, 1902; Desprelles, 1902). One influence here was probably the assumption that domestic work was "natural" for girls, part of their training for adult life, whereas waged work could never be natural for children; the labor market belonged to the adult world, and primarily indeed to men. Another concerned the sanctity of the home: There was a realistic reluctance to pursue intrusive investigations too far. (This should not be given to much weight however, as the working-class family was already subject to various forms of intervention, most notably through the operation of compulsory schooling.) In any case, it is clear that the ideological basis of the campaign in this period for the "protection" of childen meant that they were to be protected out of the labor market, not from low wages, long hours, or even from heavy work, if the work was done in the home.

Such attitudes were not dominant in the working class, where children's usefulness was taken for granted, along with their fairly rapid transition from dependence to responsibility and even wage earning. Survival was always at least potentially a collective enterprise, and one in which individuals became active from an early age. In the poorest families children's time and labor might play an essential part. But in others, too, their contribution would be valued and encouraged. Work, especially alongside an adult, or under adult supervision, was regarded as training, either in skills or in proper habits, or both. It was fostered well before the child's efforts could be of any real use. Even where the father was able to ensure the entire subsistence of the family unaided, girls and probably boys would be involved in child care and domestic labor from early on (four or five), while if the parents worked at home, in a domestic workshop or as outworkers, the children would also learn to help at that work and to do odd jobs and errands connected with it. As the youngsters grew older (say eight or ten) it was taken for granted that they would try to find Saturday jobs and other work, paying what they earned into the family exchequer. At the same time, they would continue contributing informally through housework, child care and errands, and by bringing back anything useful that they could forage. Once they left school they would most likely find work and continue handing over their earnings; though in some cases family need might instead require a girl (or even occasionally a boy) to stay at home as mother's auxilliary or replacement.

If the family could afford it, partial dependence might be prolonged as an investment while a school leaver trained as pupil teacher or apprentice (this was most likely to be possible if older siblings were already making substantial contributions to the domestic budget, and there were no younger ones to follow, or if the number of children was small anyway); but they would remain within the family economy during and perhaps after any training. In almost all cases, whatever the poverty level, they would stay at home once in regular work, and continue paying in much of their wage for ten years and more, until they married. This might mean even greater overcrowding of already cramped homes, but that was unimportant beside the increased security of having several wage earners. In much of the working class some cash contribution would be needed well before children left school, though when and how much would vary. For working-class children, generally childhood was not a sheltered time of make-believe; "real life" was the present as well as the future; work and responsibility were not the separate province of adults but co-existed with growth and play and school.

As the social worker Alexander Paterson put it, writing on South London in the 1900's, "The difference between a child and an adult is everywhere regarded as one of degree rather than of kind" (Paterson, 1911: 58). Material needs (actual or potential) and ideology are here closely intertwined, but the pattern is clear, as is the contrast it presents with middle-class norms and assumptions.

Working or Helping?

It will be clear that the family-based households I have been discussing depended on a range of input—in labor, cash, and kind—to which members contributed variously. Generalizations are difficult, given the diversity and fluidity of arrangements. But by and large, and especially by the end of the century, if there were two adults in such a household, male and female, neither of them in any way disabled from work, the largest cash contribution was likely to come from the man (though always with possible intermissions during weeks of unemployment); and the largest labor contribution from the woman. In households without a male head, there would not be such a clear division: Cash and labor would be provided according to ability, jointly by any members of the household able to contribute.

In all cases children would be deployed wherever they were most useful, which would depend on such factors as the size and composition of the household (most of all whether there were babies and toddlers), the health of the mother, the degree of shortfall between the regular cash income and the demands made on it, and local opportunities for children's earning and foraging. If the family was in relatively easy circumstances, adult gender divisions would apply more to children too; the boys would probably share less in domestic labor and have more chance of earning (and perhaps of holding on to a larger proportion of what they earned, as pocket money or because they did not feel compelled to disclose their gains), while the girls would be primarily the mother's auxiliaries, engaged in child care and other domestic work, and unlikely to be paid for anything they did, though perhaps given the occasional small coin as a reward. In poorer families these distinctions would scarcely operate: Help of every kind was needed, and whoever was old enough to provide it would do so, whatever their sex.

This probably meant that both girls and boys were able to develop a sense of their own worth, and a more independent outlook. Certainly such children as the watercress girl interviewed by the journalist Henry Mayhew in the middle of the century were pretty well supporting themselves, if within a family context: "It's like a child to care for sugar sticks, and not like one who's got a living and vittals to earn. I ain't a child, and I shan't be a woman till I'm twenty, but I'm past eight, I am" (Mayhew, 1851: 151-52).

By the end of the century children's potential for independence had lessened, though undoubtedly there were still some, like Arthur Harding's
sister "Mighty", whose contributions in time and cash must have covered
their own upkeep from as young as eight (Samuel, 1981: Chs. 1-6). But
in general, rising living standards (Hobsbawm calculates that real wages
were 84% higher in 1900 than in 1850 [1968: 163]), protective legislation
designed to reduce children's employment, changes in the organization of
production which anyway lessened the demand for children's labor (along
with the spread of the telephone, which cut down their use as messengers),
and most of all the introduction of compulsory schooling in the 1870's all
contributed to the marginalization of children's waged work. School also
shortened the time available for domestic work (unpaid or paid in kind)
and for foraging. So as the father's wage (with the usual proviso: if there
was one) became more substantial and could provide a higher proportion
of household needs, it also became more difficult for children to furnish
much in the way of cash.

The mother's role was also changing. The removal of older children into
school during the day made it harder (if there were small children) for her
to go out to work. There was little formal provision of child care, and what
there was involved payment (and in any case was often reserved for the
children of widows or other married women in special need). Although often
a neighbor or local girl just out of school could mind small children, they
had to be paid. Only family labor was free, so unless a grandparent was
available, or an eldest child already out of school, it usually made better
sense for the mother to stay at home. If earnings from her were indispensable
she would then take in washing or outwork of some kind; or she would
do casual cleaning work a day or two a week, and a child (a girl if there
was any choice, because their attendance at school was less strictly enforced)
would be kept at home to mind any little ones.

By the turn of the century the working-class mother was commonly
presented in middle-class descriptions of the poor as "chancellor of the
exchequer"; one could also see her as minister of labor (not to mention
health). By custom the use of resources was determined by the mother, or
by her substitute if there was no mother. The man of the house would hand
over most or even all of his earnings on being paid, retaining or receiving
back a share for pocket money.[6] Any other wage earners would do the same,
holding back (or more likely having returned to them) an allowance (probably a quarter to a third of the whole) for daily expenses such as fares and
lunches. Pocket money also had to cover union or Friendly Society dues
(as opposed to life insurance, which was the mother's responsibility), drink,
tobacco, newspapers, and any other leisure expenditures, boots and clothes
perhaps, and, in the case of young adults, costs of courtship and savings

for a projected marriage. Payments from the combined family purse were controlled by the mother, who had to see that everyone was fed and the children clothed, the rent paid and warmth and light provided, and all emergencies somehow met, from replacing boots to the cost of a funeral.

This role gave her much authority, but it was also a heavy burden. Wherever money ran short, it was the woman's labor and ingenuity that filled the gap, or with "maternal altruism" it was the mother who went without.[7] Everyone else's needs were always put first. Old people often recall how their mothers would stint themselves:

> Oh my mother went without for us, yes, yes ... I've known her to wipe the plate around—with a drop of gravy—and tell my father she's had her dinner ... I had mine and my sister had hers. She'd say "I've had my dinner"— She never! She said, "Don't tell your father" (Walton, 1902: 13).

They remember, too, how endlessly their mothers' worked, and how rarely they rested, or treated themselves to anything requiring money. The mother's continual labor and self-sacrifice often inspired fierce loyalty and protectiveness in the children, and great eagerness to do whatever they could to help, especially by earning. (In some cases such feelings would be reinforced by contrasting the father's apparently easier life, especially if he spent much on drink or was given to treating mother roughly.) The jobs children found were thought of as "for mother", and the words of approval with which contributions were received gave enormous satisfaction. If on the other hand the relationship with the mother was less close and her "maternal altruism" weaker or less perceived, her responsibility for extracting the children's labor in the family interest could mean that she was seen by them as harsh and perpetually demanding. When they left school and started full-time work she chose their employment, and if it was not their preference this again might be resented.

Individual interest and common interest within the family-based household did not always then coincide, and where conflict did arise over the disposition of pooled resources or the demands made on members' time, the mother's position of authority meant that she would bear the brunt. This is most obvious in the struggles between man and wife (Ross, 1982) (in which children would probably be ranged alongside their mother); but children too sometimes attempted to maintain some control of their time and their earnings. It was easiest to do where earnings were irregular and therefore unpredictable, so that something could be held back without being missed. Such work was more often done by boys. It was hardest where the child was engaged in unpaid domestic labor—housework, errands, childcare—within sight and earshot of her mother. Such work was most often done by girls. (Running errands did sometimes permit some stolen time: stopping to play with friends or to watch some street spectacle, for instance.)

Age very likely played a part in determining the child's attitude here, as one study of children's property sense made in 1902 suggests. Earl Barnes, an American psychologist, reported an experiment in which 350 girls in London Board Schools were asked to write down what they would do if when out with two friends they found a shilling. He analyzed the interests taken into account in their answers as follows: "68% of the children involved in our test consider themselves; 35% consider the other 'boys' [the story to which the children were asked to respond was told of boys, though the respondents were girls]; 37% consider their parents; and 36% consider the original owner." (The overlap is because some children envisaged several possibilities, for instance trying to find the owner and then taking it home.) Even among the 68% who intended to spend it on themselves, most apparently said they would spend it or share it with others, though sometimes perhaps the intention they expressed was as much lip-service (itself, however, significant) as real generosity:

> I should go home and ask my mother what to spend it on, and very likely she would choose something I would like for tea. Because it would be sharing it between all that was at tea.

Barnes identified an interesting relationship between the age of the child and the impulse to take home the found shilling: the younger the child, the stronger the sense of family need. Thirty-seven percent of the eight-year-olds said they would take the money home, but the proportion then declines (29% of nine-year-olds, 28% at ten, eleven, and twelve, 20% at thirteen) to zero at fourteen. No doubt, as Barnes suggests, the older child would be "more used to spending small sums independently of parental direction." But the significance of the complete drop at age 14 must lie in the imminence of the shift from school child to wage earner (probably already in part anticipated). The wage of school leaver would go to the family and would presumably be considered a sufficient contribution, so that no obligation would be felt to hand over an unexpected windfall (Barnes, 1902: 77-80). It is a pity that Barne's experiment was conducted with girls only, and therefore allows no comparison between girls' and boys' attitudes here.

Girls certainly had less chance of earning than boys, and less access to money of their own. They were increasingly identified with domestic work, and that was less often done for pay than were boys' usual jobs. If payment was made at all, it might go straight to the mother anyway. Any money they received, generally speaking, would (more than with boys) be pocket money, irregular and subject to conditions, rather than wage. Their labor contribution in housework and child care, heavier than what was expected of their brothers, would be taken for granted, the value of their work less perceived than where cash was handed over. This had implications both for their status within the family, and for how they spent their leisure. Less access to money restricted their choice of entertainment or treat. In any case, rules (likely to be more strictly enforced for them than for their brothers) would often limit how much time they could spend out, how far they could go, and what they were permitted to do. Moreover, a child whose hours of "leisure" were spent in charge of a baby and/or toddler, was most effectively limited in the range of her (or sometimes his) activities.

Conclusions

The family-based household economy in the late nineteenth-century London working class was based on a pooling of resources by all members. Most important were labor, cash, and kind. Children contributed in all these ways, though by the end of the century their cash contribution was increasingly marginalized, and in general they were seen as "helping" rather than working. This was still more true for girls than for boys.

Rising living standards and perhaps different aspirations were giving an increasingly domestic focus to many working-class families. This involved a sharpening of sexual divisions. Cash income was increasingly provided by the male head (where there was one), assisted by children once they left school, when they would take waged work and live at home until their own marriage. If the household needed domestic labor rather than larger income, then a daughter might be kept at home after leaving school, a son almost never. A new emphasis on the home and on the general appearance of the household and its members (reinforced by various outside pressures such as the school's demand for clean and tidy pupils), especially where greater prosperity meant more property and space, intensified the need for domestic labor. Growing concern about how children were reared had the same result. So in the households where father and children over 14 could earn enough for everybody—probably a third of working-class households in the early twentieth century—mother and younger children would no longer do paid work. Nor would children need to go out foraging, though boys especially might do so anyway, for fun and to augment either pocket money or the means of play. But the female members of the family would probably have a more substantial load of domestic labor, and the boys would be unlikely to have as much to do as the girls.

Where the general subsistence was more precarious the boys and, if necessary, the girls would look for Saturday jobs or more. As the socialist tailoress Frances Hicks commented in 1894: "From ten years of age they begin to be on the look-out—boys for places among the shopkeepers and girls to mind babies and do a little cleaning or sewing in the evenings and on Saturdays'' (Hicks, 1894). In more desperate cases still the mother would also be earning by any means she could contrive, and the children would augment her earning power by taking over ''her'' domestic work as far as possible—child care and shopping particularly, also cooking and cleaning, if necessary even washing. The over-riding expectation was that children would contribute to family subsistence in some way, in whatever degree was necessary, as long as they were part of the household. But the contribution in time and labor of the children still at school was likely to be less valued than that of the regular wage earner, able to put a weekly sum on the kitchen table and not tied to the relatively undervalued domestic chores and responsibilities.

The pooling of resources for the common good does not mean that all members of the group had equal benefit from them. Age, sex, and wage-earning capacity (closely bound up of course with age and sex) arranged adults, adolescents, and children in hierarchical order with the male wage earner at the top. This order is clearly seen in differential access to protein (meat, eggs, fish), where father, wage-earning sons, then younger sons and wage-earning daughters, took precedence in times of shortage over other children; the mother came last. Wage earners were more likely to be able to spend on themselves: Men's ''need'' for tobacco, drink, and papers was acknowledged, while no similar allowance was made for women, who could spend on themselves only by saving something out of the general budget. Males and wage earners had more control over their time than did females and schoolchildren, whose desire for time to themselves was always subordinate to household needs.

The coordination and allocation of resources according to hierarchy rested with the mother, and the authority thus afforded her by custom was often reinforced by the powerful emotional relationship between her children and her. The affective bond was strengthened by their appreciation of her incessant labor and frequent self-sacrifice. However, the power this authority gave her was rarely exercised in her own interest but, on the contrary, allowed her to dispossess herself through ''sharing and caring'' for the household.[8] She might attempt to protect her budget from excessive demands by her husband—even to have secret savings (Macdonald, 1904: 104)—but this was likely to be for the group's interest rather than her own.

Children, but especially boys, had more chance than their mothers of evading their subordination, because they could permit themselves more selfishness. By dodging the call to help or by hanging on to some of the coppers they earned, they would make time or opportunity for stolen treats. But whether in families where subsistence was assured but rules were strict, or in families with looser authority but greater needs, their time was not their own; yet the time and effort they contributed carried small reward in status or other recognition. Small wonder that they were impatient to finish with school and start earning a wage, or, as Frances Hicks put it, "It was their work and not their schooling which absorbed their interest and energy, the one being continuous, and the other being entirely dropped at the earliest possible age" (Hicks, 1894).

NOTES

1. This is the magisterial account of the London economy in the late nineteenth century.

2. The proportions have been recalculated from percentages of the whole population in Booth (1889: Vol. 1, Ch. 2).

3. See, for example, Wright (1867: 210-15), Willis (1948: 103), or from an earlier decade, David Copperfield's relationship with Mrs. Micawber (Dickens, 1981).

4. Most of the interesting work in this and related areas has been done by Ellen Ross (1981; 1982; 1983).

5. For extensive documentation of such work, see, for example, the Children's Employment Commission (1863).

6. For a sensitive discussion of the woman's domestic "wage", see Ross (1981).

7. The phrase is from Whitehead (1981: 107). See also the classic discussion of unequal distribution within the family in Oren (1974).

8. I owe this to Ann Whitehead, "I'm hungry, mum," (1981: 109).

REFERENCES

Barnes, Earl (1902). "A Study on Children's Property Sense," *Child Life*, Vol. IV, 77-80.
Booth, Charles (1809). *Life and Labour of the People in London*, Vol. I. London.
Chandler, Rev. A. (1902). "Evidence," Parliamentary Papers 1902, XXV, Q. 3500-6.
Children's Employment Commission (1863). "Appendix to the First Report," Parliamentary Papers 1903, XVIII.
Crossick, Geoffrey (1978). *Artisan Elite in Victorian Society*. London: Croom Helm.
Desprelles, (Mrs.) (1902). "Evidence," Parliamentary Papers 1902, XXV, Q. 1786-91.
Dickens, Charles (1981). *David Copperfield*. New York: Bantam.
Eliott, Sir Charles (1902). "Evidence," Parliamentary Papers 1902, XXV, question 16.
Foakes, Grace (1972). *Between High Walls*. London: Shepheard-Walwyn.
Hicks, Frances (1894). "Factory Girls," in Andrew Reid, ed., *The New Party*. London, 315-27.
Hobsbawm, E. J. (1968). *Industry and Empire*. London: Weidenfeld & Nicolson.
Holme, Ella (1902). "Evidence," Parliamentary Papers 1902, XXV, Appendix 19; questions 2171-80, 2208.
Jones, Gareth Stedman (1971). *Outcast London*. Oxford: Clarendon Press.
Kimmins, G. T. (1899). *Polly of Parkers Rents*. London.
Macdonald, Ramsay, ed. (1904). Women in the Printing *Trades*. London.
Mayhew, Henry (1851). *London Labor and London Poor*, Vol. I. London.

Neville, (Miss) (1902). "Evidence," Parliamentary Papers 1902, XXV, Q. 2646-47.

Oren, Laura (1974). "The Welfare of Women in Labouring Families: England 1860-1950," In M. Hartman & L. Banner, eds., *Clio's Consciousness Raised: New Perspectives on the History of Women*. New York: Octagon, 226-44.

Paterson, Alexander (1911). *Across the Bridges*. London.

Ross, Ellen (1981). "Domestic Sharing in Working Class London," unpubl. paper delivered at the Fifth Berkshire Conference.

Ross, Ellen (1982). "Fierce Questions and Taunts': Married Life in Working Class London 1870-1914," *Feminist Studies*, VIII, 3, Fall, 575-602.

Ross, Ellen (1983). "Survival Networks: Women's Neighborhood Sharing in London before World War I," *History Workshop Journal*, No. 15, Spr., 4-27.

Rowntree, B. S. (1901). *Poverty*. London.

Samuel, Raphael (1981). *East End Underworld: Chapters in the Life of Arthur Harding*. London: Routledge & Kegan Paul.

Thompson, W. (1902). "Evidence," Parliamentary Papers 1902, XXV, Q. 2395-99.

Walton, (Mrs.) (1902). "Interview," Essex Univ. Oral History Collection, No. 298, page 35.

Whitehead, Ann (1981). " 'I'm Hungry, Mum': The Politics of Domestic Budgeting," in K. Young, C. Wolkowitz & R. McCullagh, eds., *Of Marriage and the Market*. London: CSE, 88-111.

Willis, Frederick (1948). *101 Jubilee Road*. London: Phoenix House.

Wright, Thomas (1867). *Some Habits and Customs of the Working Classes*. London.

15

WAGES, CONSUMPTION, AND SURVIVAL
Working-Class Households in Puerto Rico in the 1930's

Maria del Carmen Baerga

Fernand Braudel Center
State University of New York—Binghamton

The reproduction of the labor force is a very important moment of the process of accumulation of capital. The daily and generational reproduction of a mass of workers who sell their labor power in the market represents the basis of the production process and capital accumulation. Nevertheless, within the general understanding of the process of capital accumulation, the intricate arrangements through which labor's reproduction takes place remain relatively obscure. Traditionally, analyses of capitalism have been restricted to the "economic" sphere: the capitalist factory and the wage worker. This results in the relegation of fundamental social relationships to a sphere of darkness, even though it is precisely that ignored sphere in which the reproduction of labor power takes place. The activities that constitute this sphere of reproduction vary immensely historically and culturally, and must be conceived as ongoing historical processes. This chapter looks at the variety of social relationships that accounted for the reproduction of the Puerto Rican labor force during the difficult decade of the 1930's and poses them within the wider perspective of the overall economic and political arena.

During the period of 1930s to 1940, the sugar and needlework industries were the two greatest sources of employment for the masses of Puerto Rican workers. The development of both industries went hand in hand, as the sugar industry worked for only five and a half months and used predominantly male workers, while the needlework industry primarily utilized female workers, most of whom were homeworkers. Other crops such as tobacco and coffee were grown on the island, though on a smaller scale than sugar, but like sugar, these too were seasonal crops. Hence, during the dead or slow time, needlework was the only source of cash income, which was so important in a widely monetarized economy. Moreover, the utilization of female homeworkers assured the performance of all the domestic chores within the household. It is clear then that the reproduction of the Puerto Rican workers was predicated upon the fact that they lived in households in which they combined incomes and pooled resources. This guaranteed their survival in periods of unemployment and underemployment. In addition, it sustained the existence of very low wages and the traditional division of labor within the household.

In terms of the workers' struggle, the decades of the 1920's and the 1930's were among the most dynamic periods in the island's history. Sugar and tobacco workers were very active struggling against the exploitative nature of the existing industries, yet the homeworkers in the needlework industry apparently represented a rather passive group. Why was this so? This inquiry examines the relationship between the structure of the industries operating in Puerto Rico, the households in which workers lived, and participation in the workers' movement. After a brief historical account of the economic and political conditions before and after the 1898 U.S. invasion, the focus here will shift to the workers' strategies for survival in the 1930's and link them to the political struggles of the period.

By the 1890's, the economy of Puerto Rico was oriented toward the production of sugar and coffee for the world market. Production took place within a hacienda arrangement with workers receiving payments sometimes in cash, but most often in kind, and obtaining the rights to land use. The structure of the hacienda usually provided work for entire families; members divided their time between production directly for the hacendado and subsistence activities on the allotted plots of land. The head of household, usually a male, would perform the largest share of the work for the hacendado and would receive all payments, even though the wife and children might be active especially in coffee production. Women and children were primarily responsible for subsistence and domestic tasks. A central feature of this arrangement was that the family was able to secure the balance of reproductive needs not provided directly by the hacendado. Through their access to the land, families were able to find the means to transform their labor into subsistence goods, in order to make up for periods of unemployment and to supplement the insufficient earnings from the hacienda.

After the U.S. invasion of Puerto Rico in 1898, the interests of U.S. sugar producers progressively dominated the subsequent economic development of the island. In 1897 sugar was produced in Puerto Rico by almost 500 small mills; in contrast, by 1930, 42 centrales ground the entire crop (Diffie & Diffie, 1931: 45), and by then 60% of those centrales belonged to absentee corporations, in their great majority American (Silvestrini, 1979: 50), controlling a total of at least 196,753 acres. As of 1929-30, just four U.S. corporations controlled by themselves eleven centrales (Silvestrini, 1979: 50) and, either through ownership or lease-holding, a total acreage of 170,675 acres (Diffie & Diffie, 1931: 52). The land devoted to sugar cane cultivation was the best of the island; the sugar plantations lay in the fertile valleys, with the less desirable mountainous areas left to the cultivation of other crops. Out of the approximate 568,000 acres of cultivated area of the island, 251,000 acres were in sugar cane (Diffie & Diffie, 1931: 52).

The history of the sudden eclipse of the haciendas by the U.S. sugar plantations is a quite complicated one that need not be detailed here. It is sufficient to note that this development had harsh consequences for the masses of former hacienda workers. The dismantling of the haciendas meant that workers lost access to the small parcels of land that had been so important in providing families with subsistence products. Families migrated to areas in which plantations and centrales were established, seeking work in the sugar industry and related occupations such as transportation, and stevedoring. Under these conditions the reproduction of Puerto Rican families was significantly changed, as they were now subjected to the low wages and unemployment of the sugar industry, but with very little or no access to the means of producing subsistence—the land (Parker Hanson, 1955: 31).

The sugar industry did not have fixed wages; frequently it hired piece workers, and the wages depended on the size of the plantation, the location, and type of work (Silvestrini, 1979: 63, 65). Because the sugar industry would provide work for only five and a half months per year, fluctuations in employment were huge; during the dead time almost everybody was unemployed and even during the busiest part of the season (January through March) there was high unemployment on the island (Diffie & Diffie, 1931: 105). Table 15.1 shows how the percentage of unemployed among the male population grew after the U.S. invasion, and that by 1929 the unemployed accounted for more than 36% of the male population (Diffie & Diffie, 1931: 167).

There were a few other industries whose existence paralleled the development and apogee of the sugar industry. Puerto Rico represented an attractive site for industrial investment due to the governmental protection for foreign interests, the accessible geographic position, and above all the abundance of cheap labor.

> Great risk there was never—the stars and stripes have always furnished ample protection to American property and have assured the Puerto Rican investor that no revolution would menace his holdings, no laws would be made unduly oppressive and no excessive taxes collected (Diffie & Diffie, 1931: 82).

TABLE 15.1

Year	Male Population 10 Years & Over	Number Employed	Number Unemployed	Percentage Employed	Percentage Unemployed
1899	322,567	267,764	54,803	83.0	17.0
1910	386,516	317,256	69,260	82.1	17.9
1920	447,777	322,466	125,311	72.0	20.0
1926	485,337	338,876	146,461	69.8	30.2

SOURCE: Bailey W. Diffie and Justine W. Diffie, *Puerto Rico: A Broken Pledge.* Copyright © 1931 by Vanguard Press. Reprinted by permission.

These conditions served as incentive for the establishment of other industries on the island such as the tobacco, fruit, and needlework industries. Of these three, only the needlework industry will be discussed here, because of its importance as a source of accumulation for foreign capital, and the crucial role that needleworkers played in the reproduction of the labor force.

The needlework industry followed the sugar industry in importance on the island, representing the major source of employment for women during the 1930's (Silvestrini, 1980: 69-70).[1] Table 15.2 shows the percentage of women integrated into the labor force for selected years; from 9.9% in 1899, women's participation rose to 26.1% by 1930. It is essential to note that the tendency towards higher rates of employed women corresponded to an increasing rate of unemployment among male workers (see Table 15.1). The importance of such a correlation will be discussed below, where I shall demonstrate how different segments of the working class came together as members of households and pooled their incomes and labor resources in order to survive periods of unemployment and underemployment.

The industry started to develop in Puerto Rico in the context of the First World War. During and after the war it became very difficult for New York and other East Coast department stores to obtain sufficient quantities of needlework from the usual sources, such as China, Ireland, France, Switzerland, the Madeira Islands, and the Philippine Islands (U.S. Dept. of Labor, 1940: 2). U.S. investors soon realized that the establishment of the needlework industry on the island could offer them a twofold advantage. Since needlework was a part of the Spanish heritage of Puerto Rican women, the work was skilled and of high quality.

One writer wrote in 1923 that the manufactures found a great advantage in the skilled hands of the Porto Rican women ready to be used in the sewing trades. The superior quality of this labor goes directly back to the time when lace-making, drawn-work, embroidery and kindred arts flourished in the house

TABLE 15.2 Women's Participation in the Puerto Rican Labor Force, 1899-1970

Year	Number of Women Employed	Percent of Increase over the Previous Year	Percent of Employed Women in Relation to the Total Population
1899	47,701	—	9.9
1910	73,596	54	21.7
1920	84,094	14	21.6
1930	122,488	46	26.1
1940	144,360	18	25.0
1950	138,517	4	21.3
1960	144,260	4	20.0
1970	212,421	47	22.9

SOURCE: Blanca Silvestrini, "La mujer puertorriqueña y el movimiento obrero en la década del 1930," in Edna Acosta Belen, ed., *La Mujer en la Sociedad Puertorriqueña*. Copyright ©1980 by Ediciones Huracan, Inc. Reprinted by permission.

of the Spanish families. . . . It represented that the garments are better made than those manufactured in this country (U.S.). Moreover, the adaptability of the skilled hand-workers in the sewing trades has become a part of the propaganda for more sweatshops in Porto Rico (U.S. Department of Labor, 1940: 26-27).

But, in addition to the high quality of its products, the needlework industry in Puerto Rico could offer investors a cheap, compliant labor force. The precarious economic situation of the working masses forced them to accept very low wages. Moreover, female labor has typically been seen as a supplementary source of household income and therefore has been generally valued more cheaply than the labor of males. So the wages of the needleworkers were particularly low, as the Department of Labor's report noted,

> The principal advantage of the needlework production in Porto Rico is a low wage, unorganized area with a large labor supply of poverty stricken people who have little bargaining power (1940: 26-27).

The needlework industry was conducted mostly through small establishments employing as few as 5 and as many as 50 workers, which served solely as centers of distribution of the materials to the homeworkers and collection of finished products to be readied for shipping. A few large factories, employing up to 400 people, had the capacity for machine work, but they also served as centers of collection and distribution. Regardless of the size of the shop, the bulk of the work was done by homeworkers (U.S. Dept. of Labor, 1940: 6).

The chain through which the work as well as the wages reached the workers was a very complicated one, but some qualifications can be made. On the top layer, one finds the U.S. investors. So far, it has been impossible to discern the identity of these investors from the data gathered; we know only that they were the owners of commercial firms, mainly from New York and other parts of the northeast coast. The investors decided what should be produced, taking into account the U.S. market demand, and controlled all aspects of production. Sometimes, they designed, cut, and made up patterns in their New York establishments, and would then ship the patterns and materials to their contractors in Puerto Rico; in other cases, the whole process took place in their plants on the island. Similarly, the finished products were sometimes laundered, boxed, and packed in Puerto Rico, while the products of other manufacturers were laundered and boxed in their U.S. establishments (Gonzalez, 1980: 71; U.S. Dept. of Labor, 1940: 2-3). The majority of these manufacturers did not have personal contact with their contractors in Puerto Rico. Occasionally, the whole process took place without contractors, in which case the investor would personally come to the island, rent a small shop, and distribute the work; after a week and a half he would collect the finished work and embark for New York (Clark, 1930: 470).

The contractors, or "workshop owners", were the ones who received all the materials and instructions for the work to be done in Puerto Rico by the homeworkers. Due to the financial organization of the North American firms, which was predominantly corporate in form, the majority of the Puerto Rican contractors used to report themselves as individual owners. So, although they appeared to be independent proprietors, they were highly dependent on the U.S. firms.

The contractors would give work to the working women who resided in the nearby neighborhoods where they ran their businesses. This facilitated the process of calling the workers to obtain the materials and, after they finished the work, to return it and receive the pay. But on large jobs the contractor was compelled to sublet part of the work to other agents who then delivered the work to the agencies and the workers. Finally, there were sub-agents in charge of the delivery and collection of the work in the hinterland and remote places. While some investors were contractors, some agents acted as contractors as well. According to Caroline Manning's (1934: 7) report, one agent that was working for three different contractors in three different towns was himself a contractor for a New York firm.

There were no written agreements stipulating the commission that either the contractors, agents, or sub-agents should charge. In reality, contractors, agents, and sub-agents were free to raise their commission at the expense of the workers' earnings. Wages in the needlework industry were among the lowest wages found in Puerto Rico, varying according to the personal policies of the contractors and agents as well as according to the type of work. In one case, for example, a contractor paid one of his agents a 10% commission, but another only a 5% commission, because one was more efficient than the other. But the agent who received the 5% commission deducted 6% of the workers' earnings, and thus actually received a higher remuneration than the more efficient agent. In another case, reliable data show that, for more or less the same amount and style of work, one contractor paid his agents $3.60 per dozen while another paid his agents $1.65 (Manning, 1934: 7-9).

Households and Workers' Reproduction

Puerto Rican workers relied mostly on cash income to secure the means of subsistence. Wages were so low (as the case of the needleworkers shows) that the members of the household had to combine their incomes and labor resources in order to survive. In 1933, adult male workers earned an average of less than 10 cents per hour in the cane fields, and an average of 4.7 cents in the tobacco fields; worse still, these were seasonal jobs that did not pay during the whole year. During the harvest season the average earnings for an adult male worker were $3.60 a week in the cane fields and $1.46 in the tobacco fields. In the same period, wages in the needlework industry were still lower. The Department of Labor reported that 31.4% of the homeworkers earned less than 1 cent per hour; 31.1% less than 2 cents; 21.2% less than 3 cents; and 10.2% less than 4 cents per hour. The average weekly earnings for a homeworker were 65 cents (Manning, 1934). The Department of Labor calculated that the cost per person per week for native food and other common and nourishing articles was, at the very least, $3.19. Figure 15.1 shows the relationship between the cost of food for a family of five and the earnings of workers in various industries on the island during the years 1933 and 1934. It is clear that their weekly earnings could not meet the cost of the food required for the daily reproduction of themselves and their families (see Figure 15.1).

The question then, is how did these people manage to survive? First of all, most of these workers lived in families that usually counted on a number of wage earners. For example, while the head of the household would have been working for the sugar industry or in some other agricultural job, the wife and/or daughter would likely have been engaged in the needlework industry. Concerning the seasonality of most of the employments in Puerto Rico, a report of the Department of Labor states,

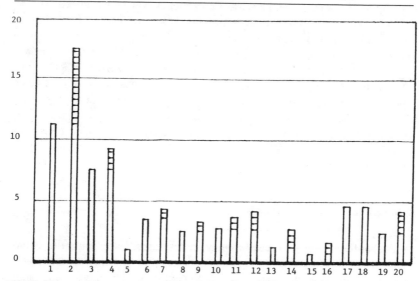

NOTE: The graph does not include the needlework industry because of the difficulty of calculating homeworkers' earnings. The Puerto Rican Department of Labor made a special report on needleworkers (see Manning, 1934).

KEY: Bars 1 and 2 represent the cost of food for a family of five for one week in 1933 and 1934, respectively; the striped bar represents the increase of food prices over the previous year. For bars 3-20, odd-numbered bars represent average weekly earnings in various industries in 1933; even-numbered bars represent average weekly earning in the same industries in 1934:

```
 3 & 4  = sugar mills
 5 & 6  = sugar cane planting–males
 7 & 8  = sugar cane planting–females
 9 & 10 = sugar cane planting–boys
11 & 12 = tobacco planting–males
13 & 14 = tobacco planting–females
15 & 16 = tobacco planting–boys
17 & 18 = tobacco stripping–males
19 & 20 = tobacco stripping–females
```

SOURCE: Rodriguez (1935).

Figure 15.1   Relationship between Cost of Food and Earnings of Workers in Various Industries in Puerto Rico, 1933 and 1934

To some extent, it is not the workers who shift employments, but rather that the family is dependent in the active season on earnings of the family head and in the slow season on earnings of subsidiary workers in other occupations (Hanson & Pérez, 1947: 96).

TABLE 15.3 Distribution of Wage-Earners Families According to Residence and Weekly Income Classes

Item	All Incomes	Under $2.00	$2.00-$3.99	$4.00-$5.99	$6.00-$7.99	$8.00-$9.99	$10.00-$14.99	$15.00-$19.99	$20.00 & Over
All families	4,999	312	626	867	853	666	888	444	343
Percentage									
All families	100.0	6.2	12.5	17.3	17.1	13.3	17.8	8.9	6.9
Urban	100.0	4.4	5.6	9.4	13.0	13.8	24.1	16.7	13.0
Rural lowlands	100.0	6.2	11.5	16.5	18.7	15.2	19.1	7.1	5.7
Rural highlands	100.0	8.1	20.8	26.4	19.2	10.7	9.7	3.1	2.0

NOTE: 4,999 families were interviewed during one week within the period January 1941 to May 1942.
SOURCE: Hansen & Pierce (1947: 11,21).

The contributions of all the members of the household were crucial for their daily reproduction. Households in which the chief earner was employed in the sugar industry, the coffee fields, or the needlework industry generally had the largest number of wage earners per family (Perloff, 1950: 168). However, wages were so low that even combined incomes could not sustain a household. The Puerto Rican Department of Labor found that in 1941, 70% of the value of food consumed by all Puerto Rican wage earners was purchased. Over 15% was received in the form of food as payment, gift, or relief, and 13% was homeproduced (Hanson & Pérez, 1947: 14). Of course, there were differences between urban workers and rural workers. While urban workers purchased as much as 90% of their food, workers in the rural highlands (coffee and other minor crop workers) and in the lowlands (sugar and fruit workers) produced more of their food. For the working class in Puerto Rico in general, expenditures for other items like clothing and housing were extremely low as compared with working-class families in the U.S.

The Puerto Rican Department of Labor interviewed 4,999 wage-earning families during the period from January 1941 to May 1942, and covered families throughout the whole island (Hanson & Pérez, 1947).[2] Table 15.3 shows the different range of earnings for the families according to residentiality.[3] The wages of urban workers tended to be the highest, followed by those of rural lowland workers and by those of workers in the highlands. Of the urban workers, 70.3% still earned less than $15.00 per week; moreover, 68.1% of the lowland workers and 85.2% of the highland workers earned less than $10 per week. In fact, the majority of all workers' families (66.4%) earned less than $10 per week. All these wages were extremely low.

TABLE 15.4 Sources of Income in One Week by Residence and for Selected Weekly Income Classes (4,999 families of Puerto Rican wage earners, one week within the period January 1941 through May 1942)

Item	All Families	All Urban Families	All Rural Families		All Families with Weekly Incomes of			
			%Lowland	%Highland	$2.00 to $3.99	$6.00 to $7.99	$10.00 to $14.99	$20.00 & over
Number of families	4,999	1,583 (31.6%)	1,851 (37.0%)	1,565 (31.3%)	626 (12.5%)	853 (17.1%)	888 (17.8%)	343 (6.9%)
Avg. no. persons per family	5.6	5.1	5.8	5.9	5.2	5.6	6.0	6.4
Average earners per family	1.2	1.3	1.2	1.2	.9	1.2	1.5	1.8
Total income	$9.21 (100%)	$12.27 (100%)	$8.88 (100%)	$6.51 (100%)	$3.10 (100%)	$6.98 (100%)	$12.03 (100%)	$26.99 (100%)
Total money income	7.47 (81.10)	10.99 (89.60)	6.97 (78.50)	4.49 (69.00)	1.68 (54.20)	5.22 (74.80)	10.09 (91.40)	24.37 (90.30)
Total income in kind	1.74 (18.90)	1.28 (10.40)	1.91 (21.50)	2.02 (31.00)	1.42 (45.80)	1.76 (25.20)	1.94 (17.60)	2.62 (09.70)
Total money income								
—wage earnings	6.54 (71.00)	9.57 (78.00)	6.22 (70.00)	3.85 (59.10)	1.53 (49.00)	4.54 (65.00)	8.85 (74.00)	21.16 (78.40)
—income from roomers	.06 (00.70)	.09 (00.73)	.06 (00.68)	.02 (00.31)	.01 (00.03)	.02 (00.29)	.10 (00.83)	.25 (00.92)

—gifts in cash	.12 (01.30)	.19 (01.50)	.11 (01.20)	.05 (00.77)	.06 (01.90)	.08 (01.40)	.15 (01.20)	.38 (01.40)
—sale of home products	.11 (01.20)	.01 (00.08)	.15 (01.70)	.18 (02.80)	.06 (01.90)	.14 (02.00)	.14 (01.20)	.06 (00.22)
—earnings from work relief	.49 (05.30)	.70 (05.70)	.37 (04.20)	.40 (06.10)	.03 (00.10)	.44 (06.30)	.77 (06.40)	.72 (02.70)
—other	.15 (01.60)	.42 (03.40)	.06 (00.68)	.00 (00.00)	.00 (00.00)	.00 (00.00)	.07 (00.60)	1.8 (06.70)
Total income in kind								
—rental value of owned house	.45 (04.90)	.65 (05.30)	.45 (05.10)	.25 (03.80)	.29 (09.30)	.37 (05.30)	.54 (04.50)	1.02 (04.40)
—home-produced food	.36 (03.90)	.05 (00.41)	.45 (05.10)	.59 (09.10)	.28 (09.00)	.38 (05.40)	.46 (03.80)	.48 (01.80)
—gifts	.60 (06.50)	.42 (03.40)	.60 (06.80)	.77 (11.80)	.53 (17.10)	.61 (08.70)	.61 (05.10)	.78 (02.90)
—goods & services as pay	.12 (01.30)	.06 (00.49)	.12 (01.40)	.19 (02.90)	.11 (03.60)	.16 (02.30)	.12 (00.10)	.15 (00.55)
—relief income	.21 (02.20)	.10 (00.81)	.29 (05.30)	.22 (03.40)	.21 (06.80)	.24 (03.40)	.21 (01.70)	.19 (00.70)

SOURCES: Hanson and Pérez (1947: 28, 32); Perloff (1950: 172).

Table 15.4 portrays the different sources of income of these 4,999 families. For urban families, wages represent 78% of all their income. This percentage decreases when one moves to the lowland households (70%), and is even lower for the highland households (59%). Incomes in kind represent as much as 31% of the total income of the rural highland household, 21.5% and 10.4% of the rural lowland and urban households total incomes respectively. If we look at the breakdown of both money income and income in kind for the selected weekly income classes, we see the same trend. Families with a lower money income had a higher percentage of income in kind, and vice versa. In the total of money income, wages accounted for the most important contribution for all the households. Although earnings from work in relief appear as the second source of money income, its importance is overstated in Table 15.4 because these were temporary jobs in defense building that were stopped by the time the U.S. entered the Second World War.

Of the different sources of income in kind, gifts were the most important for all the families, except those whose weekly income exceeded $20. Home-produced food, which one would expect to be among the most important contributions to the household, was exceeded by gifts in all cases. The nature of these gifts is not clear yet; they may have been part of a network of mutual aid within the community.

According to Charles Rogler in a study of a Puerto Rican community, Comerio, during the spring and summer of 1935, organized provision for relief of the poor was of secondary importance compared with the material benefits and comforts resulting from neighborhood cooperation. He found that the activities and functions of the family, including subsistence interest, were greatly diffused within the neighborhood. These mutual aid networks were far from being inter-class phenomena, as might be expected; in fact, they operated within the working community and were rather intra-class phenomena. Due to the instability of employment, economic advantages would shift from one family to another, and at one or another point families would be beneficiaries or benefactors. Rogler's (1940: 60) study concludes that large numbers of families depended for survival upon aid received from neighbors. Some of the statements of the poor people who were interviewed follow:

> We are just like one big family here; when we have something our friends do no have, we share it with them and our friends do the same with us.
>
> When I am hungry, my friends help me with some food.
>
> We protect each other when there is no work.
>
> My friends gave me money to bury my wife.
>
> I have one good friend who comes and helps when I am sick (Rogler, 1940: 61).

However, mutual aid within the community is just a redistributive ac- tivity, and so, although mutual aid could have been the difference between individual starvation and survival, it could not have accounted for the genera- tional reproduction of the community.

The hard time that Puerto Rican families had in making ends meet is illustrated by the large amount of their indebtedness and the impossibility of matching money income and expenditures. Table 15.5 shows that 81.2% of all the families interviewed could not keep pace with their expenditures. The outstanding debt for food alone represented more than 4% of the average annual earnings of these families, and over twice as much of their weekly cash income. Total outstanding debts for those families, excluding the mort- gage of their houses, amounted to 8% of the annual earnings—over 3 times the amount of the weekly money income. If one takes into account the mort- gage indebtedness, the figure rises to nearly 9% of annual earnings (see Table 15.6).

If indebtedness was a strategy for survival, this question remains: How in the long run did families cope with the gap between their incomes and the cost of generational reproduction?

Political Implications of the Structure of the Needlework Industry

The structure and organization of the needlework industry had impor- tant political implications. In the various documents of the Department of Labor, there are countless references to the numerous problems posed by the utilization of homeworkers. Not unlike earlier forms of cottage industry, the system at work here was very inefficient. The delivery of the work and its collection were very tedious processes, often involving the spoilage and loss of both the materials and the finished products. Although wages were paid at piece rate and the terrible economic conditions of the workers com- pelled them to work as fast as they could, productivity was affected by the fact that the workers were in their homes and were constantly interrupted by their household obligations. The physical condition of the workers' homes was another hindrance; insufficient light and ventilation, for example, were common. All this hampered the productivity of labor. The contractors themselves would have liked to have factories in which they could gather their workers; at the same time, this would have eliminated the presence of agents and sub-agents and the constant loss and spoilage of materials. And the workers would have been able to work under better conditions and in a more relaxed way. Yet petitions by contractors to set up workshops were virtually ignored by the U.S. firms that provided the capital. Why? One reason was that homework was not protected by minimum wage laws; more importantly, though, homeworkers constituted a very particular labor

TABLE 15.5 Weekly Money Expenses by Weekly Income Class and by Residence (4,999 families, Puerto Rican wage earners)

Item	All Families	Families with weekly incomes of							
		Under $2.00	$2.00-$3.99	$4.00-$5.99	$6.00-$7.99	$8.00-$9.99	$10.00-$14.99	$15.00-$19.99	$20.00 & over
Urban									
Number of families	1,583 (100%)	70 (4.4)	88 (05.5)	149 (09.4)	206 (13.0)	218 (13.7)	382 (24.1)	264 (16.6)	206 (13.0)
Total money income	$10.00	.43	1.88	4.01	5.95	7.79	10.86	15.75	26.08
Average total money expenditures	$12.06	6.77	5.62	6.41	7.96	9.15	12.47	15.28	23.01
Percentage of money income for total expenditures	120.6	1,578.2	298.8	159.9	133.8	117.9	114.8	97.0	88.1
Rural Lowland									
Number of families	1,851 (100%)	115 (6.2)	213 (11.5)	305 (16.6)	347 (18.7)	281 (15.2)	354 (19.1)	131 (07.0)	105 (05.6)
Total money income	$6.97	.33	1.61	3.41	5.22	7.00	9.72	14.54	22.44
Average total money expenditures	$7.71	4.69	4.95	4.72	5.98	7.44	10.11	12.71	17.51
Percentage of money income for total expenditures	110.7	1,441.1	308.2	138.4	114.6	106.4	104.0	84.6	80.2
Rural Highland									
Number of families	1,565 (100%)	127 (8.1)	325 (20.7)	413 (26.3)	300 (19.1)	167 (10.6)	152 (09.7)	49 (03.1)	32 (02.0)
Total money income	$4.49	.28	1.67	3.22	4.73	6.41	9.02	12.99	19.69
Average total money expenditures	$5.66	4.18	3.84	4.28	5.70	6.99	8.64	12.36	16.25
Percentage of money income for total expenditures	126.0	1,496.8	230.4	133.0	120.3	108.9	95.7	95.1	82.6

SOURCE: Hanson and Pérez (1947: 34-37).

TABLE 15.6   Average Outstanding Debts, 1941 (4,999 families)

Type of Debt	Amount (in dollars)	Percentage
Food	16.34	59.3
Rent	1.25	4.5
Clothing	1.70	6.1
Furnishings	3.94	14.3
Individuals	2.14	7.7
Other	2.15	7.8
Total for family (excluding mortgage)	27.52	100.0

force. Their prime role was linked to the realization of reproductive tasks in households. The needlework firms capitalized upon this, organizing productive processes around the traditional division of labor within the household. Women saw their inclusion in the waged sphere as the only way in which they could survive really difficult times, and so their bargaining power was diminished.

The Puerto Rican workers' struggle in the first decades of the twentieth century was a strong one, and in many cases it cost the lives of women and men committed to the transformation of bourgeois society. During those first four decades, the country faced many strikes, demonstrations, the burning of sugar cane fields, and other signs of open class struggle. The vanguard of the movement was concentrated among the sugar and the tobacco workers. Their institutional instrument was the Free Federation of Workers (FLT), whose political arm was the Socialist Party, founded in 1915. Independent of the political cooptation of the leadership of the FLT and the Socialist Party during their involvement in the colony's politics, the workers stood firm, struggling for a better life for themselves and their families. Within this very dynamic conjuncture of struggle, the needleworkers, one of the most exploited groups of the working class, remained relatively passive. It was only the factory workers, and not the homeworkers, who accounted for the majority of those workers in the industry who were at all active in the organized working-class movement.

It could be said that the homeworkers worked in isolation, without much contact with other people in their same situation. Moreover, most of these workers were so busy with their double shift of work (household chores and needlework), which confined them to their homes, that they did not have time to share and discuss their problems with other needleworkers. However, these workers lived in households in which other members were likely to be active in the workers' movement in their work places. Although these workers have been seen as a passive group within the labor force, their political role within the household and the community should be re-searched, for it may be that they were as political as the rest of the workers but that their actions were manifested differently due to the particular way in which the needlework was structured and due to their primary role in reproduction. Moreover, one could push the argument further and say that the sugar workers were at the vanguard of the movement precisely because the need workers were in a way "alienated" from it. The fact that they performed domestic tasks and earned some cash perhaps permitted other members of the household to participate in the strikes and other traditionally known activities of resistance. However, all these hypotheses have to be supported with pertinent historical research (which shall appear in a forth-coming paper).

Conclusions

It is evident that one important institution for the reproduction of the Puerto Rican working class was the household. Moreover, the division of labor within the household became the basis upon which production was organized. Men worked outside the household in agricultural tasks, and women remained responsible for the reproductive tasks within the household. The needlework industry took advantage of this situation and organized pro-duction around it. Women saw their jobs as something that they could do along with their domestic chores, which would be impossible if they held another type of job. Also, they saw their wages as a little something "ex-tra" in a period of severe economic hazard, as a complement to the sup-posedly principal earnings of the head of the household, thus permitting the existence of very low wages. What they did not see, though, was that, in the first place, their skills as needleworkers represented a great source of accumulation for the North American companies, which paid one and two cents per hour for the production of commodities later sold as luxury ones and that, in the second place, they were subsidizing capital in a dou-ble way. On the one hand, while being the ones responsible for the domestic tasks within the household, they performed an amount of unpaid labor necessary for workers to come back every morning ready to work. Fur-ther, while contributing with a "little extra" cash to the household, they not only sustained low wages in other industries but actually assumed the responsibility for the reproduction of the male workers during periods of unemployment and underemployment. Thus, Puerto Rican housewives and daughters, although absent from most of the historical accounts of the period, contributed greatly to the functioning of the whole system.

Mutual aid within the neighborhood appeared to be of importance in the daily reproduction of the workers. This raises very interesting questions as to whether or not the household sets the boundaries in which reproduction takes place. Is the household one of many sets of relationships on which the workers rely for their reproduction, or is it the central set of relationships that account for the reproduction of the labor force? This is a question that has to be answered historically. For example, the nature of mutual activities has to be researched further in order to determine if these were relations between households or individuals from the same class. Were mutual aid activities based upon class solidarity or kinship? All these questions are open for historical research.

Also, the role of the state in the reproduction of the relationship between capital and labor needs to be worked out. In the particular period covered in this chapter there is a virtual absence of any state intervention as opposed to the massive intervention in other periods. As this analysis has shown, the different strategies of survival that the Puerto Rican working class pursued—combining incomes, pooling resources, dispensing mutual aid within the community, incurring indebtedness—could not provide for their generational reproduction. How was this crisis of reproduction resolved?

After 1940, the Puerto Rican economic panorama began to change. In the following twenty years the island underwent a period of intensive industrialization. The state intervened massively, unlike in the preceding period, in organizing production and reproduction. The standard of living of the working class improved a great deal. Numerous programs of reconstruction and relief were implanted. Which were the factors that contributed to these changes in state policy towards reproduction? Did the state intervene within the household? Did the household remain as the main set of social relations for the reproduction of the working class?

This essay, then, raises more questions than it really answers, but to raise these questions is the first step necessary for a deeper understanding of the very dynamic processes discussed above.

NOTES

1. Even though the needlework industry was of utmost importance, not only as a source of employment for women, but as a very profitable enterprise for North American investors and local intermediaries, it was not until recent years that any analytical studies have appeared on the subject (see references). These are preliminary attempts to understand a very complicated chain of accumulation and exploitation that started in the hinterlands of the Puerto Rican countryside and ended somewhere in fancy department stores on the East Coast. Hence, they have concentrated mainly in trying to reconstruct the structure of the industry and the way it worked.

2. A total of 4,999 families were visited in 48 towns and 152 rural barrios. In order to limit the survey to families of wage earners, the following requirements were imposed:

(1) The family must have at least one person who has worked as a wage earner for six weeks (30 working days or 240 hours) during the past two years.

(2) Families having any clerical or professional workers are excluded.

(3) Families having any members engaged in business are excluded if:
   a. they had one or more full-time or two or more part-time employees;
   b. business income and expenditures cannot be clearly separated from family income and expenditures.

(4) Families owning farms of 10 or more cuerdas (0.97 acres) are excluded.

(5) Families owning farms of less than 10 cuerdas are included provided 50% or more of their annual cash income is derived from wages. No distinction was made between urban or rural wage earners. Many wage earners from farms were included.

Certain other requirements were imposed in order to avoid obtaining schedules not suitable for analysis. These included the following rules:

(6) The family must consist of at least two persons dependent on the same income or pooling income and sharing the same table.

(7) Families are ineligible if any person having an independent income, whose detailed expenditures cannot be obtained, is living in the household with board free.

(8) Families having no more than three boarders are ineligible.

(9) Families who moved within the past three months are ineligible.

Families were not excluded for any of the following reasons:

(1) minimum income or earnings;

(2) receipt of relief, gifts, free rent, industrial or military pensions, insurance benefits, or alimony;

(3) friend or relative dependent upon family income and living with them;

(4) homemaker working outside the home; or

(5) employed members boarding outside the home because of distance to work, but economically attached to the household.

3. Workers living in the rural lowlands were likely to be working in the sugar and fruit industries. Workers residing in the rural highlands were engaged in coffee and minor crops production.

REFERENCES

Clark, Victor S. (1930). *Porto Rico and Its Problems*. Washington, DC: The Brookings Institution.

Diffie, Bailey W. & Diffie, Justine W. (1931). *Porto Rico: A Broken Pledge*. New York: Vanguard.

Gómez, Ofelia & Reddock, Rhoda (1979). "Multinationals and Female Labour in Latin America," *Scholas Journal*, No. 1, 60-88.

Gonzalez, Lydia Milagros (1980). "La industria de la Aguja en Puerto Rico (1918-1929)," in Annie Santiago de Curet, ed., *El Arte de la Aqujia*. Fundación Puertorriqueña de las Humanidades, 63-78.

Hancock, Ralph (1960). *Puerto Rico: A Success Story*. Princeton, NJ: Van Nostrand.

Hanson, Alice & Pérez, Manuel A. (1947). "Incomes and Expenditures of Wage Earners in Puerto Rico," Puerto Rico Department of Labor, Bulletin No. 1, May 1.

Lopez Perez, Maria (1980). "The Garment Industry in New York City," unpubl. paper presented at the IDS/CEREP Seminar, La Mujer y la Produccion Social en el Caribe, San Juan, Puerto Rico.

Manning, Caroline (1934). "The Employment of Women in Puerto Rico," U.S. Department of Labor, Bulletin of the Women's Bureau, No. 18.

Morales Otero, P. & Perez, M. A. (1940). "Physical Impairments of Adult Life among Agricultural Workers," *Puerto Rico Journal of Public Health and Tropical Medicine*, XV, 4, June.

Parker Hanson, Earl (1955). *Transformation*. New York: Simon and Schuster.

Perloff, Harvey (1950). *Puerto Rico's Economic Future*. Chicago: Univ. of Chicago Press.

Pico, Isabel (1980). "Apuntes preliminares para el estudio de la mujer puertorriqueña y su participacion en las luchas sociales de principios de siglo," in Edna Acosta Belén, ed., *La Mujer en la Sociedad Puertorriqueña*. Puerto Rico: Ediciones Huracan, 23-40.

Puerto Rico Department of Labor (1927-1940). *Annual Report of the Commissioner of Labor*. San Juan.

Puerto Rico Department of Labor (1944). "Proteccion de la mujer en la industria," Manual de orientación social No. 1. San Juan: Negociado de Publicaciones y Educación Obrera.

Quintero, A. G. (1972). *Lucha Obrera en Puerto Rico*. San Juan: CEREP.

Quintero, A. G. (1980). "La Base Social de la Transformación Ideológica del Partido Popular en la Década del '40," in Gerardo Navas Davila, ed., *Cambio y Desarrollo en Puerto Rico: Las Transformaciones Ideológicas del Partido Popular Democrático*. Rio Piedras: Editorial Universitaria, 35-119.

Rivera Quintero, Marcia (1980a). "Incorporación de las Mujeres al Mercado de Trabajo en el Desarrollo del Capitalismo," in E. Acosta Belén, ed., *La Mujer en la Sociedad Puertorriqueña*. San Juan: Ediciones Huracan, 41-65.

Rivera Quintero, Marcia (1980b). "Notas para enmarcar el estudio del surgimiento de la Industria de la Aguja en Puerto Rico," in Annie Santiago de Curet, ed., *El Arte de la Aquja*. San Juan: Fundación Puertorriqueña de la Humanidades, 55-62.

Rodriguez, Aremio (1935). "A Report Dealing with Labor Statistics, Cost of Living, Housing Conditions, and Craftsmanship of Workers in Puerto Rico," Puerto Rico Department of Labor, Bulletin No. 6.

Rogler, Charles C. (1940). *Comerio: A Study of a Puerto Rican Town*. Lawrence: Univ. of Kansas Press.

Silvestrini, Blanca (1979). *Los Trabajadores Puertorriqueños y el Partido Socialista (1932-40)*. Rio Piedras: Editorial Universitaria.

Silvestrini, Blanca (1980). "La mujer puertorriqueña y el movimento obrero en la década del 1930," in Edna Acosta Belén, ed., *La Mujer en la Sociedad Puertorriqueña*. San Juan: Ediciones Huracan, 67-90.

U.S. Department of Commerce (1899). *Census*. Washington, DC.

U.S. Department of Labor (1940). "Report on Puerto Rico: The Needlework Industry," mimeo, Washington, DC.

Zeluck Stephen (1952). *The Effect of the Federal Minimum Wage Legislation upon the Puerto Rican Needlework Industry*. unpubl. Ph.D. diss., Univ. of Chicago.

16

TOWARDS A THEORY OF THE
SEXUAL DIVISION OF LABOR

Veronika Bennholdt-Thomsen

Sociology of Development Research Center
University of Bielefeld

The fact that the social sciences have no theory of the sexual division of labor at their disposal is due to that very phenomenon itself, though not to the division of labor along sex-lines as such, but rather to the specific social value that division has acquired in the present historical situation.

- The sexual division of labor is held as something natural, and this nature-like aspect is introduced not by the man, but by the woman, as if female biology itself determines the abilities and tasks of women.
- As its organizational frame is given by the family, the sexual division of labor is qualified as part of the superstructure and not as a relation of production; accordingly, the feminine tasks are not defined as work, as economy, or as production.

Because of this ideological setting, the method for developing a theory of the sexual division of labor is already established; thus, we have to start with the analysis of the present situation, and so my argument will take the following steps:

(1) A more or less descriptive panorama of the given division of labor according to sex.
(2) A critique of the usual perceptions of this relationship, using ethnographic and other material.
(3) An attempt to identify (by means of the historical materialist category of labor) the common features and the differences in the sexual division of labor.
(4) A reconceptualization of the sexual division of labor in the present.

I presume that with this basis it might be possible to work out a theory of the sexual division of labor.

A Descriptive Panorama of the Sexual Division of Labor

The relation between the housewife and the dependent wage earner is the key to the sexual division of labor in the present capitalist world-system (Wallerstein, 1974). This of course does not mean that all women are exclusively housewives and all men are wage workers; it does suggest that as society is presently organized, women throughout the world perform tasks devoted to immediate subsistence. They produce food, clothing, and housing for daily consumption needs and for the survival of the next generation, whereas men are active in production that is mediated by exchange and money. Female production is organized through the family; male production, on the other hand, follows different forms of organization: factory, craft workshop, peasant household, state administration, and so on. Furthermore, women by and large do the unpaid labor and men the paid labor. Accordingly, when women do work for remuneration, they are paid at lower rates than are men.

What is a housewife, and what does she do? In the first instance, the housewife is a mother, potentially or in actual fact. She combines many abilities, tasks, and qualifications in one person, performing manual services for the husband and children: cooking, cleaning, washing, and so on. She caters to the spiritual well-being of the family members by providing a nice atmosphere in the house, by listening to their sorrows, and by giving advice, thus performing the functions of a social worker. She is nurse and tax expert, teacher and gardener (Kontos & Walser, 1978; Oakley, 1974). The socio-economic category of housewife is relatively new, emerging together with the category of wage worker along with the rise of the capitalist world-system. The historical process, in short, is as follows: During early industrialization both men and women, and to a lesser degree children, are wage workers, at which time the bourgeois housewife emerges. This model spreads into the proletarian class in the form of a wage-earning man and an unpaid houseworker, by means of protective legislation and as a result of a struggle by the working-class organizations for a family wage (Gerhard, 1978; Bock & Duden, 1977). Along with this process of housewifization comes the development of an image of womanhood that attributes to the houseworkers manual and spiritual qualifications, naturally theirs by virtue of being female (Hausen, 1976; Kittler, 1980).

Today, the primary occupation of women is housewifery, whereas men have open access to a variety of professions. (In developed countries 70%

of women working in publicly recognized professions are concentrated in 25 professions and branches of professions where only a few men work, while men can be found in 300 different professions and branches where only a very few women work [Loufti, 1980].) In other words, male and female attributes of different tasks are not parallel or at the same level; rather, they are qualitatively different. More specifically, the tasks of women are defined by sex, whereas those of men are not. Even more, all the different occupations of women are seen in terms of the housewife, an image that persecutes women like an infectious disease, and follows them even into socially recognized professions. Women are teachers, nurses, secretaries, and workers on the assembly line who have to work on especially small objects that need special manual ability. The evaluation and remuneration of women's work is stilted as well. Thus we find that the average income of women, in virutally all countries that publish sex-specific statistics, is lower than that of men. However, the differences vary widely from region to region. In Finland, Norway, Israel, and France in the last two decades the income of women has reached 65%-70% of the income of men. In Czechoslovakia, Hungary, and Poland it is 67%, but in the predominantly English-speaking countries—Australia, Canada, the U.K., and the United States—the figure is less than 60% (Moroney, 1979: 601). (In the F.R.G. in 1979, the average income of women in industry amounted to 72.3% of that of men in 1979, according to *Frankfurter Rundschau*, 23, August 1980.)[1] Moreover, it is clear not only that women earn less on an average than men, but also that their work is given less value. An especially striking example comes from the Soviet Union, where medical doctors are predominantly women; as the proportion of female doctors increased, social recognition of the profession declined (Buckley, 1981).

The present social position of women resembles that of a caste—a low caste. The occupations they will have to fulfill are predetermined by birth, and as with outcastes or untouchables, the tasks performed by women become low-status tasks. If we finally start to take this phenomenon seriously, then two questions emerge at once: How can this fact be compatible with the capitalist system (or the industrial system or the modern society; here the concepts are really interchangeable)? And, what conclusions follow for our understanding of the capitalist system? These questions become all the more important when we consider that this description of women as born to be housewives according to their female nature emerges only with the industrial development of capitalism.

The argument for the legitimation of this description leads immediately to another question. As the argument goes, women, because of their ability to give birth and to nourish children, are destined to be housewives, since the tasks of the housewife are intimately linked to the work of the mother—namely, cooking, washing, cleaning, spiritual assistance, and so on. The question raised, then, is why it is just these tasks, seemingly developed on the basis of the ability to give birth, that are held in such low esteem. This question leads to a fundamental question about the character of society: How far is the relationship between human beings, and their attitudes towards themselves and their own bodies, structured according to this form of the social division of labor? In other words, how are sexual and social divisions of labor related to each other?

The Standard Perception of
the Sexual Division of Labor

This chapter attempts to develop the foundation of a theory of the sexual division of labor based on a critique of the dominant perceptions of this phenomenon, and so I follow this descriptive panorama of the actual state of the sexual division of labor with discussion of the main elements of the ideology that stems from this reality.

A basic assumption, common to everyday life as well as to science, is that the current prevailing form of the sexual division of labor is the only form that humankind has brought forth. One assumes, then, that either a sexual division of labor exists or it does not. This, in turn, leads one immediately to the question of whether or not, in actual fact, a difference between the sexes does exist. In other words this seemingly historic (or, better, non-historic) point of view rediscovers the entire present situation in all other historical phases. This point of view recalls the situation in classical political economy where every flint started to be called "capital"; here, every occupation performed by women starts to be seen as housework.

One example of this point of view is the standard version of how the human society has come to be organized during (more or less) the first 99% of its history (the time of the appropriative mode of production—of the hunter-gatherer complex) based on the famous model of the "man, the hunter". According to this version the man goes off to hunt while the woman must stay at home because of pregnancy and breastfeeding, spending her spare time gathering. It is historically correct that a sexual division of labor occurred in which men predominantly did the hunting and women the gathering. But it is going totally beyond a scientific analysis of facts to assume that hunting was inherently male, because it supposedly required physical strength, quick movements, and the endurance to travel long distances, or that gathering was inherently female, because it required little strength and only local movements.[2]

First, as to physical strength, there is plenty of proof to show that in societies where there were no animals and where the wheel did not exist, women did most of the carrying and, indeed, could carry even heavier loads than could the men (Murdock, 1937; Malinowski, 1932).[3] Secondly, what is the stress on brief, local movement—on women bound to a given locality? Is the cavern or the windscreen actually identified with home, sweet home? In fact, gathering, as is well known, required the traveling of long distances and the continued changing of terrain, as its yield was exhausted (Friedl, 1975: 16).[4] Thirdly,

(a) Even if it is true that hunting required agility and quickness of all those involved, is it true that women must therefore have been excluded because they were *always* pregnant and hence restricted in their movement? Probably not. Moreover, as several examples show, women often participated in hunting even when pregnant (see, e.g., Turnbull [1965] for the case of the Mbuti-pygmies).[5]

(b) Did hunting really require only the running down of, say, deer, which might indeed necessitate special quickness, or did it also require organization, cooperation, and guile? Probably so.

(c) Finally, weren't there cases in which women could be trained for speed and quickness in the same way as men, and isn't it often noted that in these cases women tended to suffer less from fatigue than did men during equivalent activities? Surely; one such case is that of the people of Tarahumara, Mexico (Benitéz, 1972).

One central feature of the ideology based on the model derived from "the man the hunter" consists in seeing female activities as inherently deficient because of the biological handicap of being a woman. Men can hunt, and women are bound to do the gathering. Meat is seen as the basic food and as being of higher value. But archeological and ethnographical material suggests that, on the contrary, vegetable food furnished the main contribution to the diet of hunter-gatherer societies, its provision being much more reliable than the hunters' luck (see Fisher, 1979).

Perhaps the most striking feature of the "man the hunter" model is that the fundamental inferiority of women is seen less in their involvement in gathering instead of in hunting, and more in their "failure" to create or to own the weapons for hunting, with the result that women do not lead wars, or even know how to kill. Typical of the view is the recent account by the well-known French anthropologist, Maurice Godelier (1981), of "the origins of male domination." "Men hunted big game and waged war," he notes, and to this was attached a "higher value, in so far as it involved greater risks of losing one's life and greater glory in taking life," whereas women only "hunted small game, gathered natural supplies, and cooked the daily food" (1981: 12). The reason put forward was that

Woman by virtue of her reproductive function is less mobile than man. She becomes pregnant, gives birth, and breastfeeds children who are weaned at a late stage (1981: 12).

In Godelier's entire paper there is no explanation of why an occupation that entails risking life has a higher value attached to it than does an occupation that brings forth new life, or of why it is more glorious to kill than to give birth.

At least Godelier does criticize the view of male dominance over women; the North American anthropologist, Lionel Tiger, in his book *Men in Groups* (1969), on the contrary, tries to show that this dominance is necessary and impossible to change. The typically male valuation that privileges aggression and violence is unconsciously implied by Godelier; Tiger consciously articulates it, even though he presents his arguments as if they were value-free. This conscious bias is typical of that strain of social biology represented by Tiger, according to which the human animal is unchangeable because the genes are programmed in a certain unique form.[6] Tiger, in his interpretation of the history of humankind, not only projects the relationship of housewife/wage worker into the past, but he then also uses the inverse argument that men, having been hunters, must also continue to act as hunters impulsively today.

Another element of the dominant ideology of the sexual division of labor is the attitude that links the male to what is socially valuable and the female to what is socially not valuable. This attitude becomes obvious when it appears in analyses of different historical periods. One striking and strange example has been gathered by Evelyn Reed; she cites the views of Julius Lippert, who pities the poor women who were not allowed to eat human flesh (Reed, 1975: 72).

This attitude of our male-dominated society underlies all other social formations; this, in turn, leads to the interpretation of different social rules and activities for men and women as signs of the disadvantage and subordination of women.

This stems from a misunderstanding of equality. The demands for equal treatment under the law and equal access to all the professions are historically necessary, and correct in the light of the bourgeois aims of liberty, equality, and fraternity. But they do not automatically apply to other historical social situations. On the contrary, there are various example of forms of sexual division of labor and of social organization that are extremely unequal and that even show a rather strict division between male and female areas and male and female life cycles, which do not, however, imply any hierarchy or even subordination of women. (For the Mundurucú in Brazil, see Murphy & Murphy [1974]; for the Jivaro and Canella in Ecuador, the Kágaba in Columbia, New Caledonia, the ethnic groups in Malekula, Melanesia, the Digul-people in New Guinea, and the Chwana in South Africa, see Baumann [1980] and Leacock, [1977]. In this context the description of the so-called sexual parallelism in Incan society drawn by Irene Silverblatt (1980) becomes interesting. The land was inherited in female and male descent lines, and there existed political and religious institutions of women, with the queen at the top, parallel to those of men. Spanish colonialism, however, changed this parallel structure to a hierarchical one. Similar (if not as striking) examples of a parallelism between the sexes, especially where property and land rights are concerned, are given by Friedl (1975) and Boserup (1970).

We therefore conclude that the existence of a sexual division of labor does not in itself reveal anything of its character. Rather, it seems that all social formations have an allocation of tasks and occupations that differentiates between the two sexes, but the sexual division of labor takes more forms than one.

Common and Unique Features of Various Forms of the Sexual Division of Labor

If we set aside the bourgeois ideology's pretensions to universality, then it is no longer problematic to state that the sexual division of labor is a constant feature of human society. Biology and nature, having once been used to threaten women, lose their threatening aspect, and we can start to see them as allies. Biological and other natural differences between the sexes are sometimes the basis of differences between the occupations each sex performs. The crucial question, however, is what kind of connection exists between the sexual nature of men and women and their different and varying occupations throughout history.

For analyzing this and related questions we need a concept that we can use to acknowledge the way biology and nature influence general and anthropological conditions, without our view becoming ahistorical and static. These requirements are fulfilled in the concept of work developed by historical materialism. One formation of Marx's definition of work comes at the start of his chapter in *Capital*, "The Labour-Process and the Process of Producing Surplus-Value":

> Labour is, in the first place, a process in which both man and nature participate, and in which man of his own accord starts, regulates, and controls the material re-action between himself and nature. He opposes himself to nature as one of her own forces, setting in motion arms and legs, head and hands, the natural forces of his body, in order to appropriate nature's productions

in a form adapted to his own wants. By thus acting on the external world and changing it, he at the same time changes his own nature (1967: 177).

This general definition of work is meant to apply to the whole of history. However, a concept of the sexual aspects of work must still be developed (though on this basis) because, astonishingly enough, neither Marx nor his interpreters have taken into account the difference between the female and the male body and their correspondingly different relationship to nature, in spite of their having *defined* the human body as the human nature (see, eg., Schmidt, 1962; Lefèbvre, 1966: 92-140). This quite fundamental anthropological question has indeed only been dealt with recently by feminist social scientists such as Leukert (1976), Maria Mies (1981) and Claudia von Werlhof (1981).

If we include in the determination of work, together with arms and legs, hands and head, also belly, breast, and sexual organs, then the crucial difference in the definition of human nature is included, namely the potential for procreation and for giving birth. In the symbiosis between the human being and nature, men and women experience themselves in different ways. The woman experiences herself as a part of nature as she produces new nature and nourishment for it out of her own body. The man on the other hand experiences nature as an exchange, mediated through hand and head. Maria Mies describes the different relationship to nature that sex imposes in the following way: The women feels her whole body as being productive, whereas the man feels himself as being productive by acting upon nature through means of instruments, namely, tools. This she argues, is the reason the man's relationship to his own and to outside nature tends to be an instrumentalist one (1981: 687).

From this point of view the concept of symbiosis, in the sense of *exchange* with nature, applies more accurately to women, whereas for men *appropriation* of nature seems the more accurate description. Women give nature something in return; they produce nature, whereas men do not. But even this statement has to be qualified as historically relative, and should not be seen as an invariable anthropological fact: It is possible only because of the experience of centuries of patriarchal history, without which our concept might be quite different. So we should not overlook ethnographical and mythological material that points to another understanding of this relationship by means of other kinds of behavior in hunter-gatherer societies. In all these societies rituals were performed after hunting and harvesting to reconcile outside nature with human nature by symbolically giving something back, establishing an equal exchange. One could say that the female and the male relationships to nature were, by means of these rituals, united.

Today this consciousness no longer exists; it is even difficult for us to understand the attitudes behind such behavior. Present society, in contrast, lives by the conquest, appropriation, exploitation, and destruction of nature instead of by cooperation with nature through an exchange. What has happened in the meantime? What has changed in nature—in both the inner, human one and the outside one? What are the cornerstones of this history?

Maria Mies, after arguing that men have etablished a relationship of power towards nature, towards women, and towards their own bodies, advances the thesis that this could occur only because men developed a productivity that seemed to make them independent from female productivity (1981: 67). This, she continues, has happened through instruments—namely, weapons. The history of male dominance is not, on her view, the history of the development of the productive forces, but rather of the destructive forces; it is a history of violence (1981: 17-19). Hers has been, so far as I know, the first and, up to now, also the only attempt to interpret the history of male dominance by means of a materialist concept of work that distinguishes between a female relationship to nature and a male one.

The common procedure in anthropological women's studies consists of trying to discover the historical moment when an original matriarchy has been transformed into patriarchy, much along the lines of the general evolutionist theory (see, e.g., Reed, 1975; Reiter, 1977; Webster, 1975). So in this literature, women continue to ask how maternal lines of descent could have been changed into paternal ones, and in which way women were forced out of religious, political, and other social positions of control and coordination.

An approach, however, that sees the sexual division of labor as an important structuring element of the overall social relationship to nature has to develop its thesis far beyond these lines. We cannot limit ourselves to examining descent, or the positions that women did or did not occupy in social hierarchy; rather, we have to clarify the direction taken by the overall social development because of the emergence of a certain sexual division of labor.

We need to pose the problem in a way similar to that in which Engels did when he argued that the existence of the state, from an evolutionary perspective, necessarily presupposes the existence of the paternal inheritance (1972). He must, however, be criticized for his exclusively male-oriented concept of work and productivity, which prevents him from fully visualizing the sexual division of labor. From the outset, he divides production and reproduction (1972: 156).[8] Then, while developing his thesis about the origins of private property,[9] he overstresses the effect of the individual appropriation of nature instead of acknowledging a possible cooperation with nature; above all, he fails to analyze the overall structural effect on social reproduction, which must go hand in hand with the change from a maternal to a paternal line of descent.[10] Engels says, "The overthrow of matriarchy has been the world's historical defeat of the female sex" (1972: 198). Couldn't it also have been the defeat of the male sex?

In Engel's earlier small pamphlet, "The Contribution of Labour to the Transformation of the Ape into Human Being" (1970), his one-sided concept of work is strikingly clear. There, "work" is equal to the "development of the hand" and this again to the "starting dominance over nature." "Work starts with the manufacturing of tools." The oldest tools are "tools for hunting . . . at the same time weapons" (1970: 70, 73).

This truly instrumentalist concept of work fails to include one important dimension of the transformation from animal to human being—namely, the conscious appropriation of human nature, the conscious acting upon the human body. Yet knowledge about procreation and birth, the menstrual cycle and pregnancy, the relationship between the human body and outside nature (stars, plants) has to be acquired. It constitutes female knowledge and skills, especially in midwifery and healing in general—a knowledge that also contributes to the organization of kinship and storing economy (Reed, 1975; Morgan, 1891).

For Engels this aspect of human labor, however, remains totally unconscious and "natural"; for him the size of population depends wholly on the conditions of outside nature and the mode of production, on the amount of food to be produced. This assumption derives from the patriarchal approach to the natural sciences typical of the nineteenth century, according to which knowledge of human physiology and about birth control was new and belonged only to the modern era. However, new writings in women's studies suggest that while ignorance about contraception and birth control was common in the Europe of 1600-1900, non-European people during these periods did possess such knowledge, which must also have existed in Europe before the beginning of the modern times (Leacock, 1977; Fisher, 1979: 203-25; Becker et al., 1980; Gordon, 1977; Honegger, 1979; Heinsohn et al., 1979).

When Engels enters into the history of class societies, he finally and irrevocably loses sight of the relationship between the social division of labor and the development of all other social institutions (which for Engels means the relationship between the kinship system and the social production) as if social classes had nothing to do with social hierarchy. Much to the contrary, it seems quite evident that a connection does exist, not only one concerning the emergence of class societies, but an overall structural relationship up to the present as well.[11]

The fact that neither Engels nor the other evolutionist authors succeeded in integrating the sexual division of labor into their analyses is due to their perception of the historical situation in which they themselves lived (Martin

& Voorhies, 1975: 145-55).[12] In both the analysis of capital and the analysis of the modern society, respectively, the specific work capacity of women has been ignored, and because of this distorted view of their contemporary situation the authors have also been unable to see the relevant historical connections. Here, a historical-materialist criticism applies to one of its creators: The anatomy of the human being contains the key to the anatomy of the ape; therefore, to the extent that the human anatomy has been ignored, the anatomy of the ape cannot be explored.

My introductory methodological remarks should be understood in the sense that we first have to explore the character of the sexual division of labor in our contemporary society in order to be able to understand its general, anthropological, historical, and ethnological dimensions.

A Few Theses on the Sexual Division of Labor and Present Capitalism

In capitalist society the relation to nature is determined by the separation of social production into two fundamental areas: subsistence production and production of commodities. By "subsistence production" we understand all production for immediate survival, such as the manufacture of basic food for direct consumption, clothing, housing, and so on—in short, what nowadays we call "basic needs".

In all prior modes of production, subsistence production is at the same time social production, and vice versa. Only capitalism gives the impression that production can be independent from its basic purpose, namely the reproduction of life. Two parallel processes are at the basis of this false impression of independence: first, the subordination of subsistence production to the production of commodities, secondly (and through), its privatization, which leads to its social invisibility. The exclusive use of concepts like "production" and "labor" to analyze the production of commodities, especially in the centers of the capitalist world-system in Marxist as well as in so-called bourgeois theories, shows how far subsistence production has become forgotten, overlooked, denied, and rendered invisible. Today it therefore becomes necessary to stress over and over again that subsistence production never disappears, but only changes its character.

If we look at the different steps of the transformation of subsistence production in the last few decades, we can see certain differences between center and periphery—between the so-called First and Second Worlds, on the one hand, and the Third World, on the other. The paths of transformation, nevertheless, are becoming ever more convergent. In the Third World, alongside the subsistence production in the cities (which is done, as in the center, mainly by housewives, maids, and other women) there is peasant subsistence production in the countryside. Here, men and women together produce a large amount of their means of subsistence (food, housing, clothing) within the peasant household itself. However, this production for thier own consumption has for a long time already been combined with the production of commodities. One way of combining wage work and subsistence production, in an almost classical form, is the combination of cash crops and subsistence crops.[13]

For nearly a decade, however, there has been a steady decrease in the subsistence crop because of a process that has been considerably accelerated by development programs that provide credit to small farmers (Bennholdt-Thomsen, 1980; Payer, 1979; Dunham, 1982). Accompanying this has been a growing tendency for a sexual division of labor with men constituting and controlling the paid, monetarized part of the peasant economies, and women performing the unpaid jobs (Rogers, 1980). In other words, the modern housewife emerges even within the peasant household.

Subsistence production, however, does not disappear with this process; rather, it changes its character. What does disappear in this change is the substance of the subsistence production, meaning raw materials for food, for textiles, and for house construction, all of which must be acquired as commodities in ever-growing amounts. But the *preparation* of food, clothes, and housing for immediate consumption remains and becomes almost exclusively women's work. While this work is time consuming and must be performed daily, it nevertheless appears as unimportant, invisible, additional work.

The peasantry as a class does not disappear with this process either; rather, it changes into a class dependent on commodity production—both as producers for the market and as consumers.

At present, the sexual division of labor on a worldwide scale takes the following shape: In the capitalism of the center, the subsistence producers are nearly exclusively women, whereas in earlier periods *all* immediate producers were at the time subsistence producers. In the periphery, as food ceases to be the immediate aim of peasant production (because of the dependency on credit for the purchase of commodities on the market), the housewife emerges even in the peasant sector.

As social production is split up and subsistence production is allotted to women, the sexual division of labor receives a fundamentally new, hitherto unknown character: Namely, sex becomes the structuring element of the social division of labor. To put the point another way, in modern society, the sexual division of labor is not part of the social division of labor; rather, the social division of labor is sexual.

In the frame of a materialist approach, the social division of labor means the division of social production into major sectors: agriculture, industry, and commerce. Furthermore, it means the division into different classes, generally understood as the producing and merely consuming classes. Finally, it means the division into different branches, like the textile industry, the food industry, and the steel industry, which need different techniques and different skills and knowledge. In comparison to this, the division of production into subsistence production and commodity production is more general and also more fundamental because it includes the other aspects of the general division; therefore it represents the social division of labor in its more proper sense.[14] The thesis that sex becomes the structuring element of the social division of labor appears most plausible when the division into subsistence and commodity production and the relegation to the respective spheres of men and women have been acknowledged. What has to be clarified, then, is whether or not this principle applies to earlier forms of the sexual division of labor as well, that is, whether or not it is really historically as new as we maintain.

The specificity of the present form of the sexual division of labor, on the contrary, becomes even clearer when we compare it with other historical forms, such as the extreme separation of the sexes in some ethnic groups of Malaysia and South America, as described earlier, and the sexual parallelism of the Inca. In these cases there are almost two societies: a male and a female one. However, although they may be separated from each other or combined in a parallel form, men and women do nearly the same things. They both provide for their own food, live in separate housing, have separate property, enjoy sex-specific rights, and combine in different political organizations. Compared to this, men and women in our present society are more intimately linked, because they need each other—since there exists no commodity production without subsistence production and vice versa.

Seen from a social point of view, however, men and women in our society are much more distant from each other than ever before, because occupations today are divided into a hierarchy. The hierarchy is impenetrable in that the male ranking system is not open to women who do not have a ranking of their own. This situation has come to be called "asymmetric", but the term is much too weak for what it describes. The hierarchical relationship exists for women only in a negative way: Men form the society, women are non-society; men are the true human beings, women are "not human-beings"; or, to put it in another form, men are the true men, women are "not-men"; women are strangers in their own society; male labor is socially visible, female labor invisible. In short, women are not social "persons". All this is due to the transformation of subsistence production from being social production in earlier periods to being private nowadays, to its exclusive ascription to women, and to the assignment of one, single, female producer to one man.

　In the European Middle Ages, this was of course different. We cannot therefore call "sexual" the social division of labor of that time. It is true that most of the branches were divided into male and female occupations. For example, all phases of textile production were women's work, and so were those of the brewing of the beer, dairy work, the rearing of pigs and hens, and a great deal of field work. However men, as well as women, had to give their special, sexually defined services to the estate; and later, when the cities arose, both men and women were artisans, also separated according to the different types of handicraft. Female guilds existed, but mistresses skilled in craftwork were allowed to produce independently only once they were widowed. In the Middle Ages there were no equal rights for men and women; on the contrary, the men had the law on their side. Nevertheless, the hierarchy that today excludes women from society did not yet exist, because they did socially equal and equally recognized work. Quite contrary to the well-known thesis, the limitation of socially recognized female professional work did not stop with the Industrial Revolution; rather, it gathered force in this period, as is clear when we compare it to the Middle Ages (Wolf-Graaf, 1981: 11, 292-396). A crucial event for the loss of women's social identity seems to have been their loss of control over their ability to give birth, a loss that has been violently imposed upon them. Their position has grown steadily weaker as the typical female occupations cease to be organized under the control of women.

　A thesis that has already emerged in discussion about the strict separation of the sexes or the sexual parallelisms can now be stated more completely: The loss of society that women suffer with the development of industrial capitalism is not in the first place a loss of participation in male society, but rather a loss and a destruction of female society; it is the separation of women from each other, without their becoming part of the male society.

　How can women's work under capitalism be defined? The characterization of the wage worker as doubly free—free from the ownership of the means of production and free to sell his labor power—is obviously insufficient to account for women's work. Because women in our contemporary society are not primarily defined as bearers of labor power that they would be free to sell as a commodity, they rather represent with their whole person a capacity to work, a capacity that is treated as a natural resource for the reproduction of others. This characterization recalls the aforestated comparison to the caste situation: By *birth*, women are ascribed determined, specific tasks. The mechanism of this ascription can also be compared to the feudal attachment of the bonded laborer to the soil, in that women are similarly inseparable from their ability to give birth and are therefore bonded.[15] It is only on this basis that the female labor force becomes a commodity; but even then, the female worker remains marked in the sense of not being the master of herself.

At this point, the objection is commonly made that the housewife relationship is a remnant of pre-capitalist society, that the generalization of wage work and the way of transforming housework into so-called "social work" has not yet been accomplished, but finally that the growing external production of consumer goods in the factories and the mechanization of the household itself are already pointing in this direction. This argument is strongly countered by three important historical facts, which are outlined below.

1. The historical development of housewife production itself is a result of industrial capitalism, and never existed in this form before.

2. Already at the turn of the nineteenth century, it was supposed that housework would become superfluous because of the mechanization and external production of all its input, but in reality it has not been reduced since then. Tasks that have in fact been eliminated have been replaced by even more time-consuming activities (Ehrenreich & English, 1975).[16] In particular, requirements concerning cleanliness and the time consumed by looking after small children have been enormously augmented. One of the most enervating and energy-consuming tasks faced by mothers of little children is to protect them from the dangers of the mechanized and chemicized environment in the house and on the street.

3. As analyses of the relations of production in the Third World show, the generalization of wage work does not include women's work, and a variety of other male and female labor relations are also left out. On the contrary, we can observe an institutionalization of non-wage forms all over the world.[17]

We can finally sum up, then, that just as housewife production is not truly pre-capitalist, the sexual division of labor, which is based on the housewife, is not truly an historical remnant or even the dominant form throughout the history of mankind. It genuinely belongs to our capitalist mode of production. Both forms of work—that of the free labor force and that of the labor force bonded by its specifically female capacity for work—belong together and constitute the basis of all capitalist relations of production. The analysis of both forms together, however, cannot consist in merely adding to the existing body of knowledge, knowledge about female labor that was hitherto lacking. Rather, much more far-reaching theoretical consequences and tasks are involved, including the reconceptualization of the labor force as a commodity. Furthermore, new concepts of social class and stratification, as well as a more fundamental reconceptualization of exploitation and accumulation, are required. This surely is no easy enterprise. The crucial point of reference, at least, has been discovered when we recognize that the sexual division of labor is the turning point of all social activities and institutions based on them, because the sexual division of labor in capitalism is not a social one, but the social division of labor is a sexual one.

NOTES

1. The low payment of women and their employment in low-status occupations are legitimized on the grounds that their earnings are only an additional income to the wage of a husband, or that their work is only the unskilled and short-term work of young women (e.g., in world market factories), who because of their later marriage need no higher training.

2. The findings of Margaret Mead (1978) are especially illustrative for these questions. She compares seven ethnic groups of the South Pacific region according to the shape and expressions that the bodies of men and women have acquired on the basis of a certain sexual division of labor, and shows how the tasks performed and the approach towards work mold the male and female physique.

3. G. P. Murdock (1937) lists 46 activities among 224 "tribes", according to whether they are predominantly performed by men or by women. The data stem from research focusing on other questions and therefore cannot yield more far-reaching conclusions. Bearing heavy loads is an exclusively male activity in 12 cases, but exclusively female, however, in 57 cases; it is predominantly male in 6 and predominantly female in 20 cases, and performed equally by both sexes in 33 cases. Bronislaw Malinowski (1932) also points to the fact that women in so-called "primitive" societies do more and harder work than the men. This knowledge, however, does not disturb his biological assumptions at all, as he immediately proceeds to say, "Heavy work ought naturally to be performed by men; here the contrary obtains" (quoted in Rogers, 1980: 15).

4. The fact that long distances have to be traveled during gathering is even used by Ernestine Friedl as a reason for the low population growth in most gathering societies (1975: 16-17).

5. In Mbuti-pygmy societies the sexual division of labor barely exists; for instance, men and women care for babies and small children equally. From our perspective, we could say that they try to minimize the difference.

6. Critiques of Tiger (1969) from feminist perspectives can be found in Reed (1975) and in Martin and Voorhies (1975: 162-77). Authors with social biologist assumptions resembling Tiger's are E. P. Wilson, Robin Fox, R. Ardrey, D. Morris, and many others. A comprehensive critique of social biology is given by P. A. Green (1981).

7. In Mundruku society the sexes are physically and socially nearly totally separated from each other. In their rites, they are even antagonistically opposed. In Malekula society, each village is divided into two halves—one male and one female; men and women live in separate houses and seldom see each other (Baumann, 1980: 346).

8.

> According to the materialist conception, the determining factor in history is, in the last resort, production and reproduction of immediate life. But this itself is of a twofold character. On the one hand, the production of the means of subsistence, of food, clothing and shelter and the tools requisite therefore; on the other hand, reproduction

of human beings themselves, repropagation of the species. The social institutions under which men of a definite historical epoch and of a definite country life are conditioned by both kinds of production: by the stage of development of labour, on the one hand, and the family, on the other (Engels, 1972: 25-26).

He starts calling remultiplication of the species "production", but then, however, changes his approach immediately and does not consider it as work, putting it instead into the category of superstructure.

9. According to Engels, private property emerges out of social wealth, which is due to favorable natural conditions such as climate, growth of plants, and multiplication of herds. Nothing seems more normal and understandable to Engels than the desire here of the male herd owners to appropriate the surplus individually and to fix it as private property by means of inheritance to their own biological children. Karen Sacks (1975) correctly criticizes this approach, stating that persons do not spontaneously produce surplus, as Engels implies. She believes too that first a power structure must exist, which forces people to produce more than they need. Social wealth that becomes a surplus to be appropriated does not emerge out of natural conditions but presupposes an existing power relationship. As the findings of Martin and Voorhies show, Engels's sequential pattern has rather to be inverted. He sees higher productivity, social wealth, private appropriation, and paternal inheritance as following each other logically; also the importance of private property as a prime mover in human history seems to be far overestimated. Martin and Voorhies, on the contrary, show how lineal horticultural societies typically do not produce surplus but provide only as much food as is needed by their own clan group (Martin & Voorhies, 1975: 234).

10. Existing ethnographic material shows that Engels has by far overstressed the importance of maternal and paternal descent, since the same lines of descent can be combined with totally different social institutions. It seems more appropriate to analyze the sexual character of a given society according to a multitude of elements and not only or primarily according to the form of descent. Different tasks performed by men and women, on the contrary, will have to play a major role. What seems particularly lacking in Engels's analysis is the connection between a change in the order of descent and the change of the persons' attitude towards their products, namely a process of alienation when the products rise as strange and forceful powers against their producers. It seems evident that the process of objectification and alienation of human relations is related to whether the children belong to the mother or to the father; in true patriarchal societies, for example, products are no longer subordinate to persons but, instead, persons, as havers, are subordinate to products. To this same line of argument can be added Morgan's (1891) proof that the change from a maternal to a paternal descent in an evolutionary perspective means that the persons no longer count simply as human beings in a kinship group, but must belong to a given territory. Engels goes even further: "The sale of his children by the father—such was the first root of father right and monogamy" (1972: 111)! Engels seems unable to analyze the process of alienation that is included in this fact as an intrinsic part of the social structures thereafter. He is unable to do so because his concept of work uncritically includes alienation.

11. Exactly this aspect, namely the "perverting influence" that the inequality between the sexes imposes on all institutions of society, has been discussed by Engels's contemporary, the liberal bourgeois writer John Stuart Mill, in his pamphlet on the topic (first published in 1869), *The Subjection of Women* (1980).

12. This critique does not only apply just to the evolutionists. Ann Oakley tries to find out the extent to which sexual differences have been acknowledged in writings on crucial topics in sociology. Needless to say, the result has been extremely negative (Oakley, 1974).

13. At present, peasant production in the Third World can be divided into two types: subsistence crop and wage work on the one hand, and subsistence crop and cash crop on the

other, including their possible mixtures. That means that, besides regions that predominantly show one or another form (e.g., subsistence crop and migrant work in the southern part of Africa, and subsistence crop and cash crop in Mexico, Colombia and the Andean region), we can also find throughout the world all types combined with each other—subsistence crop, cash crop, and wage work.

14. Even if we use Durkheim's concept of the social division of labor (1968), which distinguishes between the different social fields of work and institutions such as politics, economics, and administration, the same principle would still apply, because subsistence production and commodity production also divide and include these fields.

15. The following discussion of slave work and serfdom by Marx applies equally to women's housework in capitalism:

> It is not the *unity* of living and active humanity with the natural, inorganic conditions of their metabolic exchange with nature, and hence their appropriation of nature, which requires explanation or is the result of a historic process, but rather the *separation* between these inorganic conditions of human existence and this active existence, a separation which is completely posited only in the relation of wage labour and capital. In the relations of slavery and serfdom this separation does not take place; rather, one part of society is treated by the other as itself merely an *inorganic and natural* condition of its own reproduction. The slave stands in no relation whatsoever to the objective conditions of his labour; rather, *labour* itself, both in the form of the slave and in that of the serf, is classified as *an inorganic condition* of production along with other natural beings, such as cattle, as an accessory of the earth. In other words: the original conditions of production appear as natural presuppositions, *natural conditions of the producer's existence* just as his living body, even though he reproduces and develops it, is originally not posited by himself, but appears as the *presupposition of his self*; his own (bodily) being is a natural presupposition, which he has not posited (Marx, 1974: 489-90).

16. A common argument against the characterization of all women as predominantly housewives is that class differences are thereby obscured, since, for instance, women of the upper strata leave the housework to servants. The economist John Kenneth Galbraith, however, gives a good empirical answer to this problem:

> With higher income the volume and diversity of consumption increase and therewith the number and complexity of the tasks of household management. The distribution of time between the various tasks associated with the household, children's education and entertainment, clothing, social life, and other forms of consumption becomes an increasingly complex and demanding affair. In consequence, and paradoxically, the manual role of the women becomes more arduous the higher the family income, save for the small fraction who still have paid servants (quoted in Lloyd, 1975: 6).

17. See, for example, the research of the Working Group of Bielefeld Sociologists of Development on this topic, and their contributions to this volume.

REFERENCES

Baumann, Hermann (1980). *Das Doppelte Geschlecht: Ethnologische Studien zur Bisexualität in Ritus und Mythos*. Berlin: Reimer.
Becker, Gabriele et al. (1980). *Aus der Zeit der Verzweiflung*. Frankfurt: Suhrkamp.
Benitéz, Fernando (1972). *Los Indios de Mexico*, Vol. I. Mexico City: Biblioteca ERA.
Bennholdt-Thomsen, Veronika (1980). "Investition in die Armen: Zur Entwicklungspolitik der Weltbank," in V. Bennholdt-Thomsen, ed., *Lateinamerika: Analysen und Berichte*, Bd. 4. Berlin: Olle & Wolter, 74-96.

Bock, Gisela & Duden, Barbara (1977). "Arbeit aus Liebe—Liebe als Arbeit: Zur Enstehung der Hausarbeit im Kapitalismus," in Dokumentationsgruppe der Berliner Sommeruniversität für Frauen 1976, ed., *Frauen und Wissenschaft*. Berlin: Courage, 118-99.

Boserup, Ester (1970). *Women's Role in Economic Development*. London: Allen & Unwin.

Buckley, Mary (1981). "Women in the Soviet Union," *Feminist Review*, No. 8, 79-106.

Dunham, David (1982). "On the History and Political Economy of Small-Farmer Policy," *CEPAL Review*, Aug.

Durkheim, Emile (1968). *The Division of Labor in Society*. New York: Free Press.

Ehrenreich, Barbara & English, Deirdre (1975). "The Manufacture of Housework," *Socialist Revolution*, No. 26 (V, 4), Oct.-Dec., 5-40.

Engels, Friedrich (1970). "Anteil der Arbeit an der Menschwerdung des Affen," *Marx/Engels Ausgewählte Schriften II*. Berlin: Dietz 68-79.

Engels, Friedrich (1972). *The Origin of the Family, Private Property and the State*. New York: Pathfinder.

Etienne, Mona & Leacock, Eleanor (1980). *Women and Colonialization: Anthropological Perspectives*. New York: Praeger.

Fisher, Elizabeth (1979). *Women's Creation*. New York: Anchor.

Friedl, Ernestine (1975). *Women and Men: An Anthropologist's View*. New York: Holt, Rinehart & Winston.

Gerhard, Ute (1978). *Verhältnisse und Verhinderungen: Frauenarbeit, Familie und Recht der Frauen im 19. Jahrhundert*. Frankfurt: Suhrkamp.

Godelier, Maurice (1981). "The Origins of Male Domination," *New Left Review*. No. 127, May-June, 3-17.

Gordon, Linda (1977). *Woman's Body, Woman's Right*. Harmondsworth, England: Penguin.

Green, Phillip A. (1981). *The Pursuit of Inequality*. Oxford: Martin Robertson.

Hausen, Karin (1976). "Die Polarisierung der 'Geschectscharaktere'—Eine Spiegelung der Dissoziation von Erwerbs—und Familienleben," in W. Conze, ed., *Sozialgeschichte der Familie in der Neuzeit Europas*, Industrielle Welt, 21. Stuttgart: Hain, A/VVA, 363-93.

Heinrichs, Hans-Jurgen, ed. (1975). *Materialien zu Bachofens "Das Mutterrecht"*. Frankfurt: Suhrkamp.

Heinsohn, Gunnar, Knieper, Rolf & Steiger, Otto (1979). *Menschenproduktion: Allgemeine Bevölkerungslehre der Neuzeit*. Frankfurt: Suhrkamp.

Honegger, Claudia, ed. (1979). *Die Hexen der Neuzeit*. Frankfurt: Suhrkamp.

Joosten, Andrea (1980). *Mann, Marx spricht nicht über Hausarbeit*. Berlin: AHDE.

Kittler, Gertraude (1980). *Hausarbeit: Zur Geschichte einer "Natur-Ressource"*. München: Frauenoffensive.

Kontos, Silvia (1979). *Die Partei kämpft wie ein Mann*. Frankfurt: Roter Stern.

Kontos, Silvia & Walser, Karin (1978). "Überiegungen zu einer feministischen Theorie der Hausarbeit," *Alternative*, XXI, 120-21, 152-59.

Leacock, Eleanor (1977). "Women in Egalitarian Scoeities," in R. Bridenthal & C. Koonz, eds., *Women in European History*. Boston: Houghton Mifflin, 11-35.

Lefèbvre, Henri (1966). *Der dialektische Materialismus*. Frankfurt: Suhrkamp.

Leukert, Roswitha (1976). "Weibliche Sinnlichkeit," unpubl. Diplomarbeit, Univ. Frankfurt.

Lloyd, Cynthia B. (1975). "The Division of Labor between the Sexes," in C. B. Lloyd, ed., *Sex, Discrimination and the Division of Labor*. New York: Columbia Univ. Press, 1-24.

Loufti, Martha (1980). *Northern Women and the New International Economic Order*. Washington, DC: UNDP Division of Information.

Malinowski, Bronislaw (1932). *The Sexual Life of Savages*. London.

Martin, M. Kay & Voorhies, Barbara (1975). *Female of the Species*. New York: Columbia Univ. Press.

Marx, Karl (1966). *Pariser Manuscripte*. Berlin: Rowohlt.

Marx, Karl (1967). *Capital*, Vol. I. New York: International Publishers.

Marx, Karl (1974). *Grundrisse: Introduction to the Critique of Political Economy*. New York: Vintage.

Marx, Karl & Engels, Freidrich (1971). *Die Deutsche Ideologie*. Frankfurt: Suhrkamp.

Mead, Margaret (1978). *Male and Female: A Study of the Sexes in a Changing World*. Harmondsworth, England: Penguin.

Mies, Maria (1981). *The Social Origin of the Sexual Division of Labour*, I.S.S. Occasional Papers, No, 85. The Hague: Institute of Social Studies.

Mill, John Stuart (1980). *The Subjection of Women*. Arlington Heights, IL: Crofts Classics.

Morgan, Lewis Henry (1891). *Ancient Society, or Researches in the Lines of Human Progress from Slavery, through Barbarism to Civilization*. London.

Moroney, J. R. (1979). "Do Women Earn Less under Capitalism?" *The Economic Journal*, LXXXIX, 355, 601-13.

Murdock, George P. (1937). "Comparative Data on the Division of Labor by Sex," *Social Forces*, XV, 4, May, 551-53.

Murphy, Yolanda & Murphy, Robert F. (1974). *Women of the Forest*. New York: Columbia Univ. Press.

Oakley, Ann (1974). *The Sociology of Housework*. New York: Pantheon.

Payer, Cheryl (1979). *The World Bank and the Small Farmer*. Zürich/Rome: Rome Declaration Group.

Reed, Evelyn (1975). *Women's Evolution from Matriarchal Clan to Patriarchal Family*. New York: Pathfinder.

Reiter, Rayna, ed. (1975). *Toward an Anthropology of Women*. New York: Monthly Review Press.

Reiter, Rayna (1977). "The Search for Origins: Unraveling the Threads of Gender Hierarchy," *Critique of Anthropology*, III, 9/10, 5-24.

Rogers, Barbara (1980). *The Domestication of Women: Discrimination in Developing Societies*. New York: St. Martin's Press.

Sacks, Karen (1975). "Engels Revisited: Women, the Organization of Production and Private Property," in R. Reiter, ed., *Toward an Anthropology of Women*. New York: Monthly Review Press, 211-34.

Schmidt, Alfred (1962). *Der Begriff der Natur in der Lehre von Karl Marx*. Frankfurt: Europäische Verlaganstalt.

Silverblatt, Irene (1980). "The Universe Turned inside Out .... There Is No Justice for Us Here: Andean Women under Spanish Rule," In M. Etienne & E. Leacock, eds., *Women and Colonialization: Anthropoligical Perspectives*. New York: Praeger, 149-85.

Tiger, Lionel (1969). *Men in Groups*. New York: Random House.

Turnbull, Colin (1965). *Wayward Servants*. Garden City, NY: Natural History Press.

Wallerstein, Immanuel (1974). "The Rise and Future Demise of the World Capitalist System: Concepts from for Comparative Analysis," *Comparative Studies in Society and History*, XVI, 4, Sept., 387-415.

Webster, Paula (1975). "Matriarchy: A Vision of Power," in R. Reiter, ed., *Toward an Anthropology of Women*. New York: Monthly Review Press, 141-56.

Werlhof, Claudia von (1981). "Frauen und Dritte Welt als 'Natur' des Kapitals: Oder Ökonomie auf die Füsse gestellt," in H. Dauber & V. Simpfendorfer, eds., *Eigener Haushalt und bewohnter Erdkreis*. Wuppertal: Petra Hammer, 187-215.

Wolf-Graaf, Anke (1981). *Frauenarbeit im Abseits: Frauenbewegung und weibliches Arbeitsvermogen*. München: Frauenoffensive.

17

CONFLICTS INSIDE AND OUTSIDE THE HOUSEHOLD
A West African Case Study

Georg Elwert

Sociology of Development Research Center
University of Bielefeld

Why Focus on Conflict?

Along with common sense, traditional sociology, anthropology, and economics typically fail to consider conflicting, contradictory elements in the phenomena they study. Furthermore, when conflicts and contradictions do come under analysis in these fields, they are frequently presented as merely superficial, contingent aberrations of more basic, consistent deep structures. There are, of course, exceptions, e.g., Marx's work. But today even many Marxists seem content to explain away conflict and contradiction, following "common" sense, in the name of Marxist structuralism.

I shall try the opposite approach here: first, I shall analyze a community by focusing on the *conflicts* that exist there, and then by determining which institutions within the community serve as a frame, so to speak, and hold the opposing elements together.[1] This approach runs counter to the conventional one, which would base its description and analysis on institutions defined by superstructural thinking or on a projected framework of basic structures, and only then define conflicts on this basis. Thus, conflicts seem to be just disturbances of a basic, rigid scheme. Instead, they are seen here as channeled ways of exacting contradictions and the institutions as frameworks for clamping together diverging subsystems and groups with opposing interests within a society.[2] This methodology is, of course, not identical to its implementation in fieldwork.[3]

I shall use the following description to show that relevant parts of history can be fruitfully interpreted as processes of containment and breaking out

of conflicts—of the creation of institutions that channel the staging of conflicts or that clamp opposing parties together, and of the frailty of those
institutions. I concentrate on household-history, rather than on slave trade
or agriculture (as I have done elsewhere), because household-history is particularly thrilling: A major part of the female (and male) labor force is active
in this realm, and the conflicts over the allocation of human and material
resources in this realm are in a particular way related to global societal
conflicts. The witch hunt of the 1970's, for instance, was a national political
event in Bénin; yet it had its roots within the conflict-ridden households.
Then, too, there are interrelations of the world-system and the household,
which are essentially conditioned by international processes. For instance,
the demographic expansion of the past 90 years was generated through international economic and political transformations, the effects of which, of
course, touched the very institutions—including the household—that are
responsible for physical reproduction on the level of the village.

A History of the Ayizo "Household": Introduction

The Ayizo live in the former rain-forest belt of southern Bénin. They
make their living from a combination of agriculture (maize, cassava, and
beans) with the slash-and-burn technique (swidden agriculture) and hunting and gathering (which has been rapidly decreasing in the last 50 years).
In precolonial times they were more or less under the authority of the
kingdom of *danxomè*, which recruited the male youth to a *corvée*-type
military service for their slave raids. The dominant ethnic group of this
kingdom were the Fon. It should be clear, in what follows, why we have
chosen for study the "household-history" of the Ayizo[4] in the *République
Populaire du Bénin* (formerly Dahomey/West Africa)—a history that seems
to be just a history of conflicts.

There is no social structure in Ayizo society that falls neatly under the
common concept of household (compare the definition in Research Working Group on Households and Production Processes [1978]). There is *no*
pooling of property in the relation between a married couple, even though
there is a co-residential unit called *adòtaa* (fireplace) or *xwé* (house). Since
these terms also denote smaller patrilineal kinship groups, one has to add
on many occasions whether one includes married women; *xwé* is rather used
to denote a patrilineal lineage and *adòtaa* for a nuclear family, but neither
usage is exclusive. Still, the *adòtaa* (whose name we will translate roughly
by "household") is not a "unit of consumption and production of the labor
force" (Research Working Group on Households and Production Processes,
1978: 5). The reproduction of the labor force and its maintenance in times

of crisis depend on several overlapping networks of provision of goods and services, without which no stable reproduction would be possible (Elwert, 1980). In a year of average harvest a third of the households depend upon transfers from these networks in order to secure reproduction.[5]

The Ayizo are basically patrilineal (Elwert, 1982); they are also viri-patri-local. This means that kinship groups are reckoned according to the father's line, and that a woman has to move to her husband's house; the husband lives close to his father's house and works his land (which he will later inherit together with his brothers and—potentially—his sisters). Even after marriage women are still considered members of their lineage of origin. After her husband's death (or even when her children have grown up) a woman typically will return to "her" lineage, where she will get great respect as an old patrilineal aunt by the children of her brothers and patrilineal cousins, for these children are "her" children—children under her authority. The children she bears "to her husband" belong to his lineage, and even if, after a divorce, she keeps her younger children with her, she will have to return them to the father or to his close kin at the age of about six. Within what we would tend to see as a household, a woman will keep her property, and she may acquire new things through production on her own account.

There are obligations of reciprocity inside the lineage (Elwert, 1980): A man must share "his" property with his brothers and sisters, and a married woman must share "hers" with her brothers and sisters too, although they will seldom come to the place where she lives. Her husband, however, is not entitled to her property, and may not even use one of her knives without asking. (If one of her knives turned up missing, for instance, she would suspect that a brother, not her husband, had taken it or borrowed it.) If she sat in the village market selling soup and her husband wanted to taste some then and there, he would have to pay for it, for to give it free would be a public (quasi-obscene) signal that she wanted to sleep with him that night. At home, however, the cooking of soup with foodstuffs provided by her husband and spices provided by her for the consumption of the entire family is part of a woman's obligations.

Although most males are not actually polygamous, all may be potentially. The different wives of a polygamous man constitute several separate little households within one great household. But they do not share property, and, while they may have a relation of solidarity with each other, there might also be hatred.

A household in the larger sense of a group who eat together from the same fireplace and from the same granaries[6] potentially comprises more than just the man, his wife, and their children. For instance, it also comprises the younger unmarried brothers and sisters, if the man is the oldest living person among brothers or patrilineal cousins. Within this configuration three types of major conflicts emerge:

(a) conflicts between elder brothers and younger brothers,
(b) conflicts between husbands and wives (and between the kin group of each), and
(c) conflicts between co-wives (and between siblings from different mothers who were co-wives).

Conflicts between brothers and between co-wives[7] or their children are conflicts within the same house, and so they are dealt with routinely by a lineage head or houselord, who is the husband of the women in conflict.

A major source of social dynamics has been the husband/wife conflict, which occurs outside the household (in its basic sense) and is a political conflict involving two lineages, not just two persons. It should be noted that the Ayizo were, in spite of the loose domination by the Fon (the other ethnic group in the region), basically acephalous; there is no authority above the lineage.

The history of the Ayizo witnesses a continuous effort to *depoliticize* this alliance/conflict so as to bring it into the limits of the household;[8] that, of course, entails widening the limits of the *àdòtaa* in its strict sense in order to create something corresponding to a household in the more recognized sense. Except for a few cases of migrants to the town (and even these cases are doubtful), this effort failed due to the preservation of the separated ownership (*Gütertrennung*) within the household, the basis of women's independence.

1. What Can We Learn from Genealogies?

Until the colonial transformation the chances for reproduction cum procreation within a single dwelling are extremely unequally distributed, because the younger brothers tended to remain unmarried for a long time and thus to stay part of their elder brother's household. This inequality inside the "unit of reproduction" shall concern us here.

The number of children a male can have has depended for the last two centuries essentially upon his social status as elder or younger brother, as an analysis of genealogies bears out. The genealogies of the lineages are highly reliable,[9] and there are several possibilities for cross-checking the information contained in them. They give us, for instance, information about matrilineal descent (which is relevant for an institution to be dealt with later), from which we can easily extract information about the numbers of wives and children of a man. We can also extract information about approximate ages of various persons at someone's birth, since there is a ranking according to age and regular distance between births.

It is important here to compare the number of children of the eldest brother of a given group of brothers from the same father with the number of children of the other younger brothers. For example, going back to Saa Ahano, the founder of the quarter analyzed here, we see a typical pattern of the period. He was a younger brother and he had two sons at his birthplace. Sometime subsequent to the birth of his son's children and after a conflict with his own brother, Saa Ahano moved to a place in the wood and founded the new quarter of Hannya. In the three generations after Saa all the men who were the firstborn sons (i.e., the eldest brother) had significantly more children than did the later-born sons, as Table 17.1 shows.

This pattern changed with the following generation. In a sample of 18 brothers of four different minimal lineages born in the years between 1891 and 1929, the four eldest brothers had an average of 5.5 children, and the 14 younger brothers had an average of 3.4 children. The distinction between the number of children of first and later-born sons is still statistically significant,[10] but it is much less marked. Recently, the difference in the number of children born to older and younger brothers has tended to disappear.

These data, together with testimony from the oral tradition and observation of current practices of obligation within the kin-group, leads us to the conclusion that the eldest brother was the one who was married preferentially and who had a preferential right to food for his children (the better or worse feeding of children was a means of population control). Moreover, the younger brothers had to work for their older brother, and the number of offspring thus produced had to be in balance with the surface of land that could be cultivated.[11]

Since the village was at this time a clear island within the wood, the basic problem was to open up enough land, and clearing huge tropical trees using only axes of local African steel was very difficult and required a great deal of trained, male labor power. Only when enough land was cleared were the younger brothers allowed to marry and produce offspring. The maintenance of this and other inequalities required a control of the younger brothers by the eldest that was difficult to retain, especially once their common father had died.

In fact, there are stories of brothers who became impatient with their unmarried situation and their submission to the elder brother's authority over them, and even some stories of brothers who left the village to establish their family somewhere else.

During the precolonial period there was yet another interest in this authority relation: Strict control over young males was most helpful in the organization of defenses against slave raiders.

TABLE 17.1   Procreation of Eldest Brother and Younger Brothers

	Children of Younger Brothers		
Children of Eldest Brother	$\bar{x}$	Ratio of children to fathers	Variation
First generation=(8 sons*)	(4 sons*)		
Second generation=26	5.20	52:10	3-8
Third generation=20	2.57	36:14	0-7

*The number of daughters is uncertain for this generation.

This control over younger brothers was maintained with the help of two institutions. The first was the strict respect of the Ayizo for seniority. A kinship group's male head would always be the oldest male person, and the corresponding female head would be the lineage's oldest woman. Inside each group—even the children's play group—authority would also be organized according to age; everyone would know who was the *mexó* (oldest one) of the group. The neighboring Fon, much in contrast, have various lineage leaders both male and female, who are chosen by the ancestors through the "oracle", that is, through a disguised election. For the Ayizo we might speak about the *mexó* principle of social organization, impressive remnants of which can still be observed. The strength of the institutions associated with the *mexó* principle can be understood only in terms of the clamping together of the older/younger contradiction.

The second institution contributing to the mastery of the eldest was the mode of exchange of women between lineages, which was arranged by the eldest—the leading people of each lineage—and not on the basis of a bride-wealth system, which did not appear among the Ayizo until the beginning of this century. According to this instruction,[12] a young girl would be sent from one lineage for marriage in another only if another girl was to be sent back to the first. Most common were exchanges of sisters and daughters for brides. These exchanges might be more involved: For instance, a first lineage could send a bride to a second, which would then send a girl to a third lineage, which, in turn, would offer one of their young for marriage within the first lineage. Considerable time, up to a generation in exceptional cases, might elapse before a particularly convoluted exchange would be completed, achieving a balance. The important feature, though, of this institution was that these agreements for exchange were valid only if they were concluded between the lineage elders, upon whom young men were therefore most dependent. Household organization in Ayizo society, then, differs considerably from the more conventional model of the "household" alluded to above, according to which the household is an income-pooling unit securing the reproduction of the labor force. Among the Ayizo, both home (*xwé*) and household (*àdòtaa*) involve some pooling of the means of subsistence. But this pooling does not necessarily imply that all of its members are equally reproduced, either in the sense of individual reproduction (e.g., some children do not survive), or in the sense of procreative reproduction (e.g., males are not entitled to have children). Inside the households, then, there is a significant conflict over the allocation of the means of reproduction.

2. Technology with Politics and the New Reproductive Pattern

Demographic growth in West Africa has not been an even process. The people themselves recall a rather sudden break-through at the end of the last century, which they attribute mostly to the changed relations of reproduction "inside the house" and to technologial changes. I shall argue here that these changes can be understood only if we see them together with transformations in the world-system that caused a strengthening of the monopoly of coercion and enabled an expansion of trade inside the then French colony, Dahomey.

After 1890 the reproductive pattern changed: All brothers obtained equal access to women, and the numbers of children increased. Three technological and political developments occurring near the turn of the century were largely responsible:

(A) About this time, new trade brought the importation of axes made of European steel that were more efficient, enabling one to cut a tree in three-quarters to one-half the time needed before and lasting twice as long. This development considerably reduced the time and number of people needed to clear the wood, and also reduced the time needed to clear the bush of fallow land.

(B) As the *pax gallica* wrought by French colonial rule furthered the expansion of trade, a new type of pottery, much thinner than the older types, was imported from distant regions. Because this pottery considerably reduced the time and the firewood needed for cooking, women's work (cooking and fetching firewood) became much more efficient, and the pattern of meals changed: Now they were often cooked twice a day instead of once a day or once for two days, as before. This particular change is still an important part of old people's reminiscences. Just as the new axes reduced the amount of work time needed for the reproduction of a person, so did the new pottery.

(C) Since the end of the First World War, the Ayizo have been building huts of clay, as the neighboring Fon had done for centuries. The Ayizo had previously lived in huts of wood and bark, so that if enemies (e.g., slave hunters) should enter the village, one could flee immediately in any direction, simply breaking the wall of bark and running off. Together with other cultural elements, this building pattern formed a "culture of flight". (For example, young men were taught not to sit on their behinds; they always had to squat in a starting position.) The *pax gallica* made this culture of flight superfluous for the Ayizo; as the dominating people, the Fon never had this culture. The houses of clay have a very important advantage for the household: They moderate the fluctuations of temperature (Kinley, 1977). At noon it is cooler inside than outside, and in the night the warmth is retained. The latter fact is most important, since the cold causes a lot of respiratory diseases (e.g., pneumonia in the Harmattan Period), which are responsible for a part of children's mortality; and reduced infant mortality means higher efficiency for reproduction.

All three factors, then, combined to reduce the amount of labor needed to reproduce offspring, increasing the number of children who could be supported, so that from 1890 on the younger brothers had almost as many children as the eldest.[13] With these developments, even younger brothers could marry at an age of 35 or younger and have more than one wife; concommittantly, the age of marriage decreased for women, and it decreases still. Previously, a woman could marry only when she had large and strong shoulders (i.e., around the age of 21-25), which were not only a feature of beauty but also a sign of working capability. Now they marry earlier, at 16 to 18, "close to the start of fertility" as old women complain. The declining age of marriage (30 for today's peasant "boys") is offered as the reason for the decline in the age of circumcision (only for men), from 18 to 6 years. Although the effect of the wars deeply influenced the demographic pyramid (see Figure 17.1), there has been, from 1926 on, a marked general increase in population.

3. Conflicts around the Exchange of Women

Not only is an understanding of the conflicts arising from the custom of exchanging brides important to understanding the dominance of the eldest among the Ayizo; it is also important for the understanding of the peculiar ways they solve problems or postpone them in the form of "hidden conflicts", through the institution of the "insult dance", or by the creation of new types of marriage relations.

We have already described the women's exchange, but it goes without saying that this was not a conflict-free institution.

As we described in a previous section, the basic idea of bridal exchange is that a lineage receives a nuptial woman as wife for one of its adult young

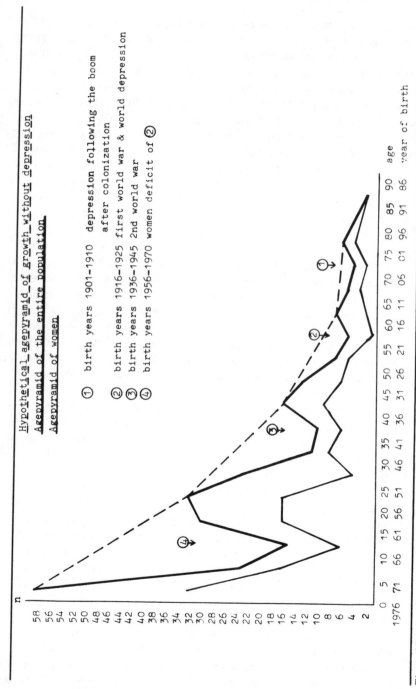

Figure 17.1 Demographic Pyramid

men if the lineage gives one of its daughters away for marriage. Of course this institution is riddled with conflicts. At first blush it might appear that the people coming together in these arranged marriages would not feel particularly happy. In fact, however, we found no report of partners refusing each other, though this is of course no proof of marital happiness. Some of the stories told for amusement may have indirectly indicated that in some cases the women reacted violently against the idea of marrying someone they did not love. Then, too, in most cases marriage forces a woman to leave her place of birth, making it more difficult for her to compensate for a troubled marriage by availing herself of the usual support networks. It must be pointed out, though, that because bridal exchange might be deferred in time or might involve a whole series of brides (see above) there is some flexibility in the determination of where and to whom a woman could be sent, which leaves room for preferences and aversions to influence the choice.

A variety of practices helps to reduce the friction between partners: the separation of spheres of action (i.e., the separation of tasks); the pre-established regulation of mutual obligations; the customary avoidance of overly close contact during the day; and last, but not least, the strict separation of property in the household.

The husband is required to provide the house, the cloth, the staple food, and the meat. The wife provides the oil, greens and spices, firewood, and water. He works in the fields and "helps" his wife, and she works on the plot cultivating vegetables and the spices, takes care of the children, and "helps" her husband in the field. But one can often see a man carrying a baby while his wife does some work that the burden of a baby might hinder, and one often sees women together with men in the fields. For example, neither sowing nor harvesting could be done without the work of wives; the notion of obligation indicates who controls the organization of work in a given sphere, but does not automatically exclude the help of kin and spouse of the opposite sex.[14]

In principle, both sexes may own the same type of things, but, due to their obligations, men tend to own fields, houses, and instruments for farmwork, whereas women tend to own kitchen utensils and instruments for the crafts. Anyway, this property is strictly separated between husband and wife.

Close patrilineal kin have a right of usufruct for their kin's belongings, but the husband has virtually no right of usufruct over his wife's belongings. Fields held in common by a minimal lineage or an extended family are considered the father's property even after his death, but only the huts for worship and the woods, part of which are holy too, are the property of the lineage. A wife has some rights: She receives a plot of whatever size she wishes for gardening and production on her own account (the size being limited only by the amount of time she has at her disposal); she has use of the house, and she may collect wild fruits and leaves in those non-sacred parts of the woods belonging to her husband's lineage.

A man or a woman may talk, tease, or joke with other women or men, but between husband and wife communication during the day should be restricted by accepted custom to the exchange of practical information. The restrictions upon chattering and joking apply as a general rule to all possible mating partners. Erotic behavior and sexuality are restricted to the night, and since husbands and wives are possible intercourse partners they are expected to respect the customary avoidance of everything that looks like a prelude to sex during the day.

Sex for itself is rarely a reason for conflict, because sexuality is not overloaded, as it is in European society, with expectations of warmth, relief of isolation, and compensation of all kinds of frustrations, which are focused on sex in Europe, and which give the double image of an over-sexed Europe and an overloaded sexuality. Sexuality in Ayizo socialization has an entirely different character; it is a joyful natural play. Children from the age of two to three start to play sex, and, according to my informants, it is their favorite game. Even the smallest ones try to have intercourse as they observe their older playmates. A year or so later they succeed with penetration or partial penetration, and they enjoy it (with erection of penis and clitoris), though they must avoid being seen by adults, who will laugh about them. Children must stop this play when they reach fertility (first ejaculation/first menstruation), and from then on they must keep "virginity".[15] This socialization process produces much less obsession with sexuality as compared to European society.

Sex is a reason of conflict only when adulterous. One speaks about adultery not only when a couple has sex, but also when a married or promised woman moves to a man's house (even if they have not had intercourse). The taking of a woman without any reciprocity towards those to whom she is linked (through her lineage of origin and husband's lineage) makes adultery synonymous with theft.

The strongest pressure upon the marital partners to keep their relation stable comes from the lineage. The reason for this pressure is the fear of a "zipper effect": If one woman goes home (by her own will or sent by the husband's family—the latter case being almost hypothetical), then the woman given in exchange for her must go home too. And if other families are also implicated in this exchange of women, each exchange reversed has another exchange reversed as a consequence. "A drama for all sides!" our informants insisted. It is not only a drama in the economic sense of a family losing an agent of reproduction and procreation, though, but also a hard blow because of all the emotional links that had been established with time. "Think of the children who lost their mother," said my informants. Understandably, members of a lineage use all the means of coercion at their disposal to avoid such a break-up.

At first glance, the lineages of the so-called "segmentary tribes" look as if they could split away from each other, raising the question of what will guarantee the stability of the bridal exchange circles if not the integrity of the lineages. In fact, unilaterial kinship systems are never as restrictive as in anthropological textbooks. The Ayizo—at least those of Ayu-Hannya we studied—also have a matrilineal institution of *vivuu* which distinguishes people of matrilineal descent stemming from the lineages of Hannya. If one's mother, father's mother, and father's father's mother came from a lineage of Hannya, then one is a *vivuu* to the Hannya people. These people meet every second year at Hannya at the ceremonial offering for the common ancestors, where they greet their kin from Hannya in a special ceremonial way and dine together. This ritual is restricted to the ceremonial greeting, the offer/dinner, and a short prayer, and it requires no other duties. Of course, the presence of these people and the special way they greet their matrilineal kin provide a source of major amusement, and the occasion reminds all the *vivuu* of their common links and alliance. Most relevant for our purposes is that this is a rare occasion when old people of lineages and sub-lineages in conflict can meet and settle issues.

4. Inherited, Hidden Conflicts

A male learns even as a child that he must respect many rules of avoidance. For instance, he must avoid going to certain places for reasons that will be revealed only when he has reached the age of 30. Although his elders—persons of authority of both sexes—try to withhold this information from him as long as possible, they would never take their knowledge with them to the grave, because these avoidances are based on conflicts that the young man has inherited from his ancestors. These hidden, inherited conflicts come from three sources:

(a) from troubled marital alliances and other failed alliances;
(b) from disputes over field limits; and
(c) from public insults.

Of the three types of hidden conflicts, those related to marriage are the most common; actually, most public insults are prompted by arguments about marriage. Field-limit conflicts, public-insult conflicts, are less common.[16]

Marital-alliance conflicts can have any of several causes: Sometimes the reciprocal sending of a daughter or sister is refused; a woman may leave her husband in order to join another one; or a man may treat his wife badly. All these cases should be brought to the "court"—a public meeting of the elders of both sexes from both of the lineages concerned, who try to settle the dispute. (Remember that a man who misbehaves against his wife or a woman who misbehaves against her husband, offends *another* lineage.) Contrary to the premise of old-fashioned functionalism, these courts do not always succeed. Furthermore, there is no superior institution that can mediate in case of non-agreement within a single court (unless both parties in the dispute belong to the same maxi-lineage), nor is there an absolute standard of harmony to be fulfilled immediately. In the case of non-agreement, both lineages mutually refuse any solidarity and stop marriage alliances; they may even threaten each other with poison, black magic, and witchcraft. Such threats, together with the risk that flirtation might end in an "impossible" alliance with the enemy who might seize this opportunity to harm the other side, are the basic reasons one has to avoid going to the quarter where the hidden enemy lives. And, because public mention of the conflict would constitute a heavy insult, thus escalating the conflict, young people are informed about the reason for the avoidances only when they are thought capable of controlling their tongues.[17]

People have to live with the conflict and, in order to avoid its proliferation, avoidance of the other side and secrecy from the less controlled youngsters is the rule.

If, in spite of her elders interdiction, a girl marries into an enemy lineage, her lineage declines, through ceremony, any responsibility for her fate. Any relations of assistance to her will end; "one will brush the dust behind her" (in the words of the ceremony's name) to sweep away even the footprints from the path she trod.

When the hidden conflicts and avoidances accumulate to such an extent that the number of possible marriages decreases noticeably, and the circulation between the hamlets constituting the village becomes difficult, the elders of several lineages seize the occasion of a ritual meeting, the *asentaa* festival held every second year, to settle the underlying disputes without requiring compensation and without declaring someone's guilt, just by making some offerings to the ancestors and of the quarreling lineages and making a public declaration that the conflict is over.

5. An Alternative Channel for Conflicts: The Insult Dance

The only alternative to the practice of hidden conflicts is the insult dance, an organized meeting with a drummer-band and singer in which one or several of the singers perform an opera-like performance and try to ridicule and insult the opposing party (which is also present). The other side can organize an insult dance too; thus both sides wage a war of songs.

Ideally, this alternative precludes the use of weapons, but some informants objected that for the last decades these meetings broadened and aggravated conflicts. Still, the insult dance is not just another conflict or way of acting out conflicts, but constitutes a channeling of conflicts (as do the avoidances). The channeling of conflicts through their containment is prescripted tracks is a powerful means of inhibiting the disruption of social relations. Thus channeled, conflicts become foreseeable and calculable, and they have defined limits, so there are fewer open conflicts.

6. Commodification and the Women's Revolution

The most visible effect of the world wide expansion of commodity economy in West Africa has been the rise of trading by women. This socio-economic phenomenon is still considered by males to be the major reason of social conflicts, the latest consequence being—according to them—the anti-female bias of the recent anti-witch movement.

Before the growth of the palm oil trade, which began with the reforms of King Gezo (about 1850) and rapidly expanded after the French conquest of 1894, there was scarcely any commodity exchange among and with the Ayizo.[18]

In this period young men had to suffer from the outside exploitation of the Dahomean kings, who recruited them every year for military service in the dry period, when there was less work on the fields. The exhausting labor required to swidden the fields (i.e., to slash and to burn weeds, stumps, and trees) fell largely upon the men. Women's work was somewhat less cyclical; theirs were continuous hard duties of which the most difficult were the fetching of water from the distant well, the pounding of oil-fruits, and the grinding of grains.

Together with the problems of outside exploitation and heavy labor, the uncertainties of weather and health comprised the major material problems that dominated the people's consciousness. So economic solidarity was very important to balance the possible risks, but solidarity was and is more available to males (Elwert, 1982). Because they live among the people with whom they have grown up, men have many more ties than do most of the wives, who typically came into a household only through marriage. This is not true of all women, since unmarried women and old women live on their birthplace together with the peer groups and have long-established ties to the place where they live. So it is not patrilineality, but the patri-virilocality, that constitutes a problem for wives, being more socially isolated than their husbands.

However, the problem faced by wives becomes an advantage with the advent of market economy. It is difficult to accumulate or even to run the accounts for one's own business when everyone around has a right of usufruct and may share for immediate consumption needs what one stores in excess. That is the case for males and for those women who stay with their own lineage, but wives staying in another lineage are mostly relieved from such claims. Theoretically, the claims still existed, but since the wives' kin cannot reach them easily, engagement in trade and crafts is much easier and more profitable for them.

Trade in food crops and craft production destined for the market (palm oil, soap, basketry, raphia cloth, and cooked and fried food) became, as in most parts of West Africa, the women's realm, and the basis for the development of a class of female merchant capitalists in those places where commodity circulation was the greatest.

Since the Ayizo villages are far from the great central markets, there has been no chance for women to gain the capitalist position of a "mammy" (as called in West Africa's English), but they could acquire some wealth and a strong independent position in petty trade and/or petty commodity production. These acquisitions meant the following gains for women:

(a)   an independent means of physical reproduction: Women could *buy* foodstuffs if their husbands could not produce enough;
(b)   an alternative means of attaining security: Women could accumulate money for hard times and thus not have to depend on economic solidarity, as was traditional;
(c)   a means of transforming wealth into prestige: Women could buy imported cotton cloth and exhibit it conspicuously at festivities; and
(d)   a means of extending their personal influence: They could offer aid to the children they had borne beyond what it was the duty of their husbands to provide; e.g., they could pay school fees and provide additional food and clothing, giving them sway over children properly in their husbands' lineages as well as over children in their own.[19]

The structural position of the wives did have a negative side too: women have had less chance to profit from solidaristic help in case of distress; and when a village's richest persons were women, the poorest ones were often women too; men's economic fate was less varied. The best chance for the accumulation of wealth came to those women who married outside the village and got a large amount of money as bride wealth, which was divided between women's patrilineal kin and themselves. Thus, young women strongly promoted the introduction of the bride-wealth marriage and abolition of the exchange marriage, a transformation beginning at the turn of the century and completed in 1951.

This emerging independence and power gave some women the chance to leave men who "treated them badly" (i.e., who did not fulfill their reciprocal obligations or shared their favors unequally among different wives); possibly, they could even look for new husbands!

This, then, is an account of economic changes from the women's perspective, an account that is, in fact, close to being a materialist reconstruction. From the men's perspective, things looked considerably different. Since they were alien to the sphere of commodity economy, men had difficulty understanding its dynamics and implications; thus they simply saw the wealth of some females, and other men "stealing" their wives, without explanation. In this same period, along with the changes wrought by commodification, came a new and threatening phenomenon: theft. Thus it was that thievery, the stealing of women, and black magic were always lumped together as new evils.

Relief from these evils was promised by the introduction of new cults (from 1890 to 1910 in Ayou). The Ayizo had always worshipped their old Hennúvodún, a god who, for the Ayizo of Ayou and surrounding villages, was Avá, a river-source god. Now, new *vodun* were introduced from the centers of century-old commodification (i.e., slave-trade centers): from the coast, *xebiosò* (thunder-*vodun*) and *dangbé* (python-*vodun*); from Porto Novo, *zàngbétó* (night-watcher—night-hunter-*vodun*—introduced in 1934); and from the Yoruba towns, *sakpatá* (smallpox-*vodun*).[20] These were ecstatic cults, based on ritual trance and spirit possession, all of which promised to cure the three evils: theft, women-stealing, and black magic. For instance, the thunder-*vodun* and the night-hunter-*vodun* (a rather secular vigilance and night-guard society) were explicitly meant to control deviant women. Women were not even allowed to become members of the *zàngbétó*, much in contrast to the straits of women in other *vodun*, where they could even hold prominent roles. The *zàngbétó* recruited less exclusively than the other *vodun*, and most of its active members were young men.

According to oral tradition, the *vodun* had no convincing success in the control of the new "evils", but they nevertheless became a stable feature of village society, mainly because of their alleged healing powers and indisputable capability for healing mental illnesses (which possibly became "epidemic" with the rapid transformation of society), and their provision of new paths toward social status (as *vodun-no* or as other *vodun-*functionaries). The failure of this effort to control the social system was, for instance, marked by an increased occurrence of divorce initiated by women. Because of the bridal-exchange system, this increase produced the "zipper effect," described above, which meant that *one* divorce produced a medium catastrophy for *several* extended families. Thus, the unsuccessful introduction of the new *vodun* was yet another reason for consciously surrendering the exchange system and adopting the bride-wealth system of the Fon.

Under this system, men and women of the immediate patrilineage of the future husband collect money, alcoholic beverages, and some gadgets (all commodities) of a value agreed upon between the two parties and hand over a part to the women's kin-group and a part to the woman herself. This wealth was at once a pawn for the woman's fidelity—it had to be repaid if she returned (with deductions for the number of children she had thus far produced for her husband's family)—and the starting capital for the woman's own trade. A divorce of this marriage based on bride wealth constituted an economic problem (a problem for trade law),[21] but not a political problem between several lineages (through the zipper effect). So, among other things, the switch to the bridal-wealth system was a successful effort to de-politicize "household" conflicts.

7. Flirting: A Class Struggle around Old and Modern Dances

The abolition of the bridal-exchange system brought a new way of arranging marriages. One of these is the individual flirt—in some instances the flirt and seduction of a girl. This arrangement introduced a class contradiction into the politics of love that has grown since independence (1960), along with the development of a new class of bureaucrats (which Hans-Dieter Evers has called a "strategic" group). This class is recruited from the ranks of those with a modern education, and so any high school student (*collégien*) is a future bureaucrat; peasants identify these *akowe*, as they call them, mostly with those national politicians and corrupt local officials who oppress and exploit them. Members of the bureaucratic class not only have an advantage in obtaining wives when increasing prices for bride wealth have to be paid, but before this the glamor of future wealth and power gives them an advantage over peasant boys when it comes to flirting. It is on this issue that young peasants focus their hatred against bureaucrats. Lolan, a 25-year-old male, said angrily,

> The peasant works under the sun without break. He works in order to feed the *akowe* [intellectuals, bureaucrats]. But they stamp him with their feet everywhere. In the offices an *akowe* is served before the peasant. If a peasant courts a girl, a *collégien* snatches her from him.

Competition for getting a particularly sympathetic and strong young woman or young man as mate is not entirely new to the mating system. In old times this competition found its expression mainly in the dances, which were similar to athletics in the European sense: As the band loudly plays a rapid rhythm, dancers (usually two in number) of either or both sexes jump into a ring formed by the spectators. They take a slightly squat position, bowed forward, and shake their torsos, shoulders, and arms as vigorously as possible until they can no longer follow the rhythms. These motions closely resemble the motions required in field labor (e.g., hoeing), so dancing was considered good training for field labor, and boys and girls who were accustomed to field labor were well prepared for these athletic dances.[22] Towards the end of this short performance (1 to 15 minutes) the applause of the spectators would signify the achievement of one or both of the actors.

The high school students disliked those dances that had the strongest appeal of an athletic contest, preferring instead new dances like the *avivi*, which were closer to European dances in which the participants can even dance as couple (and touch each other). Here, the emphasis was more on the verbal skill of the poet of the songs.

In the mid-1960's the students succeeded in bringing the conflict over the dance types to the elders and (after an initial failure) got them to judge in their favor: The athletic dances were banned. This left the peasant boys grumbling, but all they could do was adjust to the new fashion and try to imitate the *collégiens* in every aspect (for instance in wearing European-style clothes).

8. Witch-Hunting: The Noblest Duty for the Marxist-Leninist Revolution

Although commodification and the new monopoly of coercion, in short, the colonial transformation, affected the peasant society deeply, national politics as such did not interfere in village life. The peasant politics of inter-lineage disputes and the mutual obligations of men and women were neither a matter of national politics nor a subject for the (neo-) colonial courts, a situation that changed rapidly in the 1970's.

The 1972 military take-over of Kérékou and his people led to the most stable government the state of Dahomey had since its independence. After a preliminary phase of cooperation with Marxist-oriented mass organizations of school youth, rural youth, and their intellectual leaders (J.U.D.), some Marxists were sent to jail (1973), and in a presidential speech communism was declared a disease. But in 1974, when these organizations were still banned, the president declared, "Le socialisme notre voie—le marxisme-léninisme notre guide." (Socialism our way—Marxism-Leninism our guide.) A year later Dahomey was renamed République populaire du Bénin (People's Republic of Bénin).

Starting from the top, some officers and left-wing politicians (who promoted the elitist option of state socialism) founded the secretariat of the politbureau, then the politbureau and a central committee, and finally the base of a "revolutionary and proletarian" unity party.

In an effort to pick up something of the revolutionary impetus of 1972, several campaigns were launched, of which the *lutte antiféodale* (anti-feudal struggle) of 1975 had the strongest impact on the villages. This struggle was presented through the national radio as a *campagne antisorcières* (anti-witch campaign), a campaign that dug up an old latent conflict of reproduction.

The idea of witchcraft (*aze*) was not new to the Ayizo: In the past some people (only a minority) believed that the wealthy and powerful people (mostly of the neighboring Fon) and some representatives of the newly introduced *vodun* groups derived their power and wealth from the supernatural power of witchcraft.

In the 1950's there was an unsuccessful European anti-witchcraft propaganda campaign. The French Catholic priests wanted to make people aware of the dangers of communism; but to explain what is wrong with a totalitarian ideology to people who live under colonial despotism is dangerous, and so they could not speak about freedom, concentrating instead on "atheism and freemasonry".

Sixty years before, however, they had equated Le Bon Dieu with the concept of *mawu*, common to many languages of the Aja-Ewe language group. This created a problem, since *mawu* is a creator-god who is transcendental but not immanent; i.e., he does not interfere in the world. Therefore, there is no reason to discuss his reality: He once created the world; and now he has no relevance. What should an atheist think confronted with *mawu*? The problem itself did not make sense to any Fon, Ayizo, or person from a related ethnic group.

Therefore, the clergy translated "atheist/freemason" with the concept *aze* (witch). However, the witches the priests spoke about did not act in secrecy like good Dahomean witches but in the open, frankly declaring their beliefs. This story too did not seem to be particularly reasonable.

The Ayizo and Fon concluded that the Europeans in their madness spoiled their own (the European's) image, declaring that at home in Europe they had regions full of witches, a fact not very surprising to someone suffering under colonial despotism.

In 1974 some people in a quarter of Ayou attributed the frequent incidence of tetanus to witchcraft; but the majority insisted that it had something to do with the soil and wounds, and so organizing a vaccination campaign made more sense to them.

But in 1976, the same people decided that they had to beat and throw out the "witches" (all of whom were women) because outbreaks of tetanus did not stop. Meanwhile, they had heard over the radio the confessions of many witches: These witches transformed themselves into screech owls; they then bewitched children to transform their souls into animals; and then, as human persons again or still as screech owls, they ate these souls and the children died.

Torture in Ayou and the district's headquarters, Allada, produced similar confessions. The quarter-headman, mayor, or policemen would put some of the accused women in the middle of a fire circle, place a heavy stone on the belly of those who were pregnant, leave other "witches" standing upright for days in the sun at noon, or just ask someone who served in the colonial army to beat them "according to military standards". The results were usually confessions that truly reproduced the prevailing belief-system.

That belief-system, however, was itself an innovation (Elwert, 1979). The belief that witchcraft gave special power to certain prominent individuals was not generally accepted; rather, the mainstream conception of the transcendental world and of transcendental action had earlier been based upon the idea of acting *collectives*. The ancestors or a pantheon of *vodun* acted as collectives in the same way as did their living counterparts, who were elders or the leading people of a *vodun* group. This conception was not a unique feature of religion; it was just common sense, since in daily life relevant property (land) was held by collective (i.e., the extended family or household), and decisions were made by collectives.

The advent of the commodity economy, combined with the colonially enforced system of individual property, gave plausibility to models of individual action in the transcendental sphere. On this plausibility was based the belief in black magic, administered by individuals who *bought* this power, and in witchcraft, used by witches responsible to no authority but themselves and organized in witches' clubs.

The belief in the possibility of *individual* action in the transcendental field was but one aspect of the new belief-system. The other was that now the bewitched were not *powerful* (mostly male) individuals, but *marginal and poor* (mostly female) persons. We may call this type of witch-hunting the "scapegoating type", which should be opposed to the "class-struggle type", according to which the bewitched are powerful. (See, for this latter type, Kohnert [1982] and Nadel [1973].) A typical target of the scapegoating type of witchhunt was an old woman who had lost many children and therefore became isolated and depressed. Of the 29 "witches" caught in the 1975-76 campaign 26 women were between the ages of 36 and 82. (The average age was 64.8; the only two women who were younger, aged 36 and 38, were poor.)

Why poor old women? Economically, this was a period of crisis; for the Ayizo it meant the start of massive labor migration to Nigeria. In a crisis, individual as well as collective action tends either towards paralyzing depression and self-destruction or towards action, of which one possibility is class struggle. The identification, hunt, and destruction of a scapegoat is relatively easy because the required transformations of ideology and social structure are much easier to obtain as compared to those required for class struggle. (Of course, scapegoating may be presented as "class struggle".) Action is more likely than depression or self-destruction if there are still conflicts (latent or open) with scapegoats or with a group overlapping with the defined scapegoats; and action is easier still if the scapegoats are powerless.

Patrilineal principles and patri-viri-locality mean that women have fewer partners for power alliances than men do, being at their husband's place. These same principles, together with the commodity economy, made some women the most wealthy persons in their village but also made other women the poorest. The upshot of all this was that poor women made ideal scapegoats.

The witches were "detected" by a new *vodun* called *jágli* which spread all over the country, a detection that had to be confirmed by the oracle. Whether the witches confessed or not during the torture carried out by the political authorities was not relevant to the legal sentence (*corvée*, inside or outside a prison).

In two cases the accusation of witchcraft had an element of blackmail (the accused could either sleep with the head of the *jágli*, or be denounced). In principle, suspicion of witchery had to be based on the death of children in the quarter where the accused lived. If a man's children should die early while his mother still lives in his house, she must be the witch.[23] If a woman should have no children, only involuntary abortions, "she must have eaten her children" (or embryos).

The sort of conflict described here is not uncommon to this type of patri-viri-locality, which makes a woman a stranger in her husband's family. "Stranger" (*jono*) is sometimes even a personal name given to women who come to the village as wives. She is suspected of being interested only in the well-being of the children in *her* lineage of origin. If she hates the lineage she lives in, or if there is an inherited but forgotten conflict, she might seize the opportunity and kill those of the children who are closest to her. The easiest to kill would be her sons' children, her own children, or her own unborn children.

This analysis, based upon a purely legalistic ("structuralist") conception of the patrilineal social structure, is rejected by those who insist on the evidence of maternal love. These people explain the strange behavior of mothers who have lost their children as a symptom of depression, and see accusations against a mother who has lost her child as a symptom of the madness of the witchhunters.

The partial plausibility of the witchhunters' reasoning does, however, indicate a basic conflict stemming from the economically alien position of married women in the husband's "house". Since the forced incorporation of the women into the sphere of their husbands' economic interests ("housewifization")[24] is not (yet) on the agenda of the Ayizo, the tendency to channel and contain this political conflict (external to the household) finds its expression in the transference of the conflict to the criminal/juridical sphere.

Summary

The history of the household among the Ayizo shows crucial moments of interrelation between the locally developed structures and the indirect or direct effects of international transformations. The input of new commodities was one important factor enabling a demographic transformation. This commodification prompted the rise of independent trading women, whose new position caused new conflicts and brought old conflicts to the surface. The introduction of ecstatic *vodun* (voodoo) has to be understood as an attempt to channel these conflicts.

These and other developments center on the modes of allocation of brides. Still, women are economically *not* part of a minimal economic unit binding them to husband and children, as might traditionally be conceived: Even after marriage, womens' economic links with their lineage of origin are of great importance. Therefore, any conflict between husband and wife is potentially a political conflict (i.e., a conflict outside the household and the lineage), as became apparent on a national level when the (anti-female) witch-hunting movement became a matter of national politics. The tendency to contain this "husband-wife conflict" and to defuse its explosive threat can be observed throughout Ayizo history. The transference of the fear of those strangers who are married women to a juridical conflict over witches is merely its latest instance.[25]

NOTES

1. I owe this idea to Norbert Elias and was strongly encouraged by E. Terray (1977). My ideas got much clearer after confronting the chapter by Diana Wong in this volume. The help of David Miller, Law Yufei, Muctaru Kabba, and Dirk Kohnert was essential in order to formulate precisely what had hitherto been obscure.

2. In German we speak about "*die Kanalisierungen der Konflikte und die Institutionen, die die Sprengkraft der Konflikte bändigen und die Gesellschaft verklammern*".

3. For the collection of data, another approach would be suitable (since few people like to inform a fieldworker about conflicts right in the beginning): One starts with the recurring iterative processes of daily life and the representations people give of their society. Then one sees the breaks, logical contradictions, and blind spots in these pictures, which then indicate social contradictions and latent and open conflicts.

4. Data for this chapter stem mostly from my fieldwork in 1976 (supported by the Fakultät für Soziologies der Universität Bielefeld) and 1977 (supported by the Deutsche Gesellschaft für Friedens- und Konfliktforschung). I was sensitized to this subject by the young Ayizo intellectual Raymond Anato. I learned a lot from Aklii and Mehento, two old women, and from other people of Ayou. Fieldwork was done in cooperation with Raymond Anato and with the help of Ambriose Klikpo (for the genealogies), Antoine Togbsazon, and Michel Ahohounkpanzon. It is beyond the scope of this chapter to add full evidence (genealogies, testimonies from tortured "witches", and so on); therefore I restrict myself to a small selection of quotations and data in order to illustrate the argument. On the suggestion of the editors, I cut from the original information that seemed relevant only to a restricted anthropological public.

5. In another part of the same province of Bénin, Diana Wong found that wealthier persons give relatively less for the sake of economic solidarity than poor ones (Elwert & Wong, 1978: 44-46); but the absolute amount of the contribution increases with increasing wealth in the commodity economy. Thus there is no trend for the dissolution of these networks.

6. This formulation should not obscure the fact that eating has never been confined to the household; the food consumed at invitations or at festivities is not negligible, because it is there that most of the animal protein is consumed.

7. Often siblings from the same father but different mothers inherit the animosities that existed among their mothers. Such conflicts of interest between co-wives can occur when the husband does not divide his transfers equally, and they show up at the moment of the division of the heritage.

8. I think that this relation of conflicts within and without the households merits special attention for the discussion of household structures in a changing world-economy in general. Conflicts inside and outside the household (including class conflict) are interrelated. An example of a simple type of interdependence might be the following: It seems that in revolutionary periods conflicts inside the household decrease and return when the revolutionary impetus draws back. This is not valid if the revolution aims at a transformation of relations of reproduction inside the household as in a period of the Chinese Revolution. Except for this special case this interdependence can best be observed in the figures of physical violence before, during, and after revolutionary periods.

9. Genealogies are accompanied by historical accounts. One of the recurring elements in these accounts, also relevant in our context, is the story of marriages with people from the Fon. These marriages inevitably seemed to cause warlike conflicts. We cannot judge the truth of these stories, but the point in them is obvious: "Don't marry someone from outside, let's keep Ayizo endogamous!" This is also an effort to reduce the political aspect (i.e., to de-politicize the alliance conflicts).

10. The eldest brothers had 1 to 8 children (22 children for 4 fathers); the younger brothers had 1 to 7 children (48 children for 14 fathers); the difference is significant only at the 5% level (t-test).

11. One might guess that adopted children and stepchildren were added to this number, though we have no confirmation for this.

12. For a description of a very similar system of women's exchange see Huber (1969).

13. The technological factors discussed here may appear trivial to some readers. After all, is the thickness of a cooking pot really an essential technological issue? Still, any innovation that reduces the total amount of necessary labor time in a society is, in fact, essential. The preoccupation with agricultural and industrial tools, common to most of the present anthropological and historical research, is not justified from an aggregate economic perspective that includes housework; this neglect most likely has something to do with the neglect of women's work in general.

14. This separation of tasks implies that women in polygamous households have a lesser burden than their counterparts in monogamous households. Old women pointed to this as their

argument in favor of polygamy. The argument Europeans think of—the lesser share in sex—was given only by young women and raised only in combination with the problem that a husband might divide gifts in commodities unequally.

15. Some people say that a mature girl who loves (physically) a man "knows the male" (and becomes therefore rebellious against parental authority).

16. Field-limit conflicts are usually conflicts between half-brothers who share a common father. So, although their fields remain adjacent after their heritages separate, they share fewer emotional links since they are educated by different mothers and grow up with different siblings. Eventually, half-brothers may cause a lineage's segmentation, splitting off to form a new sub-lineage.

17. Those women who have returned to their lineage in old age and stay there as elders know about these cases too. The rules described here may apply to these women too, but we have no positive confirmation for this.

18. Evidence of the presence of commodities and commodity exchange is mostly absent both in the oral tradition and in material remains. They appear to have been present only in the contacts between the Ayizo and the Fon.

19. A young Ayizo male made even this general statement: "Elle arrive à se vassaliser le mari qui a besoin de soutien. . . . Il en resulte un conflit dont les retombées ne sont jamais prévisibles: empoisonnement du mari, forces occultes contre la femme et ses enfants etc."

20. In order to join these cults, some men collected money, sent a mission to places where these cults flourished, got initiated, and *bought* the secret power.

21. It is noteworthy that the commodification of the marriage relation as established through the bride-wealth system is much advanced in comparison to the European system, where marriage is still something "private and personal" and relegated to the sphere of pure use-value economics. Only the modernization of divorce law suggests the sort of commodification that exists in this "underdeveloped" economy.

22. The features of bodily beauty and the features of the beauty of motions are associated with the features of athletic constitution and physical strength for *both* sexes.

23. A very old story mentions the conflict between a man's mother and her son's offspring, though the conflict was ideally solved by means of a ceremonial avoidance.

24. For the concept of housewifization see von Werlhof (1981); for a general earlier treatment, see Mies (1979).

25. A general note on Ayizo sources: First-hand information has come from the following:

Name	Sex	Age	Sections of Chapter Based on Testimony
Anato Lolan	Male	59	4 & 5
Anato Raymond	Male	31	All sections
Ahohounkpanzon Michel	Male	27	3, 6, & 8
Klikpo Cece	Male	70	1, 2, & 8
Aklii	Female	80	2 & 8
Mehento	Female	72	2 & 8
Togbeazon Antoine	Male	35	1, 2, 3, & 6
Klikpo Asogba	Male	76	3
Klikpo Ambroise	Male	28	1 & 7
	Male	80	1 & 2
Hannyatayino Hannyamexo	Female	86	1, 2, 6, & 8

Relevant testimony for Sections 2 and 8 (and for some other sections as well) was collected from three other sources, whose names are withheld here in accordance with their wishes for strict anonymity.

For reasons of typography we could not retain the phonetic spellings of names and concepts contained in this chapter.

REFERENCES

Elwert, Georg (1979). "Alphabetisation in Ayou: Untersuchung einer bäuerlichen Selbsthilfe—Bewegung," *Osnabrücker Beiträge zur Sprachtheorie*, No. 12, 109-50.

Elwert, Georg (1980). "Die Elemente der traditionellen Solidarität," *Kölner Zeitschrift für Soziologie, und Sozialpsychologie*, XXXII, 4, 681-704.

Elwert, Georg (1982). "Traditionelle Solidarität: Überleben in Krisen und kapitalistische Maximierung," in G. Elwert & R. Fett, eds., *Afrika zwischen Subsistenzökonomie und Imperialismus*. Frankfurt: Campus, 47-69.

Elwert, Georg & Wong, Diana (1978). "Structures agraires et procès de développement dans la province de l'Atlantique," unpubl. ms., Bielefeld.

Evers, Hans-Dieter (1979). "Class Formation in Indonesia in the Southeast Asian Context," unpubl. working paper, Melbourne.

Huber, Hugo (1969). "Le principe de la réciprocité dans le marriage Nyende," *Africa*, XXXIX, 3, July, 260-74.

Kérékou, Mathieu (1975). *Libérons-nous de l'étau féodal*. Cotonou.

Kinley, David (1977). "Cement Housing in West Africa," *Food Monitor*, Sept., p. 14.

Kohnert, Dirk (1982). *Ländliche Klassenbildung im Nupeland*. Hamburg: Inst. für Afrikakunde.

Mies, Maria (1979). "Social Origins of the Sexual Division of Labour," unpubl. working paper, circulated at the Z.I.F. conference, "Underdevelopment and Subsistence Reproduction," Bielefeld.

Nadel, Siegfried F. (1973). "Witchcraft in Four African Societies," in P. F. Wilmot, ed., *Sociology in Africa*. Zaria: Ahmadu Bello Univ. Press.

Research Working Group on Households and Production Processes (1978). "Households, Labor Force, and Production Processes in the Capitalist World-Economy," Fernand Braudel Center working paper, SUNY-Binghamton.

Terray, Emmanuel (1977). "De l'exploitation," *Dialectiques*, No. 21, Aut., 134-43.

Werlhof, Claudia von (1981). "Frauen und Dritte welt: 'Natur del Kapitals'," in H. Dauber & W. Simpfendörfer, eds., *Miteinander Leben—voneinan der lernen*. Wuppertal: Petra Hammer, 187-215.